JOHNNIE JOHNSON'S
1942 DIARY

JOHNNIE JOHNSON'S
1942 DIARY

The War Diary of the Spitfire Ace of Aces

Dilip Sarkar

AIR WORLD

AIR WORLD

JOHNNIE JOHNSON'S 1942 DIARY
The War Diary of the Spitfire Ace of Aces

First published in Great Britain in 2020 by
Air World
An imprint of
Pen & Sword Books Ltd
Yorkshire – Philadelphia

ISBN 978 1 52679 170 2

Typeset by SJmagic DESIGN SERVICES, India.

Printed and bound in England by TJ Books Limited.

Pen & Sword Books Limited incorporates the imprints of Atlas, Archaeology,
Aviation, Discovery, Family History, Fiction, History, Maritime, Military, Military
Classics, Politics, Select, Transport, True Crime, Air World, Frontline Publishing, Leo
Cooper, Remember When, Seaforth Publishing, The Praetorian Press, Wharncliffe
Local History, Wharncliffe Transport, Wharncliffe True Crime and White Owl.

For a complete list of Pen & Sword titles please contact

PEN & SWORD BOOKS LIMITED
47 Church Street, Barnsley, South Yorkshire, S70 2AS, England
E-mail: enquiries@pen-and-sword.co.uk
Website: www.pen-and-sword.co.uk

Or
PEN AND SWORD BOOKS
1950 Lawrence Rd, Havertown, PA 19083, USA
E-mail: Uspen-and-sword@casematepublishers.com
Website: www.penandswordbooks.com

MIX
Paper from
responsible sources
FSC® C013056

Contents

Introduction

Air Vice-Marshal 'Johnnie' Johnson was the ultimate character from the *Boys' Own Paper*: the RAF's top-scoring fighter pilot and wing leader *par excellence* of the Second World War. A one-time household name synonymous with the superlative Spitfire, Johnnie's aerial combat successes inspired schoolboys for generations.

In those violent and uncertain times, fighter pilots were, it is true, the 'glamour boys', the aerial knights who jousted with Britain's foes, fighting a clean war. Indeed Richard Hillary, another of the Few, saw himself as an old-time duellist: 'In a fighter plane, I believe, we have found a way to return to war as it ought to be, war which is individual combat between two people, in which one either kills or is killed. It's exciting, it's individual, and it's disinterested. I shan't be sitting behind a long-range gun working out how to kill people sixty miles away. I shan't get maimed: either I shall get killed or I shall get a few pleasant putty medals and enjoy being stared at in a night club.'

Sadly, that's not how things turned out. On 3 September 1940, Hillary was blasted out of the sky by *Hauptmann* Erich Bode, baling out over the Channel, horrendously burned. Disfigured, after a long period of recovery and innumerable operations, this former Oxford scholar returned to flying – only to be killed in a night-flying accident. Such was the uncertain life – and death – of a wartime fighter pilot.

The camaraderie of the fighter pilots of the time was unsurpassed, and amongst fighter leaders Johnnie was revered. Charismatic, a superb shot and pilot with great tactical awareness, Johnnie had another great attribute, as recalled by Wing Commander Hugh Godefroy: 'Johnnie always sensed when morale was dropping in the Wing, and instinctively knew the best time for a piss-up!' Johnnie, then, was no flying and fighting automaton, devoid of emotion – far from it. Dedicated to his craft though he was, Johnnie was a well-rounded and gregarious individual who loved people – which comes through loud and clear in the following pages.

INTRODUCTION

In this diary, published here for the first time, we get a glimpse of the real Johnnie, and what it was like to live and breathe air-fighting during one of the European air war's most interesting years: 1942. This is a remarkable document on both a historical and human level. Knowing Johnnie personally, as a close friend, has enabled a truly informed reading of the diary, supplemented with interviews, correspondence and other primary sources. Comprehensively contextualised, the diary is now fixed in time and space for those of present and future generations who still want to learn about those stirring times – from the most successful Spitfire pilot ever to enter the fray in R.J. Mitchell's iconic fighter.

Dilip Sarkar MBE, FRHistS

Acknowledgements

Johnnie's youngest son, Chris, has been a personal friend for many years and has my enduring gratitude for making this diary and other material available to me.

Phil Mitzman, who now owns the diary, has also been very helpful.

As ever, my publisher and friend, Martin Mace, deserves a special mention for his constant encouragement and support, and, as always, the team at Pen & Sword were a pleasure to work with.

PART I

Prologue

James Edgar Johnson was born on 9 March 1915, at Barrow-upon-Soar in rural Leicestershire, the eldest son of Alfred Edgar Johnson and his wife, Beatrice May. Alfred was a police officer stationed at Melton Mowbray, where the family lived in Welby Lane. In due course, 'Johnnie' was joined by younger brother Ross, who later recalled his elder sibling as 'very principled'. Ross also emphasised that the great influence on young Johnnie was his maternal uncle Charlie Rossel, who had won a Military Cross during the First World War and later made a fortune in Malaya.

To the Johnson boys, Uncle Charlie was 'an exotic and romantic character'. Ross also explained, 'It was Uncle Charlie who recognised potential in Johnnie early on, and paid for him to board at Loughborough Grammar School. As our father's job as a police inspector was not well-paid at that time, this would never have been possible without Charlie Rossel's patronage.' Ross also recalled that 'as a youngster, Johnnie was always in trouble … into fast cars and equally pacey girls! That he became interested in flying was no surprise.'

After leaving school, Johnnie graduated as a civil engineer at University College Nottingham before becoming articled to the Borough Surveyor at Melton Urban Council. Aged 22 in 1938 – the year of the Munich Crisis – he took an appointment at Loughton in Essex. There Johnnie played rugby for Chingford, when, significantly, in a game against Park House he was 'brought down heavily on a frozen surface and broke my right collar-bone. Although I didn't know it at the time, the break was improperly set and nerves to the forearm were imprisoned below the bone.' Later this injury would have serious consequences – nearly ending Johnnie's epic flying career when it had barely begun.

Before Munich, Johnnie had started taking private flying lessons and applied to join the Auxiliary Air Force, a part-time reserve of amateur volunteers, based on the territorial concept – but there was a problem.

PROLOGUE

Founded in 1924, the AAF was socially elite, most pilots being extremely wealthy young men, most with their own aeroplanes, who flew for pleasure. As one auxiliary, Group Captain Sir Hugh 'Cocky' Dundas wrote of his fellows, 'they were lawyers and farmers, stockbrokers and journalists, landowners and artisans, serious minded accountants and unrepentant playboys.' What they were not, were humble policemen's sons, no matter their ability. Johnnie:

> I went along for this interview and the senior officer there, knowing that I came from Leicestershire, said, "With whom do you hunt, Johnson?"
>
> I said, "Hunt, Sir?"
>
> He said, "Yes, Johnson, hunt; with whom do you hunt?"
>
> I said, "Well, I don't hunt, Sir, I shoot."
>
> He said, "Oh, well thank you then, Johnson, that will be all!"
>
> Clearly the fact that I could shoot game on the wing impressed him not one bit. Had I been socially acceptable, however, by hunting with Lord so-and-so, things would have been different, but back then, that is what the auxiliaries were like, and do not forget that many members were of independent means, which I certainly wasn't!

After Munich it was clear that war with Hitler's Germany was inevitable, so Johnnie reapplied to the AAF, finding nothing changed: 'I was curtly informed that sufficient pilots were already available but there were some vacancies in the balloon squadrons. Was I interested in this vital part of the defence organisation? I replied, with similar brevity, that I was not at all interested in flying balloons!'

Still, there was hope, if not of flying with the AAF. By 1939 there were twenty AAF squadrons, and the University Air Squadrons provided another 500 trained officer pilots for the RAF. In 1934 the Expansion Plan had begun raising the establishment of Home Defence squadrons to fifty-two by 1940. Nonetheless, in 1936, Expansion Scheme 'F' recognised that there remained an insufficient reserve. This led to the creation of the RAF Volunteer Reserve. The official monograph on RAF Flying Training during the Second World War states that the RAFVR would 'have a wide appeal based upon the Citizen Volunteer principle with a common mode of entry and promotion and commissioning on merit... So far as aircrew training was concerned, the system was based upon local town centres for spare time ground training and upon aerodrome centres associated with the town centres for flying training at the weekend, also for a fortnight's annual camp.'

According to Air Ministry Pamphlet 101, published in November 1939, 'Entry into the General Duties (Flying) branch of the RAFVR is normally through the ranks, commissions being given by selection, either on completion of flying training or subsequently, but past or present members of UAS who hold proficiency certificates will be eligible for consideration for appointment to commissions on entry.' All volunteer aircrew were automatically made sergeants, with the possibility of a commission, based – apparently – not on an elitist background but on ability. The VR provided, therefore, a unique opportunity for many young men from ordinary educational and social backgrounds to fly. Inspired by several Chingford rugby team-mates who had already joined the VR, Johnnie applied. Unfortunately the outcome was again disappointing: for the time being there were more applicants than vacancies. Johnnie was advised that in the event of further expansion the VR would contact him.

While awaiting the call, which Johnnie never gave up hope would one day come, our hero joined the mounted Leicestershire Yeomanry, a Territorial Army unit. This was important because as a surveyor Johnnie's was a reserved occupation, and needless to say this man of action had no intention of missing the war, which everyone knew was on the stormy horizon. While happy in the saddle, having learned to ride at an early age, one day a Spitfire over-flew Johnnie's troop: 'I thought "That's more like it", if I've got to fight Hitler I'd rather do so in one of those than on the back of this bloody great horse!'

Fortunately Johnnie's prayers were answered when a letter arrived from the Air Ministry explaining that the VR was being expanded, and consequently he was invited to attend a medical. Having passed the doctor's examination, Johnnie started training at Stapleford Tawney, certain weekday evenings spent classroom-bound, studying ground subjects, while flying consumed his weekends.

In August 1939, the young surveyor left his office, never returning to the theodolite, when the VR was mobilised. Reporting to the local HQ, Johnnie was told to go home and there await orders. On 1 September 1939, Hitler invaded Poland; two days later, Britain and France declared war on Germany. Soon after hearing the Prime Minister's broadcast that fateful Sunday, Sergeant 754750 JE Johnson entrained for Cambridge along with several hundred other reservists, bound for 2 Initial Training Wing.

There the fledgling airmen were questioned regarding what, ultimately, they wished to become: fighter, bomber, reconnaissance or training pilots?

Most, sensing the opportunity for derring-do, asked to be fighter pilots. Johnnie, however, explained that given his surveying experience he might prove useful in the reconnaissance role. The interviewing wing commander agreed – but Johnnie was made a fighter pilot! It would prove a most significant stroke of the pen.

After 'square-bashing' at Cambridge, Johnnie became a pupil at 22 Elementary Flying Training School, also at Cambridge, undertaking his *ab initio* flying training on the De Havilland Tiger Moth biplane. On 10 May 1940, Hitler, at last, attacked west. With unprecedented fury, German troops smashed into Belgium, Luxembourg, the Netherlands and France, in what became an unstoppable rampage to the Channel coast. A fortnight later, Johnnie's elementary training was successfully completed, after which he reported to 5 Service Flying Training School at Sealand, there to fly monoplanes for the first time. By 3 June the battle on the continent was lost, the British Expeditionary Force evacuated from the battered port and beaches around Dunkirk. After a lull, on 10 July 1940 the Battle of Britain began with skirmishing over Channel-bound convoys, before determined attacks were made on radar installations and Fighter Command's southern airfields.

Against this dramatic backdrop, Johnnie's training continued until successfully completed on 7 August 1940 – by which time he had been commissioned as a Pilot Officer in the General Duties Branch 'for the duration of hostilities'. As Johnnie said, 'At the time, this would never have happened in the AAF. Mounting casualties, however, meant that a man's ability became more important than social class, and this was an early indication of the social change wrought by war – and the RAF's forward-thinking reaction to that.'

Next stop for Pilot Officer Johnson on the road to becoming a fighter pilot was 7 Operational Training Unit at Hawarden – where he achieved every young man's dream and flew a Supermarine Spitfire for the first time on 19 August 1940; it would be the start of a long and unparalleled association between man and machine, the Spitfire, of course, being *the* iconic fighter of the period. The flight lasted an hour and was 'one to remember'.

First flown at Eastleigh on 5 March 1936, the Spitfire had a proud lineage directly related to the Schneider Trophy-winning Supermarine racing seaplanes also designed by Reginald Joseph Mitchell. In terms of British fighter production, the Spitfire was an advanced design. Uniquely, Mitchell's curvaceous monoplane fighter was built around a clever leaf-spring, was of monocoque construction, and was all-metal covered. With an enclosed cockpit, retractable undercarriage and eight machine guns, hurtling through the skies at over 350 mph the Spitfire was a totally different machine to the biplanes which it, together with the Hawker Hurricane, replaced in 1938. Indeed the Spitfire was directly comparable to Germany's new monoplane fighter, the Messerschmitt 109, although it would be wrong to imagine that the Spitfire Mk I was either perfect or superior to its Teutonic adversary.

With typical German technical excellence, the Me 109E boasted certain advantages. For example, the Spitfire's Rolls-Royce Merlin engine had a float carburettor, meaning that in a dive, owing to the force of gravity the powerplant was temporarily starved of fuel. The 109, conversely, had fuel injection, so did not suffer this problem and could, therefore, either catch a Spitfire in the dive or escape from it in that attitude.

The 109 also had a constant-speed propeller, the rotating blades of which enabled the pilot to select the best optimum pitch for any given situation (akin to gear-changing in a car). The first Spitfire had a fixed-pitch, two-bladed, wooden airscrew, although this was soon replaced with the De Havilland two-pitch propeller providing 'coarse' and 'fine' pitch. Eventually an emergency field modification fitted during the Battle of Britain converted the De Havilland twin-speed units to constant-speed, and the new Spitfire Mk IIs reaching squadrons at that time were fitted with the Rotol constant-speed airscrew as standard.

In another area the early Spitfire was also significantly deficient: armament. Although eight .303 machine guns were an improvement on the usual one or two forward-firing guns of biplane days, aircraft were becoming increasingly armoured and therefore more difficult to shoot down. The German fighter was armed with two nose-mounted 7.92mm machine guns and a pair of hard-hitting 20mm Oerlikon cannons, one in each wing, the pilot able to choose either weapon, or fire both simultaneously.

The Germans enjoyed the advantage of having proved their weapons and tactics during the Spanish Civil War, and more recently during the fighting over Poland and the West. The 109's superiority over the Hurricane was demonstrated during the Battle of France, but the Spitfire, having been carefully preserved for home defence, only met the 109 for the first time during the Dunkirk evacuation – when these technical deficiencies were exposed.

In one crucial aspect the Spitfire was superior to the 109: it could turn tighter, and fighter combat was about height, sun, surprise – and turning, tighter and tighter, to turn the tables on an assailant. As Johnnie said, however, 'You can't keep turning forever, so these deficiencies needed sorting out PDQ.'

During the last week of August, postings began appearing on the board: Pilot Officer Johnson was to join 19 Squadron at Duxford. The RAF's first Spitfire-equipped squadron, 19 was actually based at Fowlmere, the Duxford sector station satellite, and it was there that Johnnie reported on 3 September. It was, though, a difficult time for this premier 12 Group fighter squadron.

On 26 May 1940, 19 Squadron's commanding officer, Squadron Leader Geoffrey Stephenson, had been shot down over the French coast and captured at the start of Operation *Dynamo*, the Dunkirk evacuation. Thereafter, responsibility for temporarily leading the squadron in the air fell to the commander of 'A' Flight, Flight Lieutenant Brian Lane, whose exceptional abilities as both a fighter pilot and leader were recognised with an early DFC. In those days, however, promotion was disconnected from all-important operational experience.

Instead, what counted was seniority on the Air Force List – hence why formal command of the squadron passed to Squadron Leader Phillip Pinkham AFC, whose experience comprised having flown biplane fighters during peacetime and Hurricanes as an instructor. Sensibly, given this lack of combat experience, Pinkham initially left command of 19 in the air to Brian Lane, busying himself with a major issue: introducing 20mm cannon to the Spitfire.

To 19 Squadron had fallen the task of trialling the experimental Spitfire Mk IB, fitted with a 20mm Hispano-Suiza cannon in each wing. This, however, was proving somewhat problematic. Owing to the Spitfire's thin wing section, the cannon could not be mounted upright, as the manufacturer intended, but side-mounted, with an improvised ammunition feed and cartridge ejection system. Unfortunately during combat the flexing of the wing led to frequent stoppages, which was a huge problem given that this Spitfire, the Mk IB, had no back-up machine guns. Situated in 12 Group, action was hard enough to come by, and when it did, Pinkham's pilots were increasingly frustrated by their jammed weapons – and defenceless.

Eventually the pilots lost all confidence in the Mk IB, leading to Pinkham arguing the case that they be replaced by machine-gun-armed Mk IAs. When Johnnie arrived this was preoccupying the squadron. As he said, 'With 23.50 hours on the Spitfire I wasn't really going to be any use to 19 Squadron until I had fifty. And because these chaps were engaged in active operations against the enemy, and struggling with their cannon Spitfires, they had neither time or inclination to train replacement pilots.' Two days after Pilot Officer Johnson's arrival, the Mk IBs had been replaced with IAs, and Squadron Leader Pinkham led his now machine-gun-equipped unit into action over Kent for the first time – only to be shot down and killed.

As command now formally passed upon promotion to Squadron Leader Brian Lane DFC, Johnnie learned that he would not be remaining with 19 but joining 616 'South Yorkshire' Squadron at Coltishall. It would be the start of a long and happy association.

It is worth noting that 616 was an auxiliary squadron, but now because of the casualties suffered at Dunkirk and in the Battle of Britain it included few auxiliaries but various reservists, foreign nationals and regular airmen. Already these auxiliary squadrons bore little resemblance to their pre- and early war identities of locally raised, socially elite, territorials.

Based at Leconfield, 616 had seen little action when it arrived at Kenley on 19 August 1940 – but by 3 September the 'South Yorkshire' Squadron had lost eleven Spitfires destroyed, three damaged, five pilots killed, six wounded and one captured. Pulled out of the frontline, when the unit arrived at Coltishall, there to rest and refit, only eight of those pilots who had served at Kenley remained operational. The squadron also had a new CO, Squadron Leader H.F. 'Billy' Burton DFC, a veteran and successful fighter pilot whose task it was to rebuild this battered unit – the morale of which, unsurprisingly, was low.

Johnnie: 'I did not like the atmosphere. The veterans kept to themselves and seemed aloof and very remote. Even to my inexperienced eye it was apparent that the quiet confidence of a well-led and disciplined team was missing from this group. There was a marked difference between the bunch of aggressive pilots I had met at Fowlmere and these too silent, apprehensive men.'

Burton, however, immediately impressed: 'Billy was a regular officer who had won the Cranwell Sword of Honour in 1936 … he was an outstanding product of the Cranwell system. Exacting in his demands, he was always full of vitality and enthusiasm. I liked him at first sight and have never served under a better or more loyal officer.'

In addition to the Spitfire's technical deficiencies having been exposed by the recent fighting, Fighter Command's tactics had also been found fatally flawed. Before Hitler's unanticipated lightning advance to the Channel coast, it was assumed that any aerial attack on England would be by bombers operating from bases in Germany, unescorted by fighters owing to their limited range.

The RAF tacticians, therefore, decided that the primary tactical formation would be the close formation 'vic' of three fighters, squadrons divided into two flights each of two sections of three. With vics in line astern, the leader would attack with his section of three, simultaneously bringing twenty-four machine guns to bear on the slower and less manoeuvrable target, which would cooperatively continue flying straight and level, taking no evasive action. The lead section would then break away, each following section completing their attack in turn.

In the event, with French airfields available to the Luftwaffe, even London was within the Me 109's range – which changed everything. Indeed, there were those who believed that fighter-to-fighter combat was no longer possible owing to the 'G' forces to which the human body was subjected in violent high-speed manoeuvres. This was not, however, the case. In Spain, the Germans had rapidly worked out that modern fighter combat required early sighting of the enemy and flexible formations.

Whereas the RAF's 'vic' required pilots to concentrate more on formation flying than searching for the enemy, conversely the Luftwaffe developed the *schwarm*, a section of four fighters, subdivided into two pairs – *rotten* – comprising leader and wingman. The *schwarm* was spread out in line abreast, the aircraft stepped up, some 200 metres apart, like the fingers of an outstretched hand. With no fear of collision, the pilots could search for the enemy, and in action the *schwarm* broke into the two *rotten*, the leader's job being to make the kill while his wingman, or *rottenhund*, protected his tail.

Johnnie: 'No-one, so far, had really talked to us about tactics. We were, of course, very keen to know what it was like fighting the Me 109, and how to best shoot one down. At training school we virtually had to cajole instructors into imparting knowledge, and while at Duxford had listened keenly to what the Spitfire pilots of 19 Squadron and the Czech Hurricane pilots of 310 had to say – but this was all in the informal environment of either dispersal or the Mess. Billy Burton talked to me about the difficulties of deflection shooting and the technique of the killing shot from the line-astern or near line-astern positions; the duty of the number two whose job was not to shoot down aircraft but to ensure that the leader's tail was safe; the importance of keeping a good battle formation and the tactical use of sun, cloud and height. Here was a man, I thought, who knew what he was about, and under whose leadership we might actually get somewhere.'

Over the next few days, Johnnie flew various training flights, including aerobatics, formation practice, practice attacks, and air-to-ground firing. His log book also clears up an ambiguity: Pilot Officer J.E. Johnson did indeed qualify for the coveted Battle of Britain Bar to the 1939-45 Star. For reasons shortly to be explained, Johnnie saw no action during the Battle of Britain, which lasted from 10 July until 31 October 1940. When later assessing the criteria for the award of the Battle of Britain Bar, the Air Ministry decreed that eligibility was dictated by having been on the strength of one of the seventy-two units deemed to have participated, making at least one operational flight between the relevant dates.

On 11 September 1940, Johnnie flew Spitfire X4330 on a fifteen minute 'X-Raid Patrol', thus qualifying for the Battle of Britain Bar and therefore inclusion amongst the names of Churchill's fabled 'Few'. An X-Raid was an unidentified radar plot, as yet unconfirmed as either hostile or friendly. Frequently the 'bogey' turned out not to be a 'bandit', i.e. an enemy aircraft, but a friendly machine going about its legitimate business. A patrol in pursuit of an X-Raid, therefore, could have three outcomes: interception of either an enemy or friendly aircraft, or no contact whatsoever. In this case it is assumed that the patrol was inconclusive. Nonetheless this was an operational patrol which therefore qualifies Johnnie as a *bona fide* Battle of Britain pilot.

On 14 September 1940, Pilot Officer Johnson and a number of his squadron mates were enjoying a few pints in the Bell public house at Norwich. The party was abruptly ended by the arrival of RAF policemen, recalling all RAF personnel to their airfields immediately. Back at Coltishall Johnnie discovered that Alert No 1, 'invasion imminent and probable within twelve hours', had been issued. The nation's defences were being brought to the highest state of readiness, and an atmosphere of confusion prevailed at Coltishall.

The whereabouts of Squadron Leader Burton was unknown, so Johnnie left the crowded anteroom to telephone dispersal, where he thought the CO and his flight commanders may be. As he hastened along the hallway to use the telephone, he almost collided with a squadron leader who purposefully stomped along with an awkward gait. It was to prove a most significant meeting. Johnnie:

> His vital eyes gave me a swift scrutiny, at my pilot's brevet and one thin ring of a pilot officer. "I say old boy, what's all the flap about?" he exclaimed, legs apart and putting a match to his pipe.

PROLOGUE

"I don't really know, Sir," I replied. "But there are reports of enemy landings."

The Squadron Leader pushed open the swing doors and stalked into the noisy, confused atmosphere of the ante-room. Fascinated, I followed in close line-astern because I thought I knew who this was. He took in the scene and then demanded in a loud voice, and in choice, fruity language, what all the panic was about. Half a dozen voices started to explain, and eventually he had some idea of the form. As he listened, his eyes swept round the room, lingered for a moment on us pilots and established a private bond of fellowship between us.

There was a moment's silence while he digested the news. "So the bastards are coming. Bloody good show! Think of all those targets on those nice flat beaches. What shooting!" And he made a rude sound with his lips which was meant to resemble a ripple of machine-gun fire.

The effect was immediate and extraordinary. Officers went about their various tasks and the complicated machinery of the airfield began to function smoothly again. Later we were told that the reports of enemy landings were false and that we could revert to our normal readiness states. But the incident left me with a profound impression of the qualities of leadership displayed in a moment of tension by the assertive Squadron Leader. It was my first encounter with the already legendary Douglas Bader.

Douglas Bader was legendary indeed – and from that meeting onwards would have a profound influence on Johnnie.

A Cranwell graduate, Bader, a gifted but overconfident aerobatic pilot, had crashed at Woodley airfield near Reading on 14 December 1931, while attempting a slow roll in a Bristol Bulldog. In his log book, Bader simply wrote 'Bad show'. The 21-year-old pilot was so badly injured in the crash that both legs were amputated – one above, the other below, the knee. Incredibly, Bader overcame this disability, learning to walk on 'tin' legs and even passed a flying test at the Central Flying School. Unfortunately, King's Regulations did not provide for limbless pilots, and so Bader was offered a chair-borne role.

This he was unprepared to accept, and so, with a heavy heart, left the service he loved so much. At the time of Munich, Bader, by then a married man, offered his services to the Air Ministry as a trained pilot. This was declined. In March 1939, when Hitler invaded the remainder of Czechoslovakia, Bader tried again. Although another refusal ensued, this time the decision was tempered with the possibility of acceptance in the event of war. Britain and France's declaration of war against Germany on 3 September 1939 was, therefore, Bader's salvation. On 18 October 1939, Bader passed the required flying test, the following month reporting to the CFS Refresher Squadron. On 20 December 1939, Flying Officer Bader soloed on the Hawker Hurricane. On conclusion of the course, Bader's ability as a pilot was assessed as 'Exceptional'.

While at the CFS, Bader flew over to Duxford in a Hurricane. There he rekindled acquaintance with the station commander, Wing Commander A.B. 'Woody' Woodhall, who introduced him to the 12 Group Air Officer Commanding, Air Vice-Marshal Trafford Leigh-Mallory. According to Woodhall, 'Over lunch Douglas used all of his considerable charm to persuade "LM" to take him into one of his operational fighter squadrons. After lunch Douglas put on a most finished display of aerobatics, and this finally decided "LM". Douglas was posted almost at once to 19 Squadron at Duxford, which was commanded by his old Cranwell friend Geoffrey Stephenson. Douglas impressed us all with his terrific personality and amazing keenness and drive. I have never known his equal. Flying was his supreme passion and his enthusiasm infected us all.'

On 7 February 1940, Flying Officer Bader joined 19 Squadron, converting to the Spitfire before being promoted on 16 April 1940 to Acting Flight Lieutenant and posted to command 'A' Flight of 222 Squadron. Bader was serving with 222 when Operation *Dynamo* began a few weeks later. Operating from Hornchurch on 1 June 1940, Bader claimed his first victories when he destroyed an Me 109 and damaged a 110 over the French coast. Afterwards, his CO, Squadron Leader 'Tubby' Mermagen, and station commander, Wing Commander Woodhall, recommended to Air Vice-Marshal Leigh-Mallory that the buccaneering and energetic Bader was just the man to restore the morale of the Canadian 242 Squadron – a Hurricane unit suffering badly during the Battle of France. On 2 July 1940, Bader was therefore promoted to Acting Squadron Leader, taking command of 242 at Coltishall.

On arrival at Coltishall, the disgruntled Canadians were unimpressed to discover that their new CO had no legs. Bader's response was typical of his dynamic and aggressive personality: for the next hour and ten minutes he provided a daredevil demonstration of aerobatics over the airfield. After that there was no suggestion that this legless officer was a passenger. On 9 July 1940, 242 Squadron was declared fully operational. Two days later, it was the CO who chalked up 242's first aerial victory – a Do 17 reconnaissance bomber destroyed off Cromer.

At Coltishall, Bader soon became frustrated at the lack of action and monotonous patrols over convoys chugging around the east coast. Off the south-east coast, however, the action was becoming increasingly fierce, as the fighter forces of both sides clashed over Channel-bound convoys. As the enemy air assault continued, 11 Group became stretched, but Air Vice-Marshal Park maintained his policy of intercepting raids with small formations of fighters. This was to preserve his fighters, preventing them being destroyed *en masse*. It was also in compliance with Air Chief Marshal Dowding's System of Air Defence. So a situation developed where the pilots of 11 Group were hotly engaged, sometimes several times a day, while those in 12 Group, including Bader, awaited the call to scramble – which rarely came. And so, while Spitfires and Hurricanes were embroiled in deadly combat over southern England, 12 Group had no choice but to continue their monotonous convoy patrols, occasionally intercepting small formations or lone German bombers.

They were, however, providing an essential reserve. Fighter Command had always to maintain a substantial reserve to counter any threat to the Midlands and industrial north. Indeed, the System also provided for 12 Group's fighters to move forward and patrol 11 Group's airfields in the event of Park's fighters being committed to battle further south. This was essential, as the airfields had to be kept secure. To Bader, however, this scenario was unacceptable – as he was just not getting the action he so craved.

On occasions, 242 Squadron flew south, to Duxford, and there awaited the call to reinforce 11 Group. On 30 August 1940, 242 was patrolling at 15,000 feet over North Weald as a precautionary measure, as sixty He 111s of I/KG 1 and II/KG 53 had crossed the coast north of the Thames. The bombers soon separated, I/KG 1 heading for the Vauxhall Motor Works and aerodrome at Luton, while II/KG 53, being the larger formation, flew west towards the Handley Page Aircraft Factory at Radlett. Vectored towards II/KG 53, 242 Squadron soon saw the biggest raid it had so far encountered – this aerial armada being nothing like the small numbers of bombers encountered thus far.

Attacking from the tactically advantageous up-sun position, 242 Squadron engaged. After the 'party', Bader's pilots claimed seven Me 110s destroyed and three probables, and five He 111s destroyed. It was an impressive score, leading to numerous congratulatory signals. Air Vice-Marshal Leigh-Mallory telephoned 242 Squadron's CO personally, during which conversation Bader put to his AOC that if he had commanded more fighters then the execution would have been greater. Leigh-Mallory agreed. Arrangements were then made for 242 Squadron to operate in future out of Duxford, Bader leading a formation comprising not only his Canadians but also the Czech 310 Hurricane Squadron and the Spitfires of 19 Squadron.

The theory was that a wing of thirty-six 12 Group fighters would sally forth to engage the enemy over 11 Group. The problem was that Bader's thinking was flawed from the outset: contrary to his belief, 242 had not in fact been the only RAF fighter squadron engaged on 30 August 1940, in the action which convinced him that had he more fighters available then greater damage to the enemy would have been achieved. In reality, the Hurricanes of 11 Group's 1, 56 and 501 squadrons were all also engaged and scored kills, as did the Spitfires of 222 Squadron.

Indeed, recent research indicates that only two Me 110s were definitely destroyed by 242 Squadron. Although the confused air fighting involved makes it impossible to be certain regarding any further claims, Bader's pilots certainly did not destroy anything like the number with which they were credited without question. The reason for this is because the greater the number of fighters engaged, the more confused the fighting becomes – several pilots, for example, can attack the same enemy aircraft oblivious to the presence of their comrades, meaning that a particular enemy aircraft can become multiplied on the balance sheet. Nonetheless, both Leigh-Mallory and Bader were convinced that large fighter formations were the way forward – as it certainly was from the purely parochial perspective of getting 12 Group into the battle.

On 7 September 1940, Bader led the so-called 12 Group or Duxford Wing into action for the first time. On this day the Germans began bombing London round-the-clock. Bader's Duxford fighters were ordered off to patrol North Weald and sighted another large enemy formation. Bader's Wing, however, was below the raiders and forced to climb over the Thames Estuary at full throttle to intercept. While at this tactical disadvantage, the 12 Group fighters were attacked by Me 109s.

Under such an attack it proved impossible to maintain cohesion. The Wing split up, Bader's pilots attacking individually. Once more, 12 Group's claims were impressive on paper: twenty destroyed, five probables and six damaged, offset against two Hurricanes destroyed (one pilot killed), and three more damaged. Again, though, research indicates that the destruction of but six enemy aircraft can definitely be accredited to the Duxford Wing, representing an over-claiming factor of 3:1. This pattern continued throughout the Battle of Britain – providing a completely false impression of the value of 'Big Wings'.

At the time, however, the tactic found favour with influential officers of air rank and politicians, all keen to defeat the Luftwaffe in the most efficient possible way. Bader's Duxford Wing – to which was soon added another two squadrons – appeared to provide that opportunity. By comparison, 11 Group's claims were much smaller – suggesting that mass fighter tactics were more effective than the tactics employed by Air Chief Marshal Dowding's System and used by 11 Group's Air Vice-Marshal Park.

The evidence, now that historians have had the time and opportunity to cross-reference combat claims with actual German losses, confirms that 11 Group's claims were fairly accurate while 12 Group's claims were highly inflated. This means that the tactics used by Dowding and Park were entirely correct – while those propounded by Douglas Bader – a comparatively junior and inexperienced squadron leader – supported by his AOC Air Vice-Marshal Leigh-Mallory – were not. Nonetheless, the 'Big Wing' concept, howsoever flawed, would soon underpin RAF fighter strategy, which would, along with Douglas Bader, impact on the story of Johnnie Johnson.

Fighter Command's greatest test during the Battle of Britain came on 15 September 1940 when the enemy launched repeated raids on London and other targets. On that day, away from the frontline, Johnnie flew three training flights – but there was a problem, one threatening to destroy his flying career:

> At this time my right shoulder was causing me a great deal of anxiety. I had a minor crash at Sealand during training which had wrenched it badly. The old rugby injury collar-bone break was very sore. I had to be careful when donning my parachute and tightening the cockpit harness. I started packing the shoulder with cotton wool, but that wasn't all: the fingers in my right hand sometimes felt cold and life-less. The Spitfire's fabric ailerons, however, dictated that stick pressure in a dive was so high that it took a lot of strength to control the aircraft. This aggravated the shoulder injury.
>
> Whenever I could I held the control column in my left hand, usually used for controlling the throttle, but if the CO or Ken Holden, the senior pilot officer, gave me dog-fight practice I had

also to use my right hand – as this was very much a two-handed business. I began landing the aircraft with my left hand, but this was dangerous because sometimes you needed a quick burst of throttle to ease her down. It was a difficult situation. Every day the condition got worse, while daily acceptance by the veterans increased – the formal "Johnson" had by now changed to the warmer "Johnnie", which stuck with me ever after. So I didn't want to see the doctors for fear of being taken off the squadron.

I remembered that before playing rugby again I had a course of massage and heat-treatment, and hoped revisiting this might do the trick. So I took a young doctor into my confidence in the Mess. He kindly took me to sick quarters for an off-the-record examination – but while this was in progress the Senior Medical Officer (SMO) appeared. They both told me to continue packing the shoulder with cotton wool, and were charming – but I went away with an uneasy feeling. The following day Billy Burton sent for me and, in frosty silence, accompanied me to the Station Commander's office. He, Stephen Hardy, told me that the doctors had reported the fact that I was supposedly suffering from an unspecified affliction to the right shoulder. As this had clearly not troubled me during training, he was considering transferring me to instruct on genteel Tiger Moths at an EFTS. Disaster. The matter was clearly distasteful to him and I immediately realised why: I was suspected of being "lacking in morale fibre" (LMF) – cowardice, effectively. Hardy gave me a choice: become an instructor or go under the knife. Without hesitation I said "When can I go into hospital, sir?" This broke the tension.

Arrangements were made immediately for Johnnie to have treatment at the RAF Hospital in Rauceby, Lincolnshire. Pilot Officer Johnson left for Rauceby on 20 September 1940, undergoing a painful but successful corrective operation soon afterwards. Before leaving Kirton, Squadron Leader Burton had promised to take Johnnie back once he was fit: 'It was a second chance. All I wanted was to live and fight with men like Billy Burton and Ken Holden, so I was very grateful and happy indeed to return to 616 Squadron on 28 December 1940.'

By the time of Johnnie's return to 616 Squadron, much had changed. The Battle of Britain was over, the enemy having been forced to abandon plans to invade England, and its bomber force unable to continue sustaining such heavy losses by day, the weight of attack had shifted to nocturnal operations targeting British cities. Moreover, Dowding and Park were replaced as Commander-in-Chief of Fighter Command, and AOC 11 Group, by Air Chief Marshal Sholto Douglas and Air Vice-Marshal Leigh-Mallory – both new men endorsing wings becoming standard operating procedure, in attack and defence.

During late 1940, they decided on a new offensive policy of 'Leaning into France', taking the war across the Channel to the Germans. These sorties were initially very limited. The first was flown by two Spitfires of 66 Squadron on 20 December 1940, which attacked an enemy airfield at either Berck or Le Touquet on the French coast. The idea was that these operations, called simply *Rhubarbs*, were to be carried out by either single fighters or formations not exceeding six, using low altitude and cloud cover to escape detection. The purpose of *Rhubarbs* was to 'attack and destroy enemy aircraft, or, if impractical, suitable ground military objectives.'

Although the tempo of such operations increased, the RAF fighters failed to draw the Luftwaffe to battle. *Rhubarbs* were therefore used simply for opportunist 'seek and destroy' missions.

On 9 January 1941, five RAF fighter squadrons swept over France in wing formation. The enemy very sensibly failed to respond, German fighter tacticians appreciating full-well that an enemy fighter is only dangerous if intercepted. Nonetheless, these early offensive operations in wing strength, and the fact that home-based fighter squadrons were practising flying together in such formations, provide an indication of what lay ahead.

On 15 January 1941, Flying Officer Hugh 'Cocky' Dundas, one of 616 Squadron's original auxiliaries, was on the board to lead Red Section. At 1342 hours the section was scrambled, with Johnnie flying Red Two, to patrol a convoy passing thirty to forty miles off North Coates. At 15,000 feet over the convoy, the Controller alerted Red Section that an enemy aircraft was approaching from the East. Cleverly, the controller climbed the pair of Spitfires to 16,000 feet and positioned them to attack from out of the sun.

Johnnie's combat report described events: 'The enemy aircraft (E/A) was sighted at about 1420 hours and Red One ordered line astern and dived to attack E/A. The latter went into a steep dive, turning towards the East. As soon as Red One had delivered his attack, I followed in and gave two bursts of five and four seconds, from astern and starboard, allowing for deflection and aiming for the nose of the aircraft. During this time I experienced return fire and broke away at 200 yards to starboard and climbed round to position my second attack. I again opened fire at 300 – 100 yards from the same position as before, and gave a five second burst and broke away to port. This time I experienced no return fire. After breaking away from this attack I lost sight of the E/A and Red One, so returned to base, landing at 1446.'

Back at base, the squadron 'Spy', Flight Lieutenant E.P. Gibbs, credited Flying Officer Dundas and Pilot Officer Johnson with a half share each of a damaged Do 17. Years later, Johnnie added, 'Already, our listening services had intercepted a distress signal from the Dornier to its base in Holland, and it seemed doubtful that it could struggle back to the Dutch coast. As we had not seen it crash into the sea, we couldn't claim it as destroyed or, indeed, probably destroyed. So we had to content ourselves with sharing a "damaged" Do 17.' In his logbook, Johnnie conciliatorily added, 'Believed destroyed'.

Whatever the enemy bomber's fate it had been a significant engagement, given that, as Johnnie wrote, 'this incident marked the beginning of my personal score against the Luftwaffe.' It would be the first of many combats with German aircraft – but the only time Johnnie would engage an enemy bomber. With this experience under his personal belt, and another 16.35 flying hours on Spitfires recorded in his log book that first month of 1941, Johnnie and his fellows in 616 Squadron looked forward to the fast-approaching 'season' of better weather. Little did they know how dramatic the months ahead would be.

In late February 1941 came exciting news: the squadron was moving – south. Johnnie: 'Billy Burton told us that we were going back into the line, and if all worked out we would remain in the south for the spring and summer – which, due to the better weather, was the air-fighting "season" we all looked forward to. Speculation was rife as to our destination: would it be Kenley, Biggin Hill, North Weald or Hornchurch? No. It was Tangmere, a famous fighter station on the South coast, near Chichester and on the Channel coast.'

On 26 February 1941, 616 Squadron flew south, relieving 65 Squadron at Tangmere. The two units exchanged aircraft: in a secondary role, 616 Squadron had flown obsolete Spitfire Mk IAs of Battle of Britain vintage, while at Tangmere 65 were operating the new Mk IIA. By this time Johnnie had flown 10.40 operational hours and had fired his guns in anger: 'We very much welcomed the prospect of getting stuck in from Tangmere. Billy told us that if the Germans resumed their air assault on Britain we would "have our work cut out". If not, then we would be taking the war to them, across the Channel.'

Throughout this winter, Fighter Command was reorganised for the coming season. At the end of 1940, Fighter Command's strength was 1,243 pilots. By early 1941 that figure had increased to 1,665. The huge Castle Bromwich

Aircraft Factory was also producing Spitfires at full capacity. Spitfire production in 1940 had totalled 1,246, increasing to 2,518 in 1941. Moreover, the Hurricane's deficiency as a high-altitude fighter meant that the Spitfire now ruled supreme: the Hawker fighter was withdrawn for use in secondary roles at home or service overseas, while the Spitfire became the mainstay.

As previously mentioned, Fighter Command's new masters, Douglas and Leigh-Mallory, were keen to encourage an offensive outlook; as the latter said, 'We have stopped licking our wounds. We are now going over to the offensive. Last year the fighting was desperate. Now we are entitled to be cocky.' Although Fighter Command's new chiefs were exponents of mass fighter tactics, there was no formal arrangement as to who would lead each wing. During these early sorties wings were generally led by the senior squadron commander, but there was no dedicated wing leader or wing mentality.

Leigh-Mallory recognised that change was required. On 7 December 1940 he short-listed suitably experienced officers for appointment as the first formal wing leaders. This new post would be officially known as 'Wing Commander (Flying)'. Each sector station was to have its own wing of three Spitfire squadrons, under the overall control of the wing commander. When 616 Squadron arrived at Tangmere, the new Wing Leader had yet to be appointed.

On 17 March 1941 there was exciting news. Johnnie: 'Billy Burton strode into dispersal with some momentous news. "Listen, you chaps. Fighter Command is appointing wing commanders to lead the wings. The first two have been selected. 'Sailor' Malan is going to Biggin and Douglas Bader is coming here! He has just been on the blower and will fly with us. We shall be in the thick of all the scrapping. He arrives tomorrow".'

The other Spitfire squadrons at Tangmere were 145, commanded by Squadron Leader Jack Leather, and Squadron Leader John Ellis's 610. Although collectively 145, 610 and 616 squadrons were known as the Tangmere Wing, they were not actually based at that sector station but dispersed at nearby satellites: 610 and 616 at Westhampnett (now Goodwood), and 145 at Merston. Sergeant Alan Smith was at readiness in 616 Squadron's dispersal on 18 March 1941:

> I heard the roar of a Spitfire. It dived low, climbed, did a half-roll, lowered its undercarriage while inverted, rolled out, side-slipped and made a perfect landing. Out of the cockpit climbed Wing Commander Douglas Bader – who walked with his distinctive gait into our dispersal. He announced himself, said that he would be leading the Tangmere Wing, and would do so

with 616 Squadron. He knew Flying Officer Cocky Dundas and Pilot Officer Johnnie Johnson, and said: "You'll be Red Three, Cocky, and you, Johnnie, will be Red Four." Looking around he caught my eye and said "Who are you?"

"'Sergeant Smith, sir."

"'Right, you fly as my Red Two and God help you if you don't watch my tail!" I couldn't believe my ears! It was like God asking me to keep an eye on heaven for him!

The following day, Wing Commander Bader led his new Wing on a Channel Sweep. Johnnie flew as Red Three in 'Dogsbody Section', recording in his log book 'Look Out!!', which requires explanation. Johnnie:

We flew in line-astern formation, each squadron in sections of four. Cocky was Red Two, Bader, of course, Red One, and Pilot Officer "Nip" Heppell brought the rear as Red Four. As we climbed across the Channel I spotted three 109s only a few hundred feet higher than us, travelling in the same direction. They hadn't seen us and 145 Squadron, which was higher than the 109s, were perfectly positioned to attack. I should have calmly reported over the R/T the number, type and position of the enemy. I did not do so.

In my excitement I simply shouted "Look out, Dogsbody!" (this being the Wing Commander's radio call sign). This represented a warning of utmost danger, of being bounced. The other pilots took rapid evasive action, breaking in all directions. Our tight formation was reduced to a shambles, and we returned to Tangmere individually. Bader came into our dispersal and angrily said "Now who's the clot who shouted 'Look out'?" I admitted that it was me. "Very well. Now tell us what we had to 'Look out' for?"

"Well sir, there were three 109s a few hundred feet above …"

"Three 109s! We could have clobbered the lot! But your girlish scream made us think there were fifty of the brutes behind!" This humiliating public rebuke hurt deeply, but it was well justified. Douglas, though, was always quick to forgive and gave me an encouraging grin as he stomped out of dispersal. It was a lesson in leadership that I never forgot.

PROLOGUE

Due to Johnnie's error, the Tangmere Wing's first operation had been a dismal failure. Suffice to say that in future the warning 'Look out!' would not be used.

On 15 April 1941, the Tangmere Wing once more swept high over the Channel, escorting bombers back from France, but did not meet the enemy. Such operations would become an increasing feature of the Tangmere Wing pilots' lives. Fighter sweeps over north-west France had failed to provoke the required reaction from the Luftwaffe, so it was therefore decided to add a small force of light bombers, usually Bristol Blenheims of 2 Group, Bomber Command, to the formation. Raids were to be mounted against such targets as enemy airfields, power stations and railway marshalling yards, meaning that the German fighters would have to respond. The RAF bombers were to be escorted by great numbers of Spitfires, which would, it was hoped, destroy the enemy en masse.

Codenamed *Circus*, these were complex operations requiring much planning and coordination at Fighter Command level, because fighters from 10, 11 and 12 Groups were involved. This was in direct contrast to the so-called *Rhubarb*, which could simply be initiated by a flight commander. In the *Circus* scenario, fighter wings were given specific responsibilities:

Close Escort	This wing literally surrounded and remained with the bombers at all times.
Escort Cover	A wing which protected the Close Escort.
High Cover	Positioned to prevent enemy fighters bouncing the Close and Escort Cover wings.
Top Cover	Geographically restricted to the bombers' route, but with a roving commission to sweep the sky in advance of the main formation.
Target Support	Independently routed fighters flying directly to and covering the target area.
Withdrawal Cover	Fighters supporting the return flight, by which time escorting fighters would be running low on fuel and ammunition.
Fighter Diversion	A wing, or even wings, engaged on a diversionary sweep to keep hostile aircraft away from the target area during 'Ramrod' operations – similar to a Circus but aimed at the destruction of a specific target, as opposed to a mere nuisance raid.

Circus No 1 had been undertaken on 10 January 1941. Two RAF fighters were lost; although there were several claims for the destruction of German fighters, not one Me 109 was in fact lost. It was an ominous start to the 'Non-Stop Offensive' and would soon become an all too common scenario. Involving so many aircraft, which milled around over Beachy Head as squadrons and wings formed up, these huge formations became appropriately known as 'Beehives'.

Johnnie: 'As previously explained when I began flying Spitfires no-one seemed to want to talk about tactics. Although Billy Burton had given basic advice after our first flight together, even he later rebuked me for talking "shop" in the Mess when once I began inquiring how best to get on the tail of a 109. Douglas Bader, though, was different.'

On the morning of 5 May, Johnnie was at dispersal preparing to fly a couple of air tests, when Wing Commander Bader came in. After a discussion concerning the relative night-flying merits or otherwise of the Spitfire and Hurricane, the Wing Leader decided that he and Pilot Officer Johnson would slope off on an impromptu flight across the Channel to 'see if we can bag a couple of Huns before lunch'.

A few minutes later the two Spitfires were streaking towards France in line abreast formation. Johnnie: 'I could hardly believe that I was flying as wingman to this legendary pilot. But there he was only a few yards away with his initials and wing commander's pennant painted on the fuselage of his Spitfire. There would be no reporting mistakes this time.'

Unfortunately Group Captain Woodhall, now station commander and 'Boss Controller' at Tangmere, vetoed the unauthorised sortie, recalling 'Dogsbody' who 'uttered a strong oath that stung the ears of the Controller and startled the WAAF plotters!' Instead, Wing Commander Bader taught Johnnie, at last, how to get on the tail of a 109. Indeed, as Johnnie later wrote, according to the 'Wingco', there was 'Nothing to it. A piece of cake!'

Tactics remained a vexing issue for Fighter Command. Johnnie: 'We had seen, of course, the Germans flying in these loose, strung out, line abreast formations, like a pack of hunting dogs, lean and hungry looking.' On the evening of 7 May 1941, Bader and his pilots sat up late into the night, discussing tactics in the Mess.

Flying Officer Cocky Dundas: 'We expressed our dissatisfaction with formations adopted in the past … the half pints went down again and again while we argued the toss. I suggested that four aircraft flying in line abreast, each at least fifty yards apart, could never be bounced from behind. The Spitfires on the right would cover the tails of those on the left, and vice versa.

PROLOGUE

No enemy could therefore approach unseen, but if attacked the formation could break upwards, one pair to port, the other to starboard. This was, of course, similar to the tactics worked out by Mölders in Spain.'

The following morning found Dundas nursing a hangover at breakfast, when in strode the teetotal Bader in rude health: 'He told me that he had been thinking about my idea and had decided to try it out. I nodded in weak agreement but was somewhat startled when Bader added "This morning"!'

Soon two pairs of Tangmere Spitfires – Squadron Leader Woodhouse and Sergeant Maine (of 610 Squadron), and Wing Commander Bader flying with Flying Officer Dundas, were prowling up and down, 26,500 feet above the Dover Strait. This effort to provoke an attack from marauding 109s succeeded: six 109s of *Stab*/JG 51 – coincidentally led by Major Werner Mölders himself – approached the Spitfires from the rear and at the same height. Bader held the formation together, the Spitfires continuing as if blissfully unaware of their peril. At what he considered the optimum moment, Bader shouted 'BREAK!'

The Spitfires immediately whipped round, the pilots nearly blacking out so steep was the turn. Dundas levelled out but there was no sign of the enemy. The break had, in fact, been mistimed, as the manoeuvre was intended to reverse the antagonists' position. Suddenly Dundas's Spitfire was raked with cannon fire. Thick smoke immediately engulfed the cockpit, the Spitfire pilot taking what evasive action his damaged aircraft permitted. Protected by Woodhouse, Dundas limped back across the Channel to the coastal airfield at Hawkinge, where he safely crash-landed. It was the second and final time that Dundas was shot down by the so-called 'Father of German Air Fighting'. Sergeant Mains had fared better, damaging a 109 before hitting a second which crashed in the sea.

After Dundas had been collected from Hawkinge in the station Magister, Bader held a debrief at Westhampnett. In spite of Dundas having been shot down, the benefits of the line abreast formation in helping to prevent a surprise attack had been proven. The fault on this first occasion lay with the Wing Leader, who had mistimed the break. Consequently one or more enemy fighters remained behind the Spitfires when they had come out of their turn. The Tangmere Wing now started experimenting with this idea, which was soon perfected and known as either the 'Finger Four' or 'Crossover Four', on account of the fact that in plain view the fighters occupied positions similar to the fingers of an outstretched hand, and because the pairs literally crossed over in the turn. Eventually the formation was adopted universally throughout Fighter Command – for which Wing Commander Bader and

Flying Officer Dundas can take credit. This was a significant development so far as RAF air fighting was concerned. As Johnnie said: 'We all learned a tremendous amount from Douglas, who had the ability to impart his knowledge and ideas on tactics.'

On 15 May 1941, Johnnie flew his usual mount, Spitfire P7837, on a 'Nuisance Raid – France' with Squadron Leader Burton. This was essentially a *Rhubarb*, during which operation the Spitfire pilots swept over the French coast at 4,000 feet. Their intention was to find a suitable ground or sea target, but no suitable opportunity presented itself. The Germans had been quick to implement counter-measures against these sorties. Decoy targets were common, the unwary suddenly being fired upon by numerous well-hidden flak guns.

The Spitfire's mighty Merlin engine was cooled by glycol, stored in a small tank, which, together with the all-important radiator was exposed to ground-fire during these low-level attacks. Just one rifle-calibre machine-gun bullet hitting either the glycol tank or radiator resulted in a seized engine. *Rhubarbs*, therefore, were hazardous indeed.

Johnnie: 'I loathed *Rhubarbs*. In addition to the obvious dangers presented by flak, we had also to consider letting down through low cloud over France – with no accurate knowledge of the cloud base's altitude. To me the great risk seemed disproportionate to whatever damage we inflicted on these stupid raids.' Indeed, many pilots and experienced leaders were lost on *Rhubarbs*, including such aces as Wing Commander Paddy Finucane and Flight Lieutenant Eric Lock, both of whom were killed, and Wing Commander Robert Stanford Tuck, who was captured. These were all men that Fighter Command could ill afford to lose, so it is unsurprising that Johnnie viewed *Rhubarbs* with a 'deep, dark hatred'.

June 1941 saw the tempo of fighting increase. On 17 June, Johnnie was leading Yellow Section and intercepted a pair of Me 109Fs. Although both Johnnie and his Yellow Two opened fire, the combat was inconclusive and no claims were made. This was just a few days before Hitler's surprise invasion of the Soviet Union on 22 June 1941. By this time only two German fighter groups remained on the Channel coast, the rest sent eastwards for the next assault.

Oberleutnant Adolf Galland was *Kommodore* of JG 26, based in and around the Pas-de-Calais, and Major Wilhelm Bathasar's JG 2 was located near Cherbourg. Between them these *Kanaljäger* were responsible for defending the Nazi empire from the Netherlands south to the Bay of Biscay. In overall command was the *Kanalfront Jagdfliegerführer* General

Theo Osterkamp – who had achieved the rare distinction of having already become an ace in both world wars. Osterkamp's brief to both of his *Kanaljagdgeschwadern Kommodoren* was simple: inflict maximum losses upon the enemy while preserving their own limited forces in the process.

Although due to the presence of bombers RAF Circus operations could not be ignored by the Luftwaffe, there were no targets in France of sufficient importance to lure the enemy into a rash charge. Instead the German fighter pilots had the luxury of only engaging when they possessed the tactical advantage of height, sun and numbers. Moreover, unlike during the fighting over England of the previous summer, it was now the RAF fighter pilots undertaking a two-way sea crossing and operating at the limit of their range. Also, when shot down or forced to land in France for whatever reason, more often than not RAF pilots were captured. The Germans, like Fighter Command's pilots fighting over England in 1940, were operating over territory they controlled.

The new Me 109F was an excellent fighter aircraft. It had redesigned radiators, flaps and ailerons, and a slightly greater wingspan than its predecessor, with rounded wingtips, a streamlined nose profile, and no tail-struts. The DB601E used a lower octane fuel, producing a top speed of 390 mph at 22,000 feet, a service ceiling of 37,000 feet and a range of 440 miles. An ingenious nitrous oxide injection pack, known as 'Ha Ha', was added to the Me 109F-2, giving exceptional emergency boost. The *Franz* was armed with two-engine mounted MG 17 machine guns, their rate of fire being 1,180 rounds per minute, and provision was made for a single 15 or 20mm cannon to fire through the propeller boss. Such weapons had a much slower rate of fire however. That of the 15mm Mauser MG 151 cannon, for example, was 700 rounds a minute. The benefits of cannon had long been recognised by the Luftwaffe, and in this respect the RAF had only recently caught up.

After 19 Squadron's trials and tribulations with the unsuccessful cannon-armed Spitfire Mk IB during the Battle of Britain, the difficulties of mounting cannon in the Spitfires thin wing section had at last been overcome. As a precaution against stoppages, and to provide pilots with the benefit of both the higher rate of fire provided by machine guns, which required less accuracy to be effective, and hard-hitting but slower firing cannon, the Spitfire Mk IIB was armed with four machine guns and two cannons.

Johnnie: 'My job as one of two wingmen in Dogsbody Section was to protect the remainder of the Section from a flank or stern attack.

Sergeant Alan Smith was the other wingman and did likewise from his position on the port side. My head, therefore, was usually turned to the left or strained right round so that I could watch our vulnerable rear We had little idea of what lay ahead, but knew from radio chatter and our own manoeuvres when Bader was wading into a gaggle of 109s. We had to watch our leader, and resist the natural instinct to personally break formation to chase a 109. The Squadron's total of kills and the scores of certain individual pilots increased. A combination of my role as a wingman and the fact that it seemed as if there just wasn't time to single out an opponent from the maelstrom of fighters as we jockeyed and vied for an opening, meant that I was slow to score. It was an acutely frustrating time.'

Alan Smith, Dogsbody Two, adds: 'If you cannot be a leader then be the best possible number two, and that means several things. The protection of your leader is paramount. His job is to shoot down the enemy while you must protect his tail. Stick to him like glue. Be constantly alert for the "Hun in the sun". Early warning equates with longer life. The "Finger Four" formation introduced by Douglas Bader was ideal for cross-over and a vast improvement on previous formations.' As Johnnie said, 'We number twos were actually serving a privileged apprenticeship under the Master himself.'

On 26 June 1941, Wing Commander Bader led his Wing to Redhill in Surrey, from which sector station the Tangmere Spitfires participated in Circus 24. Crossing the French coast at Gravelines, 'Dogsbody' was warned of twenty-four Me 109s to the south-east. Simultaneously these 'bandits' were sighted in front of the Wing, in the usual loose line abreast formation. The 109s then turned, climbing to attack 610 Squadron from the rear.

Immediately the battle was joined, Johnnie, flying as Dogsbody Four, reported that after the initial contact 'I became detached from Wing Commander Bader's Section at 15,000 feet, through watching three Me 109s immediately above me. I saw them dive away to port and almost immediately afterwards saw an Me 109E coming in from my starboard side, which flew across me about 150 yards away, turning slightly to port. I immediately turned towards the E/A and opened fire, closing to 100 yards. After two one second bursts, the E/A jettisoned hood, rolled over and the pilot baled out, his parachute opening almost immediately. I then broke away as there were other E/A about. I estimated I was over Gravelines when I was in combat.... I then joined up with Flying Officer Scott of 145 Squadron and landed at Hawkinge for re-fuelling.'

Johnnie's victory – his first 100 per cent confirmed personal kill – had been witnessed by several pilots of 145 Squadron. He had fired 278 machine-gun rounds (his Spitfire Mk IIA, P7837, having no cannon). His victim was one of five Me 109Fs lost that day by JG 2.

On 1 July 1941, the Tangmere Wing swept inland over France as far as Béthune, another long flight of an hour and a half. Johnnie attacked a 109F that was 'squirting' at Dogsbody Section but saw no apparent result. Three days later the Wing orbited St Omer on Circus 32. Johnnie reported having 'heard Wing Commander Bader instruct his Section to break. As I was immediately behind, I broke away steeply to the left and after two tight turns saw an Me 109E firing at me, but no fire hit me owing to the tightness of the turn. The E/A broke away to port in a fairly medium dive. I followed him down and gave him a short burst and observed glycol coming out of it. I then broke away as there were other 109s in the vicinity, finally returning to base at 1600.' Having expended eight-nine rounds, Johnnie was credited with a 'damaged'.

On 4 July 1941, Johnnie scored again. On that day the Tangmere Wing provided Target Support to six Stirlings bombing Lille. Johnnie:

> I was Yellow Three returning from Lille… when I became separated from the rest of the Section. I then joined up with Wing Commander Bader and Sergeant Smith. We were attacked separately by 109s on the journey out and on one occasion I saw a 109E about 300 yards behind us, coming up to deliver an attack. I shouted to the Section to break and did a steep climbing turn to the right.
>
> The E/A climbed straight up and I came down from his starboard side, underneath him. I pulled the stick back and delivered an attack into the underside of the E/A at about seventy-five yards range (slight deflection). Just as I was on the point of stalling, the E/A exploded into bits with black and yellow smoke coming off it. I later re-joined Wing Commander Bader and Sergeant Smith, and we were attacked again. After breaking up, as instructed by Wing Commander Bader, I saw a 109 going down with glycol flames and black smoke pouring out. This was probably the E/A Wing Commander Bader attacked as I did not shoot at it.

On 8 July 1941 the Tangmere Wing flew Target Support once more, this time on Circus 38. Johnnie wrote in his log book, 'One Stirling shot down by ack-ack.' Four Stirlings had split into two pairs, each attacking a different target. The Stirling destroyed was hit by flak on the way out – only two of the crew baled out before their big bomber crashed on houses. Next day, Bader led the Wing on yet another Circus; 616 Squadron was engaged by 109s – Johnnie fired at an enemy fighter during the swift punch-up but made no claim.

Johnnie scored again on 14 July 1941, when the Tangmere Wing flew on Circus 48 to St Omer. A section of 610 Squadron Spitfires were attacked over St Omer without loss, as was 145 Squadron, the CO of which, Squadron Leader Turner, engaged three 109s, damaging one.

Johnnie: 'I became separated from the squadron when over the target so decided to fly with the Beehive during the return flight. When about twenty-five to thirty miles from the French coast and flying at 1,500 feet above and behind the Beehive, I saw three aircraft in line astern to the south-west. I then turned inland, above and behind the three aircraft which I then identified as Me 109Fs. I made a quick aileron turn and attacked number three from below and behind, when I was climbing. I gave a second burst with cannon and machine gun at 150 yards range and saw the tail blown off. The E/A went into an uncontrollable spin. I am claiming this E/A as destroyed. I then broke away as my Number Two had lost me. When over the French coast at 10,000 feet I saw an Me 109E over Étaples, diving steeply. I gave chase. It pulled out at 2,000 feet and flew straight and level. I drew up and gave a short burst at 150 yards range. I thought I saw something break away from the starboard wing of the E/A, but cannot be certain as my screen was covered in oil from the E/A in the first engagement. I therefore make no claim in this second engagement.' The 109 that Johnnie definitely destroyed was probably that flown by *Unteroffizier* R. Klienike of III/JG 26, who was reported missing.

By now Johnnie was an established member of Wing Commander Bader's 'inner sanctum':

> Douglas and his wife, Thelma, rented the "Bayhouse", some five miles from Tangmere and their door was always open to us. About once or twice a week we motored there and always found the Wing's inner-sanctum gathered about our leader. The conversation rarely strayed far from our limited world of fighters and air fighting. Sipping his lemonade, Bader analysed our recent fights, discoursed on the importance of straight shooting, on the relative merits of machine guns and

cannons, on the ability of our opponents (whom he always held in contempt), on the probable destiny of the pilot who flew with his head in the office and of our own dreadful fate should we ever lose sight of him in combat. He was dogmatic and final in his pronouncements – nobody argued with him.

It was a great privilege for us junior officers to be taken into the confidence of a wing commander, and in this fashion the three squadrons were blended into the Tangmere Wing. It was a very exciting and inspiring time down at Tangmere that unique summer. Bader, the great man with both DSO and DFC, I was just a mere pilot officer, but he treated us all as equals. He was a great leader. It was certainly inspirational being led by this dynamic and aggressive man, possessed of incredible energy and drive.

Over France he would be chatting away to "Woody" on the R/T, organising squash courts ready for his return – and this from a man without legs! On some occasions when we were homeward bound from an operation, Bader would get out his pipe, light a Swan Vestas match on the dashboard, and sit there puffing away with the hood open – this while flying an aircraft full of highly inflammable 100 octane petrol! You could see him, sat there, puffing away. Incredible. When he lit up we used to veer away and keep our distance, I can tell you!

Such disregard for danger was perhaps reckless – but served only to raise morale and convince the Tangmere Wing's pilots that their legendary leader was indestructible. Johnnie:

He'd come stomping into dispersal and say to Billy Burton "What are we doing today then, Billy?"

Billy might respond, "Well the Form 'D' [operational order] has come through, Sir, but we're not on it. The other wings are but not us."

Bader would say, "Right, we'll see about that! I'll have a bloody word with 'LM'." He would then personally ring the AOC and, lo and behold, we would be on ops!

The afternoon of 21 July 1941 saw the Tangmere Wing engaged on Circus 55, its second escort mission of the day. After making landfall at Le Touquet, the three squadrons split up and swept independently. Johnnie was flying as Red One, his number two being Sergeant Sidney 'George' Mabbett. Near the target area, 24,000 feet over Montreuil, Johnnie positioned his section to starboard and slightly above and behind Dogsbody Section. Six Me 109s were sighted, flying east. Wing Commander Bader swung his section around so as to attack the enemy fighters from the rear.

Johnnie: 'I then brought my Section slightly below and almost abreast of Dogsbody Section, and at this stage my Number Two was with me. When about 250 yards from the enemy formation I saw Dogsbody Four (Pilot Officer Heppell) open fire at the right-hand 109 – which emitted glycol fumes but continued to fly straight, carrying out gentle swings to port and starboard. Unfortunately I did not hear the order to break and pressed home my attack on the right-hand E/A from 150-200 yards. After two short bursts (eight machine guns) the nose of E/A dropped slowly and it eventually went into a vertical dive, the white glycol fumes giving way to thick black smoke. I then broke away and did not see E/A again. My Number Two was not seen again after this engagement. Very accurate flak experienced when crossing on return journey.' Pilot Officers Johnson and Heppell were credited with a shared probable.

During the evening of 23 July 1941, Wing Commander Bader and the Tangmere Wing were up on yet another Circus, again their second operation that day. From the point of crossing the French coast over Le Touquet, the Spitfires came under constant attack from JG 26 Me 109s. The Spitfires were immediately split up into their fighting pairs. As the usual scrap commenced, another fifty 109s could be seen holding off in the distance, their leader awaiting the perfect moment to join the fray. 610 Squadron's diary records that 'all engagements were terrific dogfights'.

Wing Commander Bader and Flight Lieutenant Dundas – now commander of 616 Squadron's 'A' Flight – shared a 109 destroyed, Flying Officer 'Buck' Casson destroyed another while Pilot Officer Johnson damaged a third. 616 Squadron had scored its fiftieth combat claim in this fight, and the Tangmere Wing's 500th. Johnnie wrote in his log book that there were 'More 109s about than ever before. Wing engaged almost whole time over France.'

On the morning of Monday, 9 August 1941, the teleprinter clattered away at Tangmere. The daily Form 'D' came through from 11 Group HQ detailing the wing's task for that day. This was another complex Circus, No.68, involving many aircraft to Gosnay. The Tangmere Wing was to provide Target Support. Sergeant Alan Smith, Wing Commander Bader's usual 'Dogsbody Two', had a head cold and so was unable to fly. Imminently to be commissioned, and as his name was not 'on the board', Smith prepared to go into London and buy a new uniform. His place as Bader's wingman was taken by a New Zealander, Sergeant Jeff West, a pilot with one-and-a-half Me 109s destroyed and one damaged to his credit.

For this Target Support sortie to Gosnay, 'Dogsbody' Section therefore consisted of:

Dogsbody:	Wing Commander Douglas Bader
Dogsbody 2	Sergeant Jeff West
Dogsbody 3	Flight Lieutenant Hugh Dundas DF
Dogsbody 4	Pilot Officer 'Johnnie' Johnson

Also leading 'Finger Fours' within the 616 Squadron formation of three sections would be the squadron commander, Squadron Leader Billy Burton (Yellow Section), and 'B' Flight's commander, Flight Lieutenant Buck Casson (Blue Section). Across the other side of the airfield, Squadron Leader Ken Holden DFC and his 610 Squadron also prepared for the morning sortie.

Take-off came at 1040 hours, Dogsbody Section leading Westhampnett's Spitfires on yet another sortie into very hostile airspace. Over Chichester, Squadron Leader Holden swiftly maneuvered 610 Squadron into position above and slightly to port of 616. As Target Support, the Wing had no bombers to meet before setting course for France, although the Spitfires were still routed out over Beachy Head. As the wing left Chichester, however, there was no sign of 41 Squadron.

The Beachy Head Forward Relay Station recorded the Tangmere Wing's R/T messages that day. As the wing neared 'Diamond', 41 Squadron had still not appeared. Group Captain Woodhall, at Tangmere, was the first to speak, making a test call:

'Dogsbody?'
'OK, OK.'
Bader then made R/T test calls to the commanders of both 610 and 41, using their Christian names as was his usual practice:
DB: 'Ken?'
Ken Holden (KH): 'Loud and clear.'
DB: 'Elmer?'

There was no response from Squadron Leader Gaunce of 41 Squadron, which provoked an acerbic remark from the Wing Leader to 'Woody'. Unable to wait, 616 and 610 Squadrons set course for France and Gosnay, adopting their battle formations in the process. Still climbing, Wing Commander

Bader waggled his wings insistently, indicating that 'Dogsbody 3', Flight Lieutenant Dundas, should take the lead. Dundas slid across, tucking his wing tip just two or three feet from Bader's.

From this close proximity, Dundas saw the wing leader mouth two words: 'Airspeed Indicator', meaning that the instrument on Spitfire Mk VA W3185 was unserviceable. The wing had to climb at the right speed to ensure Time on Target (ToT) at the appointed time, which was crucial. Dundas gave a 'thumbs up' and moved forward to lead the Spitfires to France. On the rear of his hand he had fortunately written the time at which the wing was due over the French coast, in addition to the speed which had to be maintained.

Dundas later recalled that the 'sun was bright and brilliant, unveiled by any layer of high haze or cirrus cloud'. Realising that the white cumulus cloud below provided a background which would immediately reveal the silhouettes of any aircraft, Dundas correctly anticipated that under such conditions 'Dogsbody' would wish to climb as high as possible, and so adjusted both his throttle setting and rate of climb accordingly, taking the Spitfires up to 28,000 feet.

Then, more radio messages:

DB   'Ken and Elmer, start gaining height.'
KH   'Elmer's not with us.'
      Unidentified, garbled voice on the R/T, believed to be Squadron Leader Gaunce.
DB   'Elmer from Dogsbody. I cannot understand what you say, but we are on our way. You had better decide for yourself whether to come or go back.'

Following the last radio transmissions, at least the Wing was now aware that more Spitfires were bringing up the rear, even if some distance away. The Spitfires cruised over the Channel, towards France, with 610 Squadron above and behind 616. Dundas led the wing over the French coast right on cue (although there is conflicting evidence regarding whether the coast was crossed south of Le Touquet, known as the 'Golf Course', or Boulogne, slightly further north). This crucial timing observed, Bader accelerated ahead and informed Dogsbody Three over the R/T that he was resuming the lead. The Spitfires' arrival over the coastal flak belt was greeted by dangerous little puff-balls of black smoke, making the formation twist and turn. 'Beetle' then called Dogsbody, informing Wing Commander Bader that the Beehive itself was 'on time and engaged'. As the Spitfires forged inland, therefore, some distance behind them the bombers and various cover wings were now bound for France and action.

PROLOGUE

Slightly below the condensation trail level, a 610 Squadron pilot reported seeing contrails 'above and to our left'. Squadron Leader Holden consequently led the squadron higher still while 'Beetle' (B) reported:

B   'Dogsbody from Beetle. There are 20 plus five miles to the east of you.'

DB   'OK, but your transmitter is quite impossible. Please use the other.'

B   'Dogsbody is this better?'

DB   'Perfect. Ken, start getting more height.'

KH   'OK, Dogsbody, but will you throttle back? I cannot keep up.'

DB   'Sorry Ken, my airspeed indicator is u/s. Throttling back, and I will do one slow left-hand turn so you can catch up.'

KH   'Dogsbody from Ken, I'm making "smoke" [contrails] at this height.'

DB   'OK, Ken, I'm going down very slightly.'

'Beetle' then advised 'Dogsbody' of more bandits in the vicinity. 616 Squadron's Flying Officer Roy Marples (RM) saw the enemy first: 'Three bandits coming down astern of us. I'm keeping an eye on them, now there are six.'

DB   'OK'.

B   'Douglas, another 12 plus ahead and slightly higher.'

RM   'Eleven of them now.'

DB   'OK, Roy, let me know exactly where they are.'

RM   'About one mile astern and slightly higher.'

B   'Douglas, there is another 40 plus 15 miles to the north-east of you.'

DB   'OK Beetle. Are our friends where they ought to be, I haven't much idea where I am.'

B   'Yes, you are exactly right. And so are your friends.'

RM   'Dogsbody from Roy. Keep turning left and you'll see 109s at nine o'clock.'

DB   'Ken, can you see them?'

KH   'Douglas, 109s below. Climbing up.'

By this time, 616 and 610 Squadron had progressed into a very dangerous French sky indeed, Beetle having already reported some seventy-two bandits, representing odds which outnumbered the Spitfires by nearly 3:1. Clearly this was not to be an uneventful sortie. Tension mounted, the Spitfire pilots switched on their gunsight reflectors and gun buttons to 'Fire'.

Anxiously they searched the sky, an ever-watchful eye being kept on the 109s positioned 1,000 feet above the Wing, waiting to pounce. Bader himself dipped each wing in turn, scrutinising the sky below for the 109s reported by Ken Holden.

DB   'I can't see them. Will you tell me where to look?'
KH   'Underneath Bill's section now. Shall I come down?'
DB   'No, I have them. Get into formation. Going down. Ken, are you with us?'
KH   'Just above you.'

As Dogsbody Section dived on the enemy, Flight Lieutenant Casson followed with three other aircraft of 'B' Flight. Dogsbody Three, Flight Lieutenant Dundas, had 'smelt a rat' in respect of the *schwarm* of 109s that Dogsbody Section was now rapidly diving towards. Finding no targets to the Section's right, Dogsbody Four, Pilot Officer Johnson, skidded under the section and fired at an Me 109 on the left. By this time the whole of Dogsbody Section was firing, although Dundas, still unhappy and suspecting a trap, had a compelling urge to look behind. Suddenly Pilot Officer 'Nip' Heppell shouted over the R/T: 'Blue Two here. Some buggers coming down behind, astern. Break left!'

The Spitfire pilots hauled their aircraft around in steep turns. The sky behind Dogsbody Section was full of Me 109s, all firing – without Heppell's warning the Spitfires would have been instantly nailed. As the high 109s crashed into 616 Squadron, Squadron Leader Holden decided that it was time for his squadron to join the fray and reduce the odds. Informing Flight Lieutenant Denis Crowley-Milling of this decision, Holden led his Spitfires down to assist. Flight Lieutenant Casson, following Bader's section, was well throttled back to keep his flight together.

Also attacking from the rear, Casson managed a squirt at a *Rotte* of 109s. Flying Officer Marples, number three in Casson's section, then shouted a warning of even more 109s diving on the wing, while Squadron Leader Billy Burton urged the Spitfires to 'keep turning' – thus preventing the 109s (which could not out-turn a Spitfire), getting in a shot. Suddenly the air became a totally confused maelstrom of twisting, turning fighters:

'BREAK! FOR CHRIST'S SAKE BREAK!'

The Spitfires immediately 'broke' – hard. Johnnie:

There was this scream of *"Break!"* – and we all broke, we didn't wait to hear it twice! *Round.* Then a swirling mass of

109s and Spitfires. When I broke I could see Bader, still firing. Dundas was firing at the extreme right 109. There was some cloud nearby and I disappeared into it as quick as possible! I couldn't say how many aircraft were involved, suffice to say a lot. It seemed to me that the greatest danger was a collision, rather than being shot down, that's how close we all were.

We had got the 109s we were bouncing and then Holden came down with his section, so there were a lot of aeroplanes. We were fighting 109Fs, although there may have been some Es amongst them. There was an absolute mass of aeroplanes just 50 yards apart, it was awful. I thought to myself "You're going to collide with somebody!" I didn't think about shooting at anything after we were bounced ourselves, all you could think about was surviving, getting out of that mass of aircraft. In such a tight turn, of course, you almost black out, you cannot really see where you are going. It was a mess. I had never been so frightened in my life, never!

Chased by three Me 109s, the closest just 100 yards astern, Pilot Officer Johnson maintained his tight turn, spiralling down towards the safety of a nearby cloud into which his Spitfire dived with over 400 mph on the clock. Pulling back the throttle and centralising the controls, the altimeter stabilised, but the Spitfire stalled. Beneath the cloud, Dogsbody Four recovered control. Having requested and received a homing course for Dover, Johnnie headed rapidly for England. Over the R/T, Pilot Officer Johnson could still hear 616 and 610 Squadrons' running battle:

'Get into formation or they'll shoot the bloody lot of you!'
'Spitfire going down in flames, 10 o'clock.'
'YQ-C [616 Squadron Spitfire]. Form up on me, I'm at three o'clock to you.'
'Four buggers above us,' this from Heppell.
'All Elfin aircraft (616 Squadron) withdraw. I say again, all Elfin aircraft withdraw.'
'Use the cloud if you're in trouble,' from Billy Burton.
'Are you going home, Ken?', also from Burton.
'Yes, withdrawing,' from Holden.
'Ken from Crow. Are you still about?'
'I'm right behind you, Crow.'

'Are we all here?'

'Two short.'

' Dogsbody from Beetle. Do you require any assistance?'

'Beetle from Elfin Leader. We are OK and withdrawing.'

'Thank you Billy. Douglas, do you require any assistance? Steer three-four-zero to the

coast.'

The silence from 'Dogsbody' was ominous, as Flight Lieutenant Casson remembered:

> I watched Wing Commander Bader and "A" Flight attack and break to port as I was coming in. I was well throttled back in the dive, as the other three had started to fall behind and I wanted to keep the flight together. I attacked from the rear, and after having a squirt at two 109s flying together, left them for a single one which was flying inland alone. I finished nearly all of my cannon ammunition up on this boy, who finally baled out at 6,000 feet, having lost most of his tail unit.
>
> The other three "B" flight machines were in my rear and probably one of the lads saw this. I climbed to 13,000 feet and fell in with Billy Burton and three other aircraft, all from 'A' Flight. We chased around in a circle for some time, gaining height all the while, and more 109s were directly above us. Eventually we formed up in line abreast and set off after the Wing. Billy's section flew in pairs abreast, so I flew abreast but at about 200 yards to starboard. We were repeatedly attacked by two Me 109s which had followed us and were flying above and behind. Each time they started diving I called out and we all turned and re-formed, the 109s giving up their attack and climbing each time.
>
> About fifteen miles from the coastline I saw another Spitfire well below us and about half-a-mile to starboard. This machine was alone and travelling very slowly. I called up Billy on the R/T and suggested that we cross over to surround him and help the pilot back as he looked like a sitting duck. I broke off to starboard and made for the solitary Spitfire, but then, on looking back for Billy and the others, was amazed to see them diving away hard to the south-west for a low layer of cloud into

which they soon disappeared. I realised then that my message had either been misunderstood or not received.

Like a greenhorn, I had been so intent upon watching Billy's extraordinary disappearance to the left, and the lone Spitfire to my right, I lost sight of the Me 109s that had been worrying us. I remember looking for them but upon not discovering their position assumed that they had chased Billy instead. I was soon proved wrong, however, when I received three hits in both fuselage and wing. This occurred just as I was coming alongside the lone Spitfire, which I could not identify as it was not from Tangmere. I broke for some cloud at 5,000 feet, which I reached but found too thin for cover, and was pursued by the 109s.

I then picked out two more 109s flying above me and so decided to drop to zero feet, and fly north and cross the Channel at a narrow point as I was unsure of the damage sustained and the engine was not running smoothly. I pressed the teat and tried to run for it, but the two Me 109s behind had more speed and were rapidly within range, while the other two flew 1,500 feet above and dived from port to starboard and back, delivering quick bursts. Needless to say I was not flying straight and level all this time!

In the event I received a good one from behind, which passed between the stick and my right leg, taking off some of the rudder on its way. It passed into the petrol tank but whether the round continued into the engine I do not know. Petrol began leaking into the cockpit, oil pressure was dropping low, and with the radiator wide open I could smell the glycol overheating.

As the next attack came, I pulled straight up from the deck in a loop, and on my way down, as I was changing direction towards the sea, my engine became extremely rough and seized up as white glycol fumes poured forth. There was no option but to crash-land the aircraft. I tried to send "Dogsbody" a hurried message, then blew up the wireless and made a belly landing in a field some 10 miles south of Calais. The 'Goons', having seen the glycol, were decent enough not to shoot me up as I was landing, but circled about for a time and gave my position away to a German cavalry unit in a wood in a corner of the field. One of the pilots waved to me as he flew overhead, and I waved back just before setting fire to the aircraft.

Due to the petrol in the cockpit, and because I was carrying a port-fire issued for this purpose, igniting the aircraft was easy. No sooner had I done this than a party of shrieking Goons armed with rifles came chasing over and that was the end of me! What eventually happened to the lone Spitfire which I went to help out I have no idea. As the 109s followed me, I assume that he got away okay, I certainly hope so.

Flight Lieutenant Casson had been the victim of *Hauptmann* Gerhard Schöpfel, *Gruppenkommandeur* of III/JG26:

My IIIrd *Gruppe* attacked a British bomber formation, after which my formation was split up. With the British on their homeward flight, I headed alone for my airfield at Ligescourt, near Crécy. Suddenly I saw a flight of Spitfires flying westwards. I attacked them from above and after a short burst of fire the rear machine nosed over sharply and dived away. While the other aircraft flew on apparently unaware, I pursued the fleeing Spitfire as I could see no sign of damage.

The British pilot hugged the ground, dodging trees and houses. I was constantly in his propwash and so could not aim properly. Because of the warm air near the ground my radiator flaps opened and so my speed decreased, it thus took me a long time to get into a good firing position. Finally I was positioned immediately behind the Spitfire and it filled my gunsight. I pressed the firing button for both cannon and machine guns, but – click! I had obviously exhausted my ammunition in the earlier air battles.

Of course the British pilot had no way of knowing this and I still wanted to strike terror in him for so long as he remained over French soil. I thus remained right behind him, at high speed. Suddenly I was astonished to see a white plume of smoke emit from the Spitfire! The smoke grew denser and the propeller stopped. The pilot made a forced landing in a field east of Marquise. I circled the aircraft and made a note of the markings for my victory report, watched the pilot climb out and waved to him. Just before being captured by German soldiers, he ignited a built-in explosive charge which destroyed the centre-section of his aircraft.

I returned to my field and sent my engineering officer to the site to determine the reason for the forced landing. He found, to my amazement, that the Spitfire had taken a single machine-gun round in an engine cylinder during my first attack. Had I not pressed on after running out of ammunition, therefore forcing the pilot to fly at top speed, he would probably have reached England despite the damage. Just a few weeks before, in fact, I myself had made it back across the Channel after two of my engine's connecting rods had been smashed over Dover. On this occasion over France, however, the British pilot, a flight lieutenant, now had to head for prison camp while I recorded my thirty-third victory.

Returning to the French coast, Pilot Officer Johnson saw a lone Me 109 below. Suspecting it to be one of the three which had chased him into the cloud just a few minutes before, Johnnie anxiously searched the sky for the other two: the sky was clear. From astern, Dogsbody Four dropped below the 109 before attacking from its blind spot, below and behind. One burst of cannon shells sent the enemy fighter diving earthwards emitting a plume of black smoke. Pilot Officer Johnson came 'out of France on the deck, low and fast', his Spitfire roaring over waving civilians, just feet above their fields.

At the coast, German soldiers ran to their guns, but in a second the fleeting Spitfire was gone. Climbing over the Channel, Dogsbody Four realised that something might have happened to Wing Commander Bader: 'As I was crossing the Channel, Group Captain Woodhall, who obviously knew that there had been a fight from the radar and R/T, repeated "Douglas, are you receiving?" This came over the air every five minutes or so. I therefore called up and said, "It's Johnnie here, Sir, we've had a stiff fight and I last saw the Wing Commander on the tail of a 109." He said, "Thank you, I'll meet you at dispersal".'

The silence from 'Dogsbody' over the R/T clearly meant one of two things, either that his radio was unserviceable, or he had somehow been brought down. Air Marshal Sir Denis Crowley-Milling, then a flight commander in Ken Holden's 610 Squadron, recalled: 'The greatest impression I have is the silence on the R/T. Douglas always maintained a running commentary. Had the worst happened? The colourful language and running commentary had suddenly ceased, leaving us all wondering what had happened. Was he alive or dead? Had his radio failed? I know we were above thick cloud on the way home and asked the Tangmere Controller to provide a homing bearing for us to steer. This was way out in accuracy, however, and unbeknown to us we were flying up the North Sea, just scraping in to Martlesham Heath with hardly any fuel remaining – it was indeed a day to remember!'

So confused had been the fighting, so numerous the aircraft in this incredible maelstrom over St Omer, that only Wing Commander Bader himself had the answers to the questions regarding his present state and whereabouts. After the first downwards charge, Dogsbody found himself alone after flattening out at 24,000 feet. In front of him were six 109s flying in a line abreast formation of three pairs. Solo, Bader knew that he should leave this enemy formation and adhere to the instructions issued to his pilots: get out and get home. He considered these 109s to be 'sitters' however, and in a split-second greed won over discipline and good judgement.

Alone over France, Wing Commander Bader stalked the middle *Rotte*. He later reported, 'I saw some more Me 109s. I arrived amongst these, who were evidently not on the lookout, as I expect they imagined the first formation we attacked to be covering them. I got a very easy shot at one of these which flew quite straight until he went on fire from behind the cockpit – a burst of about three seconds.'

As two 109s curved towards him, Dogsbody broke right, violently, although anticipating, with some bravado, that his course would take him between a pair of 109s. Suddenly something hit Spitfire 'DB'. Due to the close proximity of the enemy aircraft, Bader assumed that he had collided with a 109. The Spitfire went completely out of control, diving earthwards, its control column limp and unresponsive. As he looked behind, Bader's impression was that the entire fuselage aft of the VHF aerial had gone, although he was later to report that it was 'probably just the empennage'.

At 24,000 feet, 'Dogsbody' was unable to consider escape due to the lack of oxygen outside the cockpit at that height. His dilemma, however, was that the doomed fighter was already travelling more than 400 mph, so would soon be subjected to forces so great that baling out would become impossible. Yanking the canopy release mechanism, the hood was sucked away, the cockpit immediately being battered by the airflow. Without legs, would he be able to thrust his body upwards to get out? As he struggled to get his head above the windscreen, he was nearly plucked out of the cockpit, but halfway he became stuck – the rigid foot of his artificial right leg jamming in the cockpit, the grip vice-like. Ever downwards the fighter plunged, the pilot helpless and continuously battered by the rushing wind, half in and half out of his crashing aeroplane.

Desperately gripping his parachute's 'D' ring, Douglas Bader struggled furiously to get out. Eventually, at about 6,000 feet, the offending artificial leg's restraining strap broke. Free at last, the pilot was plucked out into mid-air; as the Spitfire continued its dive, he experienced a moment of apparently floating upwards. That terrible buffeting having thankfully ceased, in the silence he was able to think. Hand still gripping the 'D' ring, he pulled; there was a slight delay before the parachute deployed and then he was really was floating, gently to earth beneath the life-saving silk umbrella.

At 4,000 feet Wing Commander Bader floated through a layer of cloud, emerging below to see the ground still far below. Alarmed by the roar of an aero-engine, he saw a Me 109 fly directly towards him, but the bullets he must have half expected never came as the enemy fighter flashed by just fifty yards away.

It may surprise many people to know that such a parachute descent, made due to enemy action or some other mishap while flying actively, was often the first a pilot would actually make, there being no formal parachute training. Consequently, Bader had never before had to consider the practicalities of landing with artificial legs, or indeed one such leg, as he drifted earthwards. Having had some minutes to ponder this matter, suddenly French soil rushed up to meet him and he hit the ground hard, in an orchard near Blaringhem, to the south-east of St Omer. For Wing Commander Douglas Bader, the air war was over; his period of operational service had lasted eighteen months.

Johnnie recalled the scene back at Westhampnett: 'Group Captain Woodhall was waiting for me on the airfield, and when Dundas, West, Heppell and the others came back the consensus of opinion was that the Wing Commander had either been shot down or involved in a collision.' In his log book, Johnnie wrote that on this penetration over France there had been 'more opposition than ever before'. Squadron Leader Burton's log book recorded: 'Had a bad time with 109s on way out and had to get into cloud.'

As the clock ticked on, it became clear from fuel considerations that the two Spitfires reported missing during the radio chatter over France were unlikely to return to Westhampnett. Reasoning that if flying damaged machines, the pilots might land at one of the coastal airfields, Tangmere telephoned each in turn, receiving negative responses from all.

Douglas Roberts was a Radio Telephone (Direction Finding) Operator at the Tangmere 'Fixer' station which was, perhaps oddly, located on West Malling airfield in Kent: 'We were told that Wing Commander Bader was missing and so listened out for several hours. Our system was basic when compared to modern equipment today, but nevertheless very efficient. The aerial system was a double dipole which, when rotated, would indicate either a true bearing or a reciprocal. Despite our diligence, nothing was heard from "Dogsbody".'

Had either of the two missing pilots reached mid-Channel, then there was an excellent chance that they would be picked up by air-sea rescue. If their dinghies had drifted closer to the French coast then it was more likely that the Germans would get to them first, unless their positions could be discovered and a protective aerial umbrella established. Consequently Dundas, Johnson, Heppell and West were soon flying back over the Channel, searching. At Le Touquet, Dundas led the section north, parallel to the coast and towards Cap Griz-Nez. Avoiding flak from various enemy vessels, especially near the port of Calais, a steep turn at zero feet returned the Spitfires to Le Touquet. At one point Heppell broke away to machine gun a surfacing submarine, but otherwise the only item to report was an empty dinghy sighted by Sergeant West.

To Johnnie, that empty, life-saving, rubber boat was somehow symbolic of their fruitless search. With petrol almost exhausted, the section landed at Hawkinge. No news had yet been received of either missing pilot. Immediately the aircraft were refuelled, the 616 Squadron pilots took off, intending to head back across the Channel to France. Shortly after take-off, however, Group Captain Woodhall cancelled the sortie, fearing that a second trip was too risky as the enemy might now be waiting. Swinging round to the west, the Spitfires flew back to Westhampnett. For Hugh Dundas the thought of Bader dead was 'utterly shattering'. He drove back to Shopwyke House 'alone and utterly dejected'. Back at the Mess, he and Johnnie shared a whole bottle of brandy. Despair had overtaken the inner sanctum.

When on 14 August 1941 the Red Cross announced that Wing Commander Bader was a prisoner, there was euphoria at Tangmere. Group Captain Woodhall broadcast the news over the station tannoy. Sir Denis Crowley-Milling remembered that 'The loss of Douglas Bader had left us all stunned. A few of us, including Dundas and Johnson, were with Thelma Bader in their married quarters at Tangmere when the telephone rang. After speaking, Thelma came back to join us and very calmly said "Douglas is safe and a prisoner".'

The Germans had been unable to decide for certain which of their pilots had brought down this famous British war hero. Wing Commander Bader's personal view, so shocking was the damage to his Spitfire, was that he had collided with an enemy machine. Indeed, collision, due to the very great number of aircraft engaged, was Johnnie's greatest fear in this action. The reality, however, was quite different, and I would refer the reader to Flight Lieutenant Casson's account.

As we have seen, 'friendly fire' was not uncommon, and aircraft identification in such fast-moving and high stress combats was often fraught with danger. The enemy lost but one 109 in this fight, the tail of which was not shot off; the only other aircraft down was Bader's Spitfire. There can be no doubt that in the heat of the moment Flight Lieutenant Casson – an experienced and able fighter pilot – made a perfectly understandable mistake. Buck died, convinced that he had destroyed a 109 that fateful day – but the evidence confirms that was unlikely to have been the case. So it was, therefore, that the 'Master's' active war against the Germans was not abruptly ended by the shells of a German fighter – but by those from another Spitfire.

Johnnie:

When Douglas was shot down it really was his own fault. He was tired, ready for a rest. Leigh-Mallory had asked him to come off ops, as "Sailor" Malan, leader of the Biggin Hill Wing, had already done so, having recognised in himself the signs of strain. Douglas wouldn't go, of course, and so the AOC agreed to let him stay on until the end of the season, the end of September when the weather started failing. Flight Lieutenant Peter MacDonald MP, our Adjutant, who had served with Douglas since 1940, also recognised in him the signs of strain. He insisted that Douglas and Thelma should join him on a week's golfing at St Andrews. They were, in fact, booked to go on 11 August. Douglas was exhausted. Irritable. And he couldn't see things quickly enough in the air.

On the day in question, when Ken Holden sighted the 109s and Bader was unable to see them, he should have let Ken come down and attack as he suggested. In not allowing this he lost us six, maybe even seven seconds, by which time the high 109s were down on us. But of course Douglas was a bit greedy and would not, therefore, allow this. As he couldn't personally see the enemy, Douglas should have stayed put and covered Ken Holden while he attacked. Douglas was greedy, especially towards the end. Someone had seen a 109 down here and Bader would go after it with thirty-six Spitfires bounding after him, it was chaotic.

Indeed, once the Wing Leader's ASI went unserviceable shortly after take-off, he should not simply have allowed Flight Lieutenant Dundas to lead the formation across the Channel in his stead, but turned back. After battle had been joined, Wing Commander Bader had swiftly been separated from the rest of his section. At that point he should also have headed home – as per his own instructions. The whole sequence of events represented a catalogue of errors, but the prevailing press-on attitude was so typical of the man. There were also other problems generated by Bader's style of leadership. It was wrong for him to exclusively lead the Wing at the head of 616 Squadron. Johnnie:

> Yes, that was a mistake. I can understand to a degree that Douglas wanted people around him upon whom he knew he could depend, and that by flying with the same pilots in Dogsbody Section we all got to know the form pretty well, what he required and how the thing worked, and so on and so forth. What I think he should have done was perhaps kept the same wingman, but rotated the squadrons with whom he flew. While we of 616 and 610, based at Westhampnett obviously saw Douglas daily, and we of 616 had a particularly close relationship with him of course as he flew with us and operated from our dispersal, those squadrons based at Merston, firstly Stan Turner's 145, then Gaunce's 41, never saw him. The other problem was that by always leading the Wing at the head of 616, Billy Burton never got to lead his own Squadron – and he, a Cranwell Sword of Honour man – was a very capable leader indeed. Once I heard Burton say "Now Douglas, could you fly with 'B' Flight today?" You can imagine where this is going, can't you? Douglas responded "No Billy, I am not flying with *fucking* 'B' Flight today, I want Sergeant Smith, Cocky and Johnnie with me and that's an *order*!" And that was that.

Nonetheless, Bader had left an inspirational and indelible impression on many of his young pilots – not least Johnnie: 'You can learn 90 per cent of the skills required for leadership, man management, being straightforward with your subordinates and so on, but that last 10 per cent, which wins the hearts and minds, is an indefinable gift given to but a few, such as the gift of a great artist or writer. Bader had that gift, make no mistake.'

The experience gained that summer was, as Air Marshal Sir Denis Crowley-Milling said, 'unforgettable' and 'stood us in good stead'. Johnnie: 'Douglas Bader had shown us the true meaning of courage, spirit, determination, guts. Now that he was gone it was our job to follow his example and signposts pointing the way ahead.'

Under Wing Commander Bader's leadership and guidance Johnnie had gained both inspiration and experience. His combat reports have a common feature: whenever possible he was getting in as close as possible before opening fire, and attacking from below and behind – the blind spot. Johnnie had flown numerous operational sorties over France, participating in complex operations and frequently engaging the enemy. His apprenticeship was coming to an end. On his Spitfire, Johnnie had painted 'Bader's Bus Company - Still Running'. And so, with Bader a prisoner, the war continued for Pilot Officer Johnson and the Tangmere Wing.

On 12 August 1941, Johnnie was transferred from 'A' to 'B' Flight, now commanded by Flight Lieutenant Darling following Buck Casson's enforced departure. Johnnie flew Spitfire W3437 on a Target Support sweep to Gosnay, the Tangmere Wing acting as Cover Wing that afternoon, protecting the withdrawal of Hampdens returning from Le Trait. On 14 August 1941, Johnnie joined 616 Squadron on an 'offensive patrol after bombing operations in Boulogne'.

In his log book he wrote: 'Attacked Me 109F. No result. Poor shooting'. Five days later, the Tangmere Wing provided Close Escort to Blenheims bombing Longuenesse. This, however, was a Circus with a difference, because an 82 Squadron Blenheim also dropped spare artificial legs for Wing Commander Bader by parachute. Johnnie's log book simply recorded 'Tin legs dropped by parachute SW of St Omer'.

Johnnie: 'Bader was replaced as Tangmere Wing Leader by a man called Woodhouse, but he wasn't in Bader's league as a leader.' On 21 August 1941, Johnnie claimed an Me 109 probable on a Circus to Béthune. It was a bad day for the Tangmere Wing and 610 Squadron in particular: over Hazebrouck 'A' Flight was bounced by 4/JG 26, four out of six Spitfires being shot down. Amongst those who failed to return was Flight Lieutenant Crowley-Milling – who escaped over the Pyrenees back to England.

The final day of August was a busy day for Johnnie. His first flight was a 'Wing escort to HM destroyer operating off French coast'. Next the wing flew a sweep to St Omer, 'B' Flight attacking 'about twenty Me 109s', but Johnnie made no claim. The final sortie was close escort to Blenheims 'attacking Trait-en-La-Seine'. Johnnie also wrote of that sortie in his log book that 41 Squadron provided top cover but lost another pilot.

The 616 Squadron diarist concluded that the month had been 'a disappointing one from the operational point of view, owing to poor weather conditions. Although sixteen offensive sweeps were carried out over France, their effectiveness was in several cases hampered by too much cloud, making it difficult for the Wing to keep together. Wing Commander Bader DSO (and Bar) DFC, and Flight Lieutenant Casson were shot down on 9 August and are now prisoners of war. This was a serious loss to the RAF, the Wing and the Squadron.' Fighter Command had lost a total of 108 fighters. The combined losses of JG 2 and 26 were just eighteen – a loss ratio of 6:1 in the enemy's favour.

On 4 September 1941 the Tangmere Wing provided cover over the Channel for bombers returning from Mazingarbe. Johnnie and Sergeant West, of 'A' Flight, both attacked the same Me 109E, claiming it as probably destroyed. Johnnie: 'We are talking about the period immediately after Bader had been brought down, by which time I had been in the Tangmere Wing for some time, certainly all that spring and summer, and I had shot down at least four enemy aircraft. Soon after Bader disappeared I was awarded the DFC and made up to flight lieutenant on the same day, which I think was one of the highlights of my career, when the CO told me that I had got the DFC, together with a chap called "Nip" Heppell from Newcastle. Another pilot called Jeff West from New Zealand had got the DFM, and then the Squadron Commander said "Oh, and by the way, I'd like you to take over 'B' Flight". My feet, I don't think, touched the ground for about two days, a feeling of great elation to have these two things. Winning the DFC and being promoted means that you are at last out of your apprenticeship and were now an experienced flight commander with upwards of 100 offensive sweeps under your belt.'

PROLOGUE

Johnnie's next big fight came on 21 September 1941, while escorting Blenheims to Gosnay. The top cover wings failed to make the rendezvous. Johnnie's combat report described the events that took place at 1515 hours, just inland of and 20,000 feet above Le Touquet:

> I was Blue One, leading my Flight … I was flying at 20,000 feet and shortly after crossing the French coast at Le Touquet we were engaged by at least thirty 109s which dived to attack my Section from above and behind. I broke my Section to the left and after maneuvering for position attacked a 109F with cannon from quarter astern and slightly below, closing from 200 – seventy yards.
>
> I observed pieces falling away from the port wing and wing root and then broke to starboard as another 109 was coming down on me. On completing my turn I saw a parachute just opening at approximately the same position in which I had seen the 109. This was also seen by my Number Three, Pilot Officer Smith, and this aircraft is claimed as destroyed. I then lost Pilot Officer Smith and as the Beehive had long since disappeared into France I decided to work my way out as there were several 109s about who seemed anxious to destroy me. I spun and spiraled down to sea level with my pursuers getting in an occasional shot.
>
> When about ten miles off Le Touquet at nought feet I saw an E/A come in from astern. And waited until he was almost within range before I carried out a steep climbing turn to the left. He pulled up to attack and I distinctly saw four streams of machine-gun fire and one of cannon, but his aim was unsteady and I wasn't hit. As I straightened out I saw another 109F just ahead of me – I opened fire and closed in from the quarter astern again, firing a long steady burst of cannon, recalculating my deflection as I closed to about fifty yards. E/A climbed steeply, stalled, and as I broke away, I saw him fall on to his back and then into the sea – this engagement taking place between sea level and 1,000 feet. This E/A is claimed as destroyed. There were still two 109s about and although I could out-turn them they seemed to possess a greater speed and caused them to abandon their attack. They eventually gave up the chase when about ten miles South of Dover.

This was great shooting: two 109s definitely destroyed. These kills also made Johnnie's tally six enemy aircraft destroyed (not counting those shared, damaged or probably destroyed) – making him officially an 'ace', such status being achieved upon a fighter pilot's fifth victory.

On 30 September, the award of Johnnie's DFC was gazetted: 'This officer has participated in forty-six operational sorties over enemy territory and has destroyed at least four hostile aircraft. Flying Officer Johnson has at all times shown great courage.' Back home, Johnnie's brother, Ross, recalled that 'the folks were as proud as punch'.

On 1 October 1941, Squadron Leader Burton was rested, after what had been a long spell on operations, and posted to 11 Group HQ as 'Squadron Leader Tactics'. As CO of 616 Squadron, Burton was replaced by a New Zealander, Squadron Leader Colin Falkland Gray DFC. Johnnie: 'Colin was a very able and successful fighter pilot, but he did not have the same qualities of leadership as Billy Burton did, he was rather a rough, aggressive, sort of man.' Five days later 616 Squadron's tour at Tangmere concluded. By this time Flight Lieutenant J.E. Johnson DFC had flown 183.40 operational hours and destroyed six enemy aircraft. The conclusion of 616 Squadron's tour at Tangmere was the end of a profound experience for Johnnie.

At Kirton, back in 12 Group, 616 Squadron, Johnnie recalled: 'Settled down to a winter of training new pilots, of convoy patrols off the East coast, a little night-flying over Hull and the industrial cities which were being bombed during that winter, but we couldn't do much from a Spitfire because of its limited vision at night and it was a tricky aeroplane to land at night because of that narrow undercarriage. Our Honorary CO was a man called Lord Titchfield, all auxiliary squadrons had honorary COs, and he had a big estate not far away at Welbeck Woodhouse which had one of the best pheasant shoots in the country. He knew that some of us were very keen on shooting, so every week or so four or five of us were invited to shoot at Welbeck, which was very enjoyable, and I loved every moment of it myself. As I say, we trained a lot of pilots, we sent a lot of pilots overseas, got a lot of new ones to replace them, and trained them too.'

The monotony of training flights was broken on 8 November 1941 when 616 Squadron formed a wing with the Canadian Spitfire squadrons 411 and 412 operating out of West Malling in 11 Group on Circus 110. This was Fighter Command's last Circus of 1941, but was a disaster. Two targets were attacked, a distillery at St Pol and the railway repair works at Lille. The sun favoured the Luftwaffe, which also hampered the Beehives forming up. The 12 Group Wing flew as the second rear support wing.

Incredibly the formation was led by Wing Commander Douglas Scott AFC, a 33-year-old without any combat experience. His formation reached the French coast in good order but had to orbit over Dunkirk, as it was too early. Heavy flak caused the formation to break up, at which point II/JG 26 fell on the Spitfires. Three Canadians of 412 Squadron were shot down, and the 'Wingco' also failed to return: his last radio message was, 'I guess I'm too old for this boys.' This ill-fated operation indicated the folly of Fighter Command's strategy throughout 1941: seventeen Spitfires were lost, fourteen pilots being killed. This disaster marked the end of the 'season'.

Significantly, *Hauptmann* Joachim Müncheberg's II/JG 26, which had taken such a toll of 12 Group Wing fighters on Circus 110, was equipped with a new fighter. After this action Flying Officer Heppell reported that the enemy fighters engaged were not 109s but had radial engines. All agreed that this new enemy machine was superior to their own Spitfire Mk V in every respect. The new menace in the sky was the Focke-Wulf 190, appropriately known by the Germans as the 'Butcher Bird'.

The 190 had first appeared in small numbers during September 1941. The radial engine caused confusion, and the possibility of a superior new German fighter was at first dismissed by RAF intelligence, which stated it more likely to be a Curtiss Hawk (some airworthy examples of which had been captured by the Germans in 1940). In October, however, cine-gun camera film definitely confirmed that this was no obsolete Hawk but was indeed a potent new enemy fighter.

The FW190 was powered by a 1,700 hp BMW 801D-2, fourteen-cylinder, radial engine. This provided a maximum speed of 312 mph at 19,500 feet; with a one-minute override boost it could accelerate to over 400 mph. The 190's operating ceiling was 35,000 feet, and it could climb to 26,000 feet in twelve minutes. Furthermore, it was extremely manoeuvrable. By comparison, the Spitfire Mk VB, with which Fighter Command's squadrons were most commonly equipped at this time, could reach 371 mph at 20,000 feet, but could not operate much above 25,000 feet (359 mph), and took some twenty-five minutes to reach that height. The Spitfire Mk V was essentially a Mk II airframe coupled with a more powerful Rolls-Royce Merlin 45 engine. Initially the Mk V was seen merely as a stop-gap, a fighter with better high-altitude performance than the Mk II.

By October 1941, over 100 FW190s had been delivered, and began engaging on an increasing basis. Initially, however, the first pilots to fly the new fighter, II/JG 26, were forbidden from operating further than the French coast for fear of being brought down over or close enough to England for a 190 to be captured and examined by the British. The German pilots were impressed with the 190s rate of roll and acceleration, but significantly it was unable to out turn a Spitfire Mk V

On 23 December 1941, Flight Lieutenant Dundas was promoted to squadron leader and left 616 Squadron, of which he was the last surviving original member still serving with the unit. Johnnie: 'Yes, I missed Cocky, of course. He went off to command 56 Squadron, which was starting to fly the new Hawker Typhoon. Although this later proved an excellent ground-attack aircraft, initially there were a lot of problems caused by carbon monoxide leaking into the cockpit – which led to fatalities. Cocky had to sort all this out, and it couldn't have been an easy job.'

Times they were now a-changing, and Johnnie's time to really shine was fast approaching. Having now explored Johnnie's experience to date, we move on to his previously unpublished 1942 diary, with extra commentary – which can now be read and understood in context.

PART II

The 1942 Diary

By the end of 1940 Hitler's plans to seize aerial supremacy over southern England as a prelude to a seaborne invasion had been thwarted by Fighter Command's victory in the Battle of Britain. Thereafter, Germany's aerial attack had switched to the night-bombing of British cities, until Hitler turned eastwards, invading Russia on 22 June 1941. On the wider stage, fighting had erupted in the Western Desert, and Yugoslavia and Greece also fell. Then, on 7 December 1941, the Japanese attacked the American fleet at Pearl Harbor in an undeclared act of war, at last bringing the United States into the war on the Allied side.

So far as the air war over north-west Europe was concerned, during 1941, in a reversal of the Battle of Britain scenario, Fighter Command had adopted an aggressive posture, taking the war across the Channel to the Luftwaffe. This had not gone well however, with heavy losses of pilots and leaders of irreplaceable experience. Of great concern was the new German fighter, the FW190, which completely outclassed the Spitfire Mk V, restricting the radius of Fighter Command's penetrations. As Johnnie said: 'The 190 drove us back to the coast.' Nonetheless, these operations were an important means of demonstrating Britain's offensive outlook to the Soviet leader, Stalin, and an attempt, albeit unsuccessful, to divert German units from the Eastern Front – where Hitler's advance had stalled at the gates of Moscow.

The Soviets were strongly urging the western Allies to open the Second Front – but this was not yet an option, as certain events in 1942 would confirm. In Britain, the worst of German air attacks had subsided, and it really remained a question of holding out while awaiting men and materiel to pour in from the United States, resources which would, one day, make the Second Front a reality. By night, RAF Bomber Command was actively pursuing a strategic bombing campaign – for which support would soon be forthcoming from the Americans. In the meantime, it was a matter of Britain continuing to weather the storm and remain in the war.

This, then, in summary, is the backdrop to the year in which Johnnie wrote his diary, which begins with a breakdown of 616 Squadron's pilots. His daily entries are supplemented by my commentary, greatly assisted by reference to Johnnie's personal Pilot's Flying Log Book and combat reports, and the Operations Record Books of 610 and 616 Squadrons. For those interested in such detail, the serial numbers of the particular Spitfires flown by Johnnie appear in brackets.

616 (Fighter) Squadron, AAF.
Sqn Ldr Gray DFC & Bar.

'A' Flight	'B' Flight
F/Lt. Heppell DFC.	F/Lt Johnson DFC.
P/O Murray.	P/O Beecham.
P/O West DFM.	P/O Bower.
P/O Ollivier.	P/O Sanderson.
P/O Langie.	P/O Ware.
P/O Smith.	P/O Crofts.
P/O Gunn.	

As previously stated, the New Zealander Colin Falkland Gray DFC had succeeded the popular Billy Burton in command of 616 Squadron. From Christchurch, Colin was a twin. His brother, Ken, successfully volunteered for aircrew with the RAF during 1937, whereas, for medical reasons, it took Colin three attempts to achieve a Short Service Commission, which he did in 1939.

After training, Pilot Officer Colin Gray joined 54 Squadron, flying Spitfires at Hornchurch, in November 1939, but sadly, on 1 May 1940, Ken was killed in a flying accident. During the air battles ahead, over the French coast and subsequent Battle of Britain, Colin became an 'ace', a highly successful fighter pilot with a string of victories to his credit, leading to the DFC being awarded on 15 August 1940. A bar followed in September 1941, in which month he was promoted to squadron leader and given command of 616 Squadron. At that time the Squadron was still at Westhampnett and part of the Tangmere Wing, withdrawing on 6 October 1941 to rest and refit at Kirton-in-Lindsey. It would be at that station that Johnnie's diary began.

Another decorated pilot was also a New Zealander, Pilot Officer Jeff West, from Palmerston North, who had been a civil servant before joining up and arriving on 616 Squadron during spring 1941. Often flying in

Dogsbody Section, Jeff destroyed a number of enemy aircraft that summer, and narrowly escaped death himself when his Spitfire was so badly shot-up that his engine seized on the return flight home, forcing him to bale out over the Channel. Fortunately, a passing fishing boat rescued him. He was awarded the DFM and commissioned on conclusion of the 1941 'season'.

Johnnie's opposite number, the commander of 'A' Flight, Flight Lieutenant Philip Whaley Ellis Heppell – more commonly known as 'Nipple' or 'Nip' – had joined the VR on his eighteenth birthday, 26 June 1939, at Newcastle. The Heppells were a flying family. Nip's father, Philip Forsyth Heppell, was a reconnaissance pilot in the Royal Flying Corps during the First World War; shot down and badly wounded, three fingers were amputated, but this trauma failed to dampen his passion for aviation. Between the wars, Philip was a founder member of Newcastle Aero Club, where he taught both his children, Nip and sister Rhoda, to fly immediately upon leaving school.

When the Second World War broke out, Nip was mobilised, commencing service flying training, while Philip was made a squadron leader and sent to America, there to work on pilot training for the duration; Rhoda became a ferry pilot in the Air Transport Auxiliary, flying a multitude of aircraft types. In September 1940, Nip was commissioned and posted to 616 Squadron, also scoring well the following year with the Tangmere Wing, his DFC being gazetted on 30 September 1941.

With Squadron Leader Gray, Flight Lieutenants Johnson and Heppell, together with Pilot Officer West providing a decorated cadre of combat experience, 616 Squadron's other pilots at this time were replacements gaining experience before the unit returned to a frontline station.

January

Thursday, 1st

Newcastle. Came to Newcastle yesterday with the Nipple – found his house damaged by a bomb and had to stay with some of his friends.

Two or three boozy parties in the Northern New Year Style.

There was no flying on this first day of 1942, owing to bad weather.

Friday, 2nd

Johnnie made no entry on this day, another of no aerial activity due to the weather.

Saturday, 3rd

Valerie up in Lincoln for the evening. The White Hart. Lincoln.

Although the weather remained bad, Johnnie flew Spitfire Mk VB AB266 twice, firstly on a 'Flight exercise' of an hour's duration, secondly on a convoy patrol twenty minutes longer.

Sunday, 4th

Kirton. Dan Barry (who has been with the Squadron almost a year) is posted away from us with effect from tomorrow. We put on a bit of a show for him in the Ladies Room, having for dinner some pheasants and partridge that had been confirmed (i.e. killed) at Lord Titchfield's shoot a few days previously. An excellent evening with the poor Dan as boozed as I have ever seen him, and everyone running around in their pants.

Squadron Leader McKenzie a guest and all went well except for Colin (Gray) who spoke too much.

Had a great stand in the bar with Bob, Derek, the Doc and Mally.

The weather improved sufficiently for new pilots to practice 'circuits and bumps', while others completed cine gun, local and formation practice flights. Johnnie flew a different aircraft, AA923, twice on this day, a weather test followed by formation practice.

A cine gun was a camera which was synchronised with the aircraft's guns to record moving footage. This permitted combats to be viewed and analysed.

The Flying Officer Barry referred to was the Squadron Medical Officer, who was posted to RAF Cosford on promotion to flight lieutenant. Barry was succeeded as MO by Flight Lieutenant D.E. Christie.

Monday, 5th

No entry made by Johnnie. A section was scrambled to intercept an unidentified raid, but nothing was seen, and a pair of sergeants provided convoy escort. Interestingly, Squadron Leader Gray and other pilots paid a morale-boosting visit to address workers producing Spitfires at Birmingham's Castle Bromwich aircraft factory.

Johnnie flew AD266 twice, an 'Air Test' followed by formation practice.

Tuesday, 6th

Kirton. Sgt Waite ('Biff') missing from an operational patrol: he lost his leader (Sgt Strouts) in cloud which was down to 300 feet over the sea and unfortunately was not seen again. I can only conclude that he spun into the drink. Carried out a search for him with Sanderson but did not see any sign except foul weather.

To round off the day Sgt Davidson landed a couple of fields away in my a/c when coming in to land after a night patrol – unfortunately he hit the telegraph wires on the Lincoln Road which threw him on the ground and damaged the a/c which was wrecked completely. He suffered no hurt other than bashing his nose on the reflector sight.

Sergeants Waite and Strouts had been patrolling over a convoy when vectored towards an unidentified raid. The pair of Spitfires climbed into cloud, but only Strouts emerged, who, after a 'good look round', was obliged to return owing to a lack of fuel. 26-year-old Sergeant Maynard Miller Waite of the RCAF was never seen again.

A/c means aircraft, u/c means undercarriage, u/s means unserviceable, r/t means radio telephone, e/a means enemy aircraft.

Johnnie had a busy day, first patrolling Convoy 'Ocean' (AB266), then flying to Scampton, before returning (in AA932) and searching unsuccessfully for Sergeant Waite (AD543).

JANUARY

Wednesday, 7th

No entry. Local flying took place, and a lecture by the Intelligence Officer.

Johnnie did not fly at all on this date.

Thursday, 8th

Kirton. As Davidson is u/s I packed him off to Ford to see Hugh Forman and to collect Robin's (out of Sally) puppy which Cocky had given to me.

A day of 'good flying weather', three convoy patrols were flown along with low-flying attack, cine gun, aerobatic and spinning practice flights.

Johnnie flew three times (AA932), a weather test followed by a climb to 30,000 feet for firing practice, before 'Cine gun and low flying attacks'.

Friday, 9th

Kirton. 6 weeks old today – The Pusher. Davidson rang up from Peterborough so I sent Derek down to collect him and the puppy in the Maggie. Arrived back at Kirton safely with the pup who is a very grand little man. We did not know what to call him so after a few suggestions named him 'the Pusher' because that is the Flight's code call-sign - and after all he's very much RAF.

'Plenty of training' took place, despite snow and sleet showers. Johnnie 'beat up RAF station' for thirty minutes (AB266).

Saturday, 10th

No entry. Two sections were scrambled to intercept an unidentified raid, making no contact, and further practice sorties were completed.

Johnnie flew four times, searchlight cooperation (AB266), formation and cine gun practice (AD543), a convoy patrol (AD543), and formation flying (AD543).

Sunday, 11th

Kirton. Flight released so I arranged transport and took the whole of my flight and a great deal of 'B' Flight into Lincoln. A very good evening – Al Porter distinguished himself by knocking down the doors of the Saracens Head after 10:30 pm.

Low mist prevented all flying except two weather tests, one of which Johnnie flew (AD375).

Monday, 12th

No entry, no flying, again due to weather, but the 'Link trainer was busy'.

Tuesday, 13th

No entry, snow prevented any flying.

Wednesday, 14th

No entry, and no flying, on a day with three inches of snow on the frozen ground. Four pilots were lucky enough to be invited by the Marquis of Titchfield for a day's shooting at Welbeck Woodhouse, while the rest sat an 'intelligence test' in the morning and trained in the gym by afternoon.

Thursday, 15th

Goxhill. After taking off from Kirton I flew to Goxhill and landed there – the runway was only partially cleared but I did not experience any difficult in getting down – the first portion of the runway (south –end) was only half cleared but two hundred yards on the whole width of the runway was serviceable: as the total length of this runway is 1600 yards I considered it safe enough to bring the whole of my pilots over, both operational and u/t. Before leaving Kirton both F/LT Heppell and P/O Bowen landed at Goxhill and considered the runway serviceable. I left Kirton with my flight (9 a/c) at 11.30 hours and ordered the flight to land immediately after me. I touched down and on coming to rest looked round and saw Blue 2 (Sgt McDermid) landing holding off well on the left-hand side of the first portion of the runway, his port wheel struck a glim lamp, this threw him into a heap of snow and the a/c was thrown violently into the air and came to rest upside down, the pilot was released after a few minutes with a bruised and cut eye – otherwise unhurt.

Johnnie's 'B' Flight was ordered to Goxhill, a new aerodrome originally constructed as a bomber station, just south of Hull, for a week or so, to assess its suitability as a fighter station. Johnnie flew over to the temporary base, returning to Kirton having checked it out, then led 'B' Flight back there (AD266).

Friday, 16th

Goxhill. Last evening in Grimsby we ran into some rather good naval types and as a result we were invited to dine with them this evening. First off all of the them came to Garhill for a dekko and tea then made are way to

Immingham Docks and went aboard – HMS *Shelldrake* – a corvette. Our party consisted of four – Sandy, Joe, Bob and I – we had an absolutely cracking evening – beer, whisky, gin, an excellent dinner, beef, steak and chips and pears, with sherry, Burgundy, Kimmel, Madeira, liquer brandy and then back to gallons of beer (Lt Wattams RN).

Once more, there was no operational flying for 616 Squadron, only practice flights, while Johnnie flew twice (AB266), formation practice and visiting Kirton.

Saturday, 17th

Goxhill. All pilots at Dispersal at 0900 hours for flight exercise – took off at 0945, eight aircraft & put in 12 hours – good start. Sgt Tilley sent solo on Mk V, experienced difficulty in landing owing (he says) to the lightness of the ailerons after having flown Mk Is. Also he had a lot of trouble getting down on the runway – parts set came in handy. Decided to send him back to Kirton where I can give him a thorough test. Managed to put in a fair amount of flying today – flight exercise, cine guns, air to ground, aerobatics, formation etc in addition to Readiness. Total 26.15 hours.
To Grimsby with Nip who was over for the evening.

Again, only training flights took place. At Kirton, two sergeant-pilots collided on take-off, seriously damaging both Spitfires. The accident, it was decreed, was attributable to 'gross negligence' on one pilot's behalf, who was consequently grounded. Johnnie flew three times, 'Flight Exercise and Drill' and air-to-ground firing (AB266), and 'Low Flying Attacks' (AA932).

Sunday, 18th

Goxhill. Managed to put seven a/c in the air immediately after lunch, but soon after all a/c were airborne Ops called up and instructed everyone to return. Sgt Bolton came into land on the long runway (north east to south west) and, according to Derek Beecham, made a very fast approach and when down on the runway suddenly swerved to the right, probably through harsh use of the brakes, ran off the runway onto the snowy ground and nosed in – a/c written off – pilot's nose hurt. 12.50 hours today.
    Derek Beecham volunteered for flight commanders post – Middle East.
    Tea Dance in the Mess, scheduled from 4 – 6 pm finished up at 3 am with bacon & eggs, drunk as owls.

In addition to the training flights, two convoy patrols were flown, although Johnnie's three flights were non-operational, formation and cine gun practice before returning from Kirton (AA932), and aerobatics (AB266).

Monday, 19th
Goxhill. Only 2.55 hours flying today – snowstorms etc. Beecham, the Trapper and I fired our guns off North Coates. W/C Walker over here for lunch.

Another day of poor weather, although air-to-ground-firing and formation practice sorties were made, Johnnie flying once on an air-to-ground firing practice sortie (AB266).

Tuesday, 20th
Goxhill. Arrange to take six a/c to Sutton Bridge for air firing but S.B. rang up and cancelled this; fired all our guns into the sea … gun beat up, cine gun, aerobatics and dog fight all carried out. Sandy, when taking off in my a/c (YQ-U), had to hold the thing right down as Derek was beating him up and chipped the props on the runway – landed at Kirton.
    Last night the troops beat up Barton-on-Humber and were accused of pissing in the streets, fighting and assaulting the Police, damaging public property etc. Rang up the Police Inspector and squared things (Baker again).
    An ENSA show came this evening and after the concert the girls came into the Mess – and the whisky started - the Trapper out drank me and after falling face first into the snow I passed out in the mess and even bacon and eggs held under my nose had no effect!
    18.40 hours today.

Snow fell throughout the morning, but despite four inches covering the airfield by afternoon, the relentless programme of training flights continued, Johnnie undertaking firing practice and returning from Kirton (AA932).
    ENSA was the Entertainments National Service Association, providing entertainment for British service personnel, involving many of the period's leading stars, including force's favourite Vera Lynn.

Wednesday, 21st
Goxhill. 4 a/c only serviceable. Bowen, Campbell, Smithson and Davidson airborne at 0930 cine gun etc. Davidson landed and taxied in with flaps down. Self and Davidson carried out a weather test, u/s over the North Sea, landed at Kirton and saw W/C Walker and CO. In Kirton, Friday and

Saturday, Derek Ware and Crappé local formation. Two sections at readiness for dusk state – after take-off we land at Kirton.

Campbell, Smithson, Winter and Strands – day off. Bolton and McDermid sent back to Kirton.

Had a few beers with Bob, Derek and S/L Lantens at East Malton. The landlord being a miserable specimen (he had eight beers with us and never offered to push the boat out) we smartly helped ourselves to the whisky bottle while he was having a pee. Lantens a very good type, ex balloons, nearly ditched the car on the return. Bacon & eggs in front of the ante-room fire on returning at 1305 hours today.

Further training flights were made, including drogue and cine gun firing. Johnnie flew a weather test and returned from Kirton (AA932).

Thursday, 22nd

Goxhill. Dawn Readiness. P/O Bowen and Crofts scrambled for Convoy Patrol. P/O Ware and No. 2 scrambled for X Raid off North Coates. One week today since we arrived at Garhill – should log the 100 mark today. Five aircraft serviceable, no replacements for S or T have arrived yet. Blue section near the Hun but were controlled badly. Ops making a complete balls up. Managed to keep five a/c in the air, cine gun, low level attacks, section reccos etc. W/C Walker arrived at 4 pm in the Maggie to spend the last night with us, and Nip popped in about 6 pm so the party was complete. After dinner we sped down to the "Six Bells" at Barrow on Humber with S/L Lantens and F/Lt Holmes and spend the evening on some excellent draught Worthington, quite the best I have tasted in some years. Left the pub at 11.30, and after bacon and eggs and an amazing game of snooker pool, negotiated the level crossing and on arriving at the site found all beds arse about face, undoubtedly the work of the Sgts. Promptly attacked their quarters and had them on the floor in no time at all. Sgt Smithson last seen amongst the wreckage of their beds and a door. 16 hours 35.

Three convoy patrols were flown, in addition to further air-to-air firing practice, in which Johnnie participated once (AA932).

Friday, 23rd

Weather u/s and unable to return to Kirton so I pushed off in the Standard Van leaving Derek i/c. Had a bloody good bath, changed into a clean shirt and best blue and felt 100 per cent. Expect Mother Booth over tomorrow.

No flying at all owing to bad weather.

Saturday 24th
Kirton. Transport collected Neville from Doncaster, played squash and had a chat, managed to rack up a couple of pheasants for dinner. Had several beers and lost the usual amount of money to the old bugger.

Only one flight was made by 616 Squadron, a 'sector recco'.

Sunday 25th
Kirton. Flight arrived back from Garhill more dead than alive, made my report and to Group Capt. Woolhams (tbc). In the evening Neville, Nip, Derek and I slipped down to the Royal and met old Nat, pushed along to the "Jolly Sailor" and had several more beers and the odd brandy. Lovely night with almost a full moon and Nip decided he was going to fly; tried to persuade him not but the bugger was very obstinate and moved quietly off in my van; rang up Kimby and told him to tell Nip that the CO's instructions were that he was not to take off, Dicky Stafford also refused him permission from Ops – no use, he took off and after beating up the Mess pranged when landing – stalled from about 20 feet. Hell of a row, CO talking about a Court Martial and the Nip walking about as white as a ghost.

On this day, according to the ORB (Operations Record Book), there were no training flights due to winds up to 50 mph, but in his logbook Johnnie recorded having flown low flying practice (AB266) for just fifteen minutes. Flying Officer Derek Beedham, one of the squadron's oldest serving members, left for the Middle East, while Sergeants Tilley and Campbell were posted to India. According to the ORB, 'At 0200 Flight Lieutenant Heppell crashed on landing. He took off without permission. He was uninjured.' This reckless act would have far-reaching consequences for Nip, as we shall see.

Monday, 26th
Kirton. Things very sticky here today over Nip's effort, the CO after his balls without a doubt. Interviewed by Wing Commander Walker about the incident, he's rather browned off with the Nip.

Johnnie flew aerobatics for over an hour (AB266).

During the evening, a signal was received at Kirton notifying 616 Squadron that it was to relieve 266 at King's Cliffe, the Wittering satellite, the latter unit being re-equipped with the new Hawker Typhoon fighter-bomber at Duxford.

Tuesday, 27th

Kirton. Court of Inquiry commenced into the crash, gave evidence, but as I was on the flare path can say very little to help him. Today we heard that we are moving to King's Cliffe, satellite of Wittering, which is a good thing - but I expect the accommodation will be very similar to Goxhill. Master Booth still here and giving me useful thrashing at squash each day.

There was no flying on this day.

Wednesday, 28th

Kirton. Farewell party in the mess with the usual bullshit. Had to make a bit of a speech so told everyone to cut out the talking and get on with the drinking. I am afraid that this time we are not leaving Kirton with the same feeling that was expressed when Billy took the Squadron away in February 1941, to go to Tangmere for the season. Colin Gray has done a great deal of harm and destroyed most of the good work that Billy created. Colin with his uncouth manners and unpleasant personality, although a grand and brave fighter pilot, is not a good CO and has actually put up a few backs here – the CO pissing in the Ante-Room fire in front of the junior officers is not a good thing for discipline and morale. This time last year, the Squadron's personnel were also far different: Ken (Holden) and Mac (Colin MacFie) as flight commanders, with such people to back them up as Cocky (Dundas), Buck (Casson) and, to a lesser extent, Roy Marples and John Brewster, the latter who was shortly afterwards killed in the West of England. In those days there was a lot of Squadron spirit and morale, and such officers as Sanderson, Strouts, Linton and Beecham, although equally good pilots, cannot be compared to the old brigade.

Johnnie's observations regarding Colin Gray – a fighter ace – are illuminating, giving a greater insight into the personality behind the combat record.

By February 1941, Squadron Leader Burton had rebuilt 616 Squadron after its Battle of Britain mauling, and his gentlemanly personality did much to quietly inspire his men. Of course, Tangmere was a premier 11 Group fighter station, on the south coast and directly across the Channel from the Germans in France – so Burton's pilots optimistically looked forward to regular action. King's Cliffe, however, was on the east coast, in 12 Group, and while the opportunity for action existed, it was hardly the same for the incarnation of 616 Squadron led by Colin Gray a year later.

On this day, Johnnie flew three times (AB266), two convoy patrols and a formation/cine gun training flight.

Thursday, 29th

Johnnie made no entry on this day, on which 616 Squadron's ground personnel moved to King's Cliffe in driving sleet and rain, which prevented flying. At the new station, 266 Squadron was found to still occupy the sleeping accommodation for NCOs and airmen, which was not a great start.

Friday 30th

King's Cliffe. The weather being u/s yesterday we flew down to King's Cliffe today to replace 266 (Rhodesian) Squadron. Group Captain Embry DSO (Bars), AFC, ADC, & Wing Commander Jameson DFC (Bar) were there to welcome the Squadron, but what a change from the Ritz atmosphere of the Kirton Mess. Cold huts without lights to sleep in, muck and filth everywhere, and dirty, cold, dispersals. But after we all became settled down in our new quarters, King's Cliffe didn't really seem too bad, and, indeed, as the weather improved and we saw a little spring sunshine, things were very rosy. Basil Embry proved himself to be an ideal Station Commander, although we did not see a lot of him, and Jamie a very stout fellow and a grand Wing Leader. All told, we had some good dos and grand parties both at Wittering and King's Cliffe.

Johnnie's only flight this day was the journey to King's Cliffe.

Saturday 31st

King's Cliffe. Nipple has managed to get himself posted to Malta, with the help of Ken Holden, and left immediately today – with Colin still on his tail – who bloody well meant to have Nip's blood at all costs, but the old Nipple has evaded him smartly! He left today and under the circumstances we couldn't give him much of a party to wish him God's speed. I had a letter from him just before his ship reached Gibraltar and he seems to be in good form, as he has found a good CO and seems to be with a good squadron: he also seemed very pleased with the price of liquor on board HM ships!

During this first half of the Second World War, control of the Mediterranean was bitterly contested, the struggle beginning when Italy joined the Axis in June 1940. The tiny island of Malta was key to that theatre, a crucial staging post for Allied reinforcements and supplies bound for North Africa, where British and Axis troops were engaged. Quickly the Italians had set about attempting to neutralise the island, the aerial defence of which initially comprised three antiquated Gloster Gladiators: *Faith*, *Hope* and *Charity*.

At the end of June 1940, four much-needed Hurricanes arrived, and throughout the following month these seven machines successfully resisting the best efforts of some 200 enemy aircraft based in Sicily. So furiously did the defenders fight, that, like the Germans during the Battle of Britain, the Italians were forced to bomb at night. More Hurricanes would arrive, but in March 1942 the Italians were reinforced by the superior and combat-hardened Luftwaffe. Spitfires were required – urgently – and Flight Lieutenant Heppell, having escaped his former CO's wrath, was off to deliver some. Becoming a flight commander in 249 Squadron, in March 1942 Nip would lead his flight off HMS *Eagle*, fifteen vital Spitfires in total landing on the battered island – incensing the enemy. Time and time again the Axis air forces attacked, and by 2 April not one complete section of Spitfires remained operational. On 15 April 1942, Malta was, uniquely, awarded the George Cross. Five days later, more Spitfires arrived, then still more, but the fierce aerial fighting persisted until Rommel's defeat in the Western Desert that autumn. According to one veteran, these battles made the Battle of Britain 'look like child's play'. Nip, and other Tangmere Wing luminaries, including Alan Smith, were there throughout this violent period, scoring well against a determined enemy – and survived. All of this, of course, is another story – but Nip's reckless flight, therefore, that cold winter's night of early 1942, did indeed have far-reaching consequences.

At King's Cliffe that last day of January 1942, Johnnie flew a 'Sector Recco' (AD543) and a similar sortie including 'Practice Homing' (AA932). This brought his personal total of flying hours to 593.05, 138 of them operational.

February

Sunday, 1st

King's Cliffe. Settling down at King's Cliffe, plenty of sector reccos and local flying. Colin (Squadron Leader Gray) seems to have put up a black when leading two sections of 'A' Flight on a dusk patrol. Apparently, he steered an erratic course, and missed the convoy. Jamie (Wing Commander Jameson) was over the following day to check the compass log book and ball him out. They don't seem to get on too well together, despite the fact that they are both New Zealanders. I shouldn't for one be in the least surprised if trouble lies ahead. My old friend Peter Clapham is here, the Group Captain's AI Operations Officer. We have 'discovered' two locals which are quite good, although the nearest one, 'The Haycock', is well-known but rather off-handish and staid, so we have abandoned it in favour of the small, cheerful, village pub at Castor where we had some really good parties.

There was no flying owing to further snowfall the preceding night, and personnel were put to work clearing it.

Monday, 2nd

King's Cliffe. 'Scruffy' Haywood is at present Squadron Leader supernumerary and attached to my flight. He has been out East for a long time and is expecting a squadron in this Group. Yesterday I motored down to London with him and he pushed off to see his girlfriend – Lady Marguerite Strickland – after he has dropped me with my old pals, the Trevallions. Spent a very pleasant evening at Loughton with ?, George, Coke and several other old acquaintants. George and I hit the whisky stakes rather hard and I'm afraid I made an unsteady course back to 'Ashberrie'.

Station personnel snow-clearing efforts enabled sector reconnaissance flights and weather tests to be made.

FEBRUARY

Tuesday, 3rd
No entry. More snow drifted across the airfield, continuing to prevent flying and occupy personnel in clearing operations.

Wednesday, 4th
No diary entry, on a day when there was some flying in bad conditions. Johnnie flew once, a fifteen-minute weather test (AA932).

Thursday, 5th
Again no entry. No flying due to further snow. The Station was visited by the Duke of Kent.

Friday, 6th
Bath. 48 hours leave, so after a lot of preliminary arrangements Joe Crofts and I slipped down to Bath after wangling ourselves a railway warrant. Stayed at the Christopher Hotel and met Joan. Fixed Joe up with another girl, and after several bars pushed along to the Pump Room where they wouldn't let us in. Called the police out and after a big talk we were invited in – free.

Walked Joan back to Larhall and staggered back to the Christopher about 4 am – starved to bloody death, but I [sic] do it again! Rather a grand old place Bath, with its Abbey, Pump Room, Assembly Room and fine old Regency buildings.

In the Pump Room I met Dan Bregay BA, now a Corporal in the RAF whom I was at school with years ago. We always used to have a good tussle in the school cross-country.

Back at King's Cliffe, the weather had much improved, and 'considerable' flying was carried out, including five convoy patrols.

Saturday, 7th
Bath. At Bath still with Joe, spot of shopping and a Turkish Bath in the morning followed by a useful couple of hours drinking with some Canadian and American types. Joan turned up at 3 pm, visited the local flicks – back to the Christopher for more beer and eventually onto the Assembly Rooms with the foursome made up by one Pamela. Saw Vernon Key there who trained with me at Marshalls and he told me that Brooken ('the faithful one') and Mardon are both with him at Hullavington. Must pop down there for a spot of lunch and a jar sometime.

Again, further training and other routine flights took place at King's Cliffe.

Sunday, 8th

King's Cliffe. Back to King's Cliffe today, walking the last few miles from Wansford to WB? Rather an enjoyable weekend but everything costs so much these days and ones month's pay is soon accounted for - although old Walter (Manager Lloyd's – MM) is more than decent to me.

Johnnie did not fly upon return, finding the squadron busy with drogue-firing and cine gun training flights.

Monday, 9th

No entry. Johnnie flew four times this day, all in Spitfire AA932, a weather test, a contactless interception patrol, cine gun and aerobatic practice. On this day another 616 Squadron stalwart left for the intense air battles over Malta, namely the New Zealander Pilot Officer Jeff West DFM, who would increase his score and survive the war.

Tuesday, 10th

No entry, but convoy patrols and training flights were made, Johnnie flying a weather test (BL345), air-to-ground cine gun and then cloud-flying practice (AA932) followed by a trip to and from Duxford (AA718).

Wednesday, 11th

Wolverhampton. To Wolverhampton with Squadron Leader Gray to talk to the war workers. Rather a dim evening in the town – no-one to meet us, the whole show very badly organised.

Johnnie did fly once on this day, climbing to height with his flight and practising cine gun (AB266).

Once more, on the wider stage this was a significant day: the German battleships *Scharnhorst* and *Gneisenau*, with the heavy cruiser *Prinz Eugen*, all heavily escorted, slipped anchor in Brest and headed for the Dover Strait. There these impressive warships had been ideally located to disrupt Allied shipping in the Atlantic, but Hitler had ordered their redeployment to the Baltic coast in response to a non-existent British threat to Norway. The German planners decided that the most direct, audacious, route provided them the advantage of surprise, and coupled with heavy air cover the risk was manageable.

A belated British reaction, however, led to a German success, and the loss of a number of RAF aircraft, although both *Scharnhorst* and *Gneisenau* were both damaged by mines in the North Sea, the former significantly; indeed, bombed in dry dock, she would never sail again. Never again, due to this strategic error, would these dangerous enemy surface vessels threaten the Atlantic route.

Thursday, 12th

Wolverhampton and Birmingham. Talked to the workers at three different sites today about our operational experiences and shot a bit of a line. Had a look round the factory and never saw such a crowd of slackers in my life, the petty little officials too, a very dreary crowd, full of self-esteem and importance. Colin and I beat a hasty retreat at the first available opportunity and met Doc Barry in Wolverhampton for tea. The Doc was with the Squadron during the whole of our stay at Tangmere and all the chaps thought a hell of a lot of him. Proceeded onto Birmingham where the three of us dined and wined at the expense of the local BSA association.

Birmingham nightlife very dull so returned to the Queens and drank brandy. Very good to see the old Doc again.

At King's Cliffe, ten 616 Squadron Spitfires flew to operate from the Coltishall satellite of Matlask, six pilots subsequently providing cover for 137 Squadron Whirlwinds tasked with attacking the German naval formation negotiating the Dover Strait. The enemy was not sighted however, so the Spitfires escorted their charges safely back to base.

Friday, 13th

Birmingham and Leicester. Today we were scheduled to talk to the BSA chaps and this show was rather enjoyable as they made us so welcome. Platform, spotlights and microphones – Colin and I shot a terrific line – but that's what they wanted, and they all seemed to like it. The CO gave me a tremendous build up and I told them about his seventeen 'confirmed'.

Heard on the news today that there had been a bit of a battle in the Straits. Apparently, the *Scharnhorst, Gneisenau,* and *Prinz Eugen* have at long last moved out of Brest, and Fighter, Bomber, Coastal commands, the Fleet Air Arm and the Navy turned out in numbers. The results do not seem very clear, except that general opinion is that they all got through.

After leaving BSA we pushed on to Leicester and contacted Judy and Kay. Had quite a pleasant evening and all finished up at Carisbrooke. I drove back via Oakham and Melton and we fried ourselves a bloody great meal in the mess at 4 am.

Back at King's Cliffe, training flights had been conducted, and it was duly noted that Squadron Leader Gray and Flight Lieutenant Johnson had returned from their visit to the Bovis Ltd aircraft factory.

Saturday, 14th
King's Cliffe. 16 hours flying today – cloud, cine gun, pp etc. Valerie came up from Nottingham and stayed at The Haycock. Rather a pleasant evening with all the boys and a 'kitty'. Wire from Joan, 2.45 Paddington – it's about, letter from Thelma, DB escaped again from Germany but was soon caught and returned. Henry Longhurst is co-writing his book, Thelma wants to borrow my diary and photographs, she is welcome to anything I have. The Pusher is growing like a bomb, Thelma has his brother – Puddle Duck.

Jeff West popped in at 9 pm, I thought he was on his way to Malta but, apparently, he missed the flying boat and now has to go by sea – *bon voyage*!

Johnnie flew twice this date, aerobatics (AB266) and practising interceptions with Ground Control (AA718). His diary entry is of particular interest, because that the *Sunday Times* golf correspondent Henry Longhurst was working on a book about Douglas's life is a revelation. Ultimately, however, this project never came to fruition, and nothing more is known about it. Bader's story would be told, though, by the canny Australian journalist, fellow Spitfire pilot and PoW Paul Brickhill, whose eye for a post-war bestseller included other popular successes such as *The Great Escape* and the *Dambusters*. Brickhill entitled his inspiring Bader tale *Reach for the Sky*, published in 1956, selling millions of copies worldwide. Made into a blockbusting movie by film-maker Danny Angel the following year, the book and film made Bader a household name long after the war, and, indeed, beyond his death in 1982.

Sunday, 15th
King's Cliffe. 30 hours flying today and topped the 150 mark, which is not so bad considering the difficulties and the beginning of the month. Valerie returned to Melton Mowbray.

In the wider war, this was a disastrous day for Britain and her Allies: in the Far East, Singapore fell – a decisive victory for the Japanese – described by Churchill as the 'worst disaster' in British military history. Certainly, it was the largest ever surrender of British and Commonwealth troops, some 80,000 British, Indians and Australians becoming prisoners, who would be appallingly treated by the brutal Japanese.

Monday, 16th

London. To London with CO. Bloody cold journey but the old V8 made good time and we arrived at the Mount Royal without mishap. Photographed the Cambridgeshire Hounds on the way down. Met Joan at Paddington. Colin went to have his photograph taken – Joan and I bogged off to the flicks – Belle Starr and rather good. Joined up at the Brasserie and saw some of the 1 Squadron boys. A little WAAF by the name of Kay made the four up, so proceeded to Wellington (Knightsbridge). Met Jeff West and one or two other types who are waiting for their conveyance overseas and spending their leisure in a business-like manner. Had a few more beers, everyone including Joan getting under the weather, and then streaked off to The Chez Moi. Repaired to the Mount Royal eventually without kicking anyone, more drunk than sober.

Johnnie made no flights between this date and 19 February.

Tuesday, 17th

London. To the Buck House with Joan, Colin and Colin's cousin Shirley to receive our gongs. Crowds of other service people there including Navy and Army types and a rather strange sight was to see an RAF officer with the DSC up – for air sea rescue in the Straits of Dover. My old Tiger Moth instructor was there to collect an AFC, also McKenna, one-time CFI at Sealand (and no pal of mine). Edwards was there too to collect his VC and DFC. After an interminable wait and being rehearsed by an exceedingly nice young man in morning clothes, we paraded in front of George and had the old gong clipped on a sort of meat hook hanging from the left breast. The King asked me how long I had been in the RAF. Afterwards saw Alexander (late Eagle Squadron) in the Brassie – just pushing off to South Africa. Saw 'Hellzapoppin' at Leicester Square in the afternoon and in the evening had several brandies with a Flight Lieutenant recently returned from Gibraltar minus one eye – good type.

Wing Commander Hughie Edwards was the Australian commander of 105 Squadron, flying Blenheims, awarded the VC for 'pressing home bombing attacks from very low heights against strongly defended targets'.

Wednesday, 18th

King's Cliffe. Saw Joan off to Bath, and after visiting Burberry's set course for King's Cliffe. CO ran a big-end outside Baldock and we limped home at 30 mph. Found 'Freddie' and several press photographers at 'B' Flight

71

taking various snaps of the pilots (Associated Press). Only two operational pilots of 'A' Flight about – remainder u/s with colds and influenza.

Nonetheless, it was a busy day for 616 Squadron with various convoy patrols and 'X' Raid interceptions (no contact), in addition to low-flying attack and cine gun practice.

Thursday, 19th

King's Cliffe. Spitfire AA842 to be collected from Squires Gate, Blackpool. Ken Holden rang up from 12 Group re Saturday's show at Hutton Cranswick, be there by 1200 hours for lunch. CO u/s today with kidney trouble – pleasing. Arranged for a Master to fly Sandy to Squires Gate to collect the Spitfire. Sandy rang up from Blackpool, weather u/s so he is staying there. Rang up Group Captain Embry about CO, u/s pilots and Huck's posting. He can't do anything about the latter as he says it is entirely political from the Canadian Government.

Sgt Philbey ('A' Flight) taxied into Joe Ollivier while on a practice scramble - due to gross carelessness on his part and I stated this on his report. Joe landed downwind at Bircham Newton but fortunately, the machine was not damaged.

26.15 hours flying today ('B' Flight).

Interestingly, two of 616 Squadron's pilots escorted 'the circus of captured German aircraft from Bircham Newton to Sutton Bridge', the latter home of the gunnery range and Air Fighting Development Unit. Johnnie flew three routine training flights (AB266).

Friday, 20th

King's Cliffe. Last night 151 Squadron (Defiants) shot down one Do 217 and damaged four other e/a on the dusk patrol; good work but they should have been our meat as 'A' Flight were on readiness - but the Controller decided to send out 151 as Huck only had three a/c. Went over to Wittering to see W/C Jameson and Peter Clapham about one or two details – dusk patrols, night sets. Arranged for a talk by the Wittering ACP at my dispersal, 1400 hours today. (Dance at Stamford Hospital this evening but don't think I will go as it's a 'day do'.)

CO still in bed and u/s.

Tess, Joe, Bob and I slipped into our best blue after readiness and after a few quick whiskeys at the Fitzwilliam pushed on to Peterborough. Few more at the Falcon and then on to a dance at the Town Hall (had to pay to gain entry for a change). Found myself with a wee young blonde by the name of Pat.

Joe finished up with a luscious tart and I gave him 12 hours off – I hope he makes the most of it.

1300 hours flying today ('B' Flight)

Stan Turner posted to Malta, about the last of the Tangmere Wing.

For 616 Squadron this was a 'busy operational day', with several patrols in addition to the usual range of training flights. Johnnie flew once (AB266), a cloud-flying practice sortie.

Squadron Leader Stan Turner DFC was a Canadian fighter ace and tough character who had flown throughout the Battle of Britain in Douglas Bader's 242 Squadron. Thereafter he became a flight commander on 145 Squadron in the Tangmere Wing, before commanding 411 (Canadian) Squadron, by which time he had earned a Bar to his DFC. Now Turner was taking command of 249 Squadron at the height of the Axis siege of Malta. Later he and Johnnie would meet again, on the continent, after the invasion (see *The Great Adventure*).

Saturday, 21st

King's Cliffe. Fly to Hutton Cranswick today to see demonstration beat up. Met Ken Holden there for lunch. Leaving early today – don't think I'll manage Hutton Cranswick today. Rang up F/O Hicks (12 Group) about Huck's posting (W/C Barraclough away). Huck not to leave until new flight commander arrives. CO up today and not looking too well, understand he is going on seven days leave tomorrow. A little cine gun practice in the afternoon but had to pancake rather hurriedly because of a snowstorm.

To the Haycock in the evening where we had a few beers and a hop in the attic – rather enjoyable. Also met a young farmer type who lives in his district and who promised us a couple of cases of onions.

Owing to low cloud, little flying took place, Johnnie only practising cine gun for 30 minutes that afternoon (AB266).

Sunday, 22nd

King's Cliffe. Beat-up Home Guard at Castle Ashby 1100 hours today, arranged by W/C Jameson. NE of the Castle, between the castle and the two lakes, objective – farm wagon marked by two blankets.

Attack from W. to E. in four phases at intervals of 2-3 minutes.

1. Over low in formation.
2. Over [illegible].
3. Various attacks.
4. In formation at 10.00! (gas).

Home Guard beaten up in poor weather, AT gun, low flying attacks, formation today. Sandy back from Blackpool after a shaky trip there. McDermid now day operational. Spoke to Wing Commander Gough and Ken Holden on the phone. Asked Gibbo to arrange a clothing parade for my Flight as their uniforms are getting very shabby.

Fighter Night: 23 Feb – 8 March inclusive (must get in plenty of night flying too).

Johnnie flew four times (AB266), the usual weather test followed by the 'beat-up' and two low-flying and cine gun exercises. Some of the pilots also went to Wittering to examine the display of captured German aircraft, which was 'very interesting'.

Reference to a period of 'Fighter Nights' is interesting. During the early days, when the Luftwaffe shifted the focus of its attack to bombing at night, Britain's nocturnal defences were ill-prepared, with no coordinated radar or purpose-built night-fighting aircraft. Consequently Spitfires and Hurricanes – both designed and intended as short-range daytime interceptors – were pressed into the night-fighting role. The Spitfire, however, was not an easy aircraft to fly at night, owing to its narrow track undercarriage and, like the Hurricane, two glowing rows of red-hot exhausts in front of the pilot, affecting night vision.

On Fighter Nights, Spitfire and Hurricane squadrons would sent aloft, passing through 'gates' over London and other cities indicated by searchlight beams, in the hope of encountering a raider. On 19 June 1940, Squadron Leader 'Sailor' Malan notched up the Spitfire's first nocturnal kill, but successes were rare, owing more to luck than anything else. The Defiant turret-fighter, beaten during daylight by the Me 109, proved an essential stop-gap night-fighter until the dedicated Bristol Beaufighter with 20mm cannon and Airborne Interception radar arrived. Then the de Havilland Mosquito, the 'Wooden Wonder', took over. By then, however, the sting had gone out of the night Blitz, the last big raid being on the night of 11 May 1941.

FEBRUARY

The following month, Hitler invaded Russia, most of his bomber units moving eastwards. Enemy air activity over England during February 1942 was slight, so it is difficult to understand why this period of 'Fighter Nights' was arranged, especially considering the improved, dedicated, night-fighting defences available at that time.

Monday, 23rd
King's Cliffe. FIGHTER NIGHT
Three pilots for muster by 1000 hours.
Visit German a/c at 0930 hours.

Weather u/s, snow and low cloud at 0800 hours, CO seven days leave – 1137 train to town.

Cleared slightly after lunch so put in an hour's air gun and low-level attacks in the low flying area. One P/O or Sgt To be posted overseas.

Day operational	Night	Morn	UT
F/Lt Johnson	F/Lt Johnson	F/Lt Johnson	Sgt. Welch
P/O Bowen	P/O Bowen	P/O Bowen	Sgt. Muler
P/O Sanderson		P/O Sanderson	P/O Sanderson
P/O Ware	P/O Ware	P/O Ware	
P/O Crofts	P/O Crofts	P/O Crofts	
P/Sgt Strands		P/Sgt Strands	
Sgt Davidson		Sgt Davidson	
Sgt Smithson			
Sgt Winter			
Sgt Bolton			
Sgt McDermid			

Joe, Tess, Gledhill and I down to the Fitzwilliam and then to the Sergeants' Dance. Terrific evening with beer, whiskey and rum, had a bloody thick head when I came to this morning.

No Fighter Night took place. Johnnie's training flight was again in Spitfire AB266.

Tuesday, 24th
King's Cliffe. FIGHTER NIGHT. CO posted to HQ 10 Group.
Bob and I at Hutton Cranswick for 1200 hours. Cancelled – sometime tomorrow.

Smithson took Spitfire 'S' over to Castle Bromwich to get it repaired but had to land at Bramcote – bad weather. Took off again after half an hour and was very nearly written off by a Wellington beating the aerodrome up. Found CB and Smithson landed there, returned to WB2 (King's Cliffe).

Convoy Patrol in afternoon – Attack - took five a/c 'B' Flight to Docking and three a/c 'A' Flight. When returning noticed some seals basking in the sunshine and sandbank in the Wash, whipped round and gave them a squirt with my Brownings – are confirmed! Shortly after this my glycol began to pour out of the port side but struggled back to Bircham Newton and made a landing with a dead motor. Left Strands at Bircham and came home with Tess and Joe, Mother Booth landed in the dusk with his Wellington. To Peterborough, met Pat and had a few beers at the Angel – she looked very charming too.

Johnnie flew to and from Bramcote, then to Docking (the satellite of Bircham Newton, a Coastal Command base, on Norfolk's East coast), from where the convoy codenamed 'Attack' was patrolled before he was forced to land at Bircham Newton leaking coolant. The Spitfire was swiftly repaired and Johnnie returned to base – fortunately not disrupting his busy social life! All flights were made in AB266.

Squadron Leader Gray's tour was up, not an unwelcome development from Johnnie's perspective, given previous diary entries. The New Zealander was replaced by Squadron Leader H.L.I. Brown DFC, from 609 Squadron at Digby, and who remained with 616 until January 1943.

Some readers may be shocked by Johnnie's reference to using basking seals for target practice. This is the first instance that such a scenario has come to this author's notice in a lifetime of research – but was not isolated so far as Johnnie and 616 Squadron were concerned. Writing in *The Guardian* on 7 November 2018, Philip Hoare, in a broader article regarding animal suffering during the world wars, claims that during the Second World War the RAF used rafts of eider ducks in the North Sea for target practice, although no evidence is provided to support this allegation. *If* this happened, it was certainly not policy and, like the seals, the result of an *ad hoc* pot shot.

Wednesday, 25th
King's Cliffe. To Kirton, formed up with Wing Commander Walker and on to Hutton Cranswick. Group Captain Handy, Wing Commander Gough, Ken Holden, Jack Adams and Scruffy. Met Crowley-Milling, who was shot

down in August and walked home from Northern France; has his old Flight in 610. Hugh Gill and he are about the sole remaining members. Lunch at Hutton and then on to Skipsey ranges to see a beat up by 610 and a flight of 253, the latter being very good – we have to put on a similar show at Lakenheath. Spot of tea and then back to King's Cliffe. Took the chaps down to the Fitzwilliam for a few noggins. Strouts commissioned today.

Ken told me that Billy Burton is now Station Commander (Wing Commander) at Hawkinge (heard on the 26th that Billy had been posted overseas. Libya).

On this day, Johnnie flew to Kirton, then Hutton Cranswick and back to King's Cliffe (all flights in AD543). The weather, however, was bad, the squadron making but one convoy patrol.

Mention of Billy Burton is worthy of extra comment. A Cranwell Sword of Honour recipient, and a successful fighter pilot in addition to being a respected leader, Billy was very likely destined for great things. Posted to Tunisia to command a Kittyhawk fighter-bomber equipped wing, he subsequently added a DSO to his DFC. After the Tunisian campaign, Billy was amongst a gaggle of fighter leaders sent home on leave.

On 3 June 1943, on the return flight to North Africa, the unarmed Hudson in which Billy was a passenger was shot down by a Ju 88 over the Bay of Biscay; there were no survivors. Wing Commander Burton left behind a young widow, Jean, who had been a camp follower, living near Tangmere during those heady days of the 1941 season. Many years later, Jean commented, 'that summer is one that remains amongst my most vivid memories, perhaps it was the first and last that Billy and I were ever to spend together.'

Thursday, 26th
King's Cliffe. Dawn readiness at 0715. Weather test, recco'd the Wash and down to Cambridge and Ely. Landed at Marshall's and had a couple of coffees at the Adjutant. Corky rang up when I arrived back, he wants to see me urgently – must try and make it sometime today. Two charges, Sgts Coldrey and Blanchard for not wearing respirators – admonished. Group Captain Hardy over for a look round the Squadron, had a long chat and volunteered to go anywhere abroad on Spitfires. Contacted Cocky at Duxford, he's going too and, undoubtedly, he's the one chap who can arrange the journey – the Trapper wants to come too and if we make landfall at Malta we shall be in good company, Paddy Woodhouse, Davy Woodhall, Stan Turner, Nipple,

Jeff West and a host of others. Huck going to 416 tomorrow so we beetled off to the Haycock returned and thrashed up the Ante Room.

Johnnie's flight to Marshall's airfield was recorded as a 'weather test' (AA932). Clearly the dull and dreary British winter was frustrating Johnnie and friends – enviously had they heard of the great air battles and rich pickings over Malta, and desperately wanted some of the action. It was not to be.

Friday, 27th
King's Cliffe. Write to Squadron Leader Gray today, Amersham 274.
HUCK POSTED TO 416 CANADIAN SQUADRON.
SGT BOLTON POSTED OVERSEAS (LIBYA)
S/LDR BROWN ARRIVED.
    Bob and I flew a couple of Spitfires over to Manby to see Cocky, but, unfortunately, he was away at a Typhoon conference. Had a chat with Ingle-Finch and returned home via the Wash where fired our guns - no seals about today! In the evening Keene (the new 'A' Flight Commander) Bob, Joe and I took Huck to Grantham and saw him off on the train, then finished up at the White Hart and left at 12 pm, Grantham to Stamford 21 miles (19 minutes). Sandy and Strouts over to Wittering for Fighter Night but the weather was u/s.

On this rare day of good weather, Johnnie flew three times, squadron formation practice (AA718), an air test and gun-firing (AA932). The reference to 'Huck' is the popular Canadian Flight Lieutenant W.W. Murray, posted to 416 (Canadian) Squadron at Peterhead.

Saturday, 28th
King's Cliffe. PARTY IN THE MESS.
The Trapper and I flew up to Kirton to try and wangle some booze from Mr Smith – succeeded and returned with two bottles of Scotch, one bottle liqueur brandy and 2 lbs of Balkan Sobranie, makes you think – can't beat the old place. Had a chat with Dicky Stafford, Derek Beecham and Johnnie Walker, arranged for Derek and Dickie to come down for the party this evening. Returned to King's Cliffe and made a safe landing with the booze. Cocky and his Flight Commander turned up about sixish, bath, a shave, few beers, some supper and down to the Haycock to meet the girls – at least ten brandies, picked up Pat and flashed back to the Mess in fine form;

W/C Jameson, Peter Clapham, David Lloyd, G/C Embry all there, polished off the whisky, rye and liqueur brandy; cock fight with Cocky. Took a party home in the Comer but they didn't like my driving so sprang out half way to Peterborough. Arrived back OK. To bed at 7 am.

TOTAL FLYING HOURS FOR FEB. 335.30

On this final day of February 1942, Johnnie flew an 'air test' to Kirton and return (AA932), on this occasion a new description for a booze run! While the pilots ended the month partying, the ORB described it as 'a cold and cheerless month, the numerous reverses in the Far East and escape of the German battleships *Gneisenau* and *Scharnhorst*, together with the battle cruiser *Prinz Eugen*, adding to the gloom.'

March

Sunday, 1st

King's Cliffe. Fell out of bed at 1030, found my way to the Mess and there discovered … over a bottle of Worthington. Took Robin to see the Pusher and Corky, the Trapper, Dicky, Joe and I made a bee line for the Haycock for some more Worthington: drank steadily from 12-2 and felt a little better – everyone admired the Pusher. Some lunch in the Mess and saw Corky off, Flight called to readiness for a convoy patrol and Tess Ware led them – the Trapper and myself being u/s. Borrowed the CO's car in the evening, met Pat and discovered the Wheatsheaf, good spot too. Took Pat home to Peterborough.

Johnnie did not fly this day, which, owing to the amount of Worthington consumed throughout the day, was perhaps no bad thing! Other pilots flew air firing and cine gun practice while three Spitfires searched the North Sea for a downed bomber crew in their dinghy – sadly fruitless.

Monday, 2nd

King's Cliffe. Ken Holden down from 12 Group to talk about low flying attacks, which we have to carry out on Sunday and Monday. No flying today – weather u/s. Steady evening in the Mess.

This was a day of low-lying fog, preventing flying. Instead pilots watched gun camera combat footage and practised blind flying in the Link Trainer.

Of Jewish heritage, Ken Holden was another former Tangmere Wing luminary. A pre-war auxiliary member of 616 Squadron, Holden first saw action over Dunkirk, destroying two and damaging two more Me 109s. Flying from Kenley towards the end of the Squadron's ill-fated deployment at that battered 11 Group station, he increased his score and was promoted to command 'A' Flight later that year.

On 26 February 1941, Flight Lieutenant Holden led his flight to Tangmere, where Douglas Bader became the Sector's first Wing Leader the following month. Shortly afterwards, Holden was promoted to squadron leader and given command of 610 'County of Chester' Squadron, which he led successfully throughout that fateful air-fighting season of 1941, destroying more enemy aircraft and earning the DFC.

After that memorable tour, Holden was posted to the staff at 12 Group HQ, in which capacity his visit to his old squadron was made this day. He would not return to operations, surviving the war as a wing commander, as did his younger brother 'Gus', who became a decorated ace flying Hurricanes with 501 'County of Gloucester' Squadron during the Battle of Britain. Having left the service in 1945, a year later Ken Holden returned to what was now the Royal Auxiliary Air Force, commanding 616 Squadron, when re-formed at Finningly on Gloster Meteor jets. He died in 1991.

Tuesday, 3rd
King's Cliffe and Melton Mowbray. Derek Beecham attached supernumerary, pending posting to Middle East. Weather test and few minutes flying at 1500 hours – landed immediately afterwards with faulty hood. Tony Gunn posted PRU Middle East. 40 hours leave – To Melton, Val over for a couple of days.

Fog had prevented flying that morning but cleared sufficiently after lunch to permit some training flights. Johnnie's weather test and low flying practice was of just fifteen minutes (BL345). In these Spitfires the canopy slid back on a runner, unlike the Me 109's, which blew off. Sliding back a Spitfire's hood safely in an emergency was reliant upon the runner being undamaged, and required strength, difficult on occasions for a wounded pilot trying to abandon the aircraft. Later high-altitude Spitfires with pressurised cockpits had locked-down canopies, which could be blown off, but these were unpopular with many pilots, some of whom, including Johnnie, preferred to fly without the canopy fitted.

Derek Beecham had also flown with 616 Squadron in the Tangmere Wing. Squadron leaders were often posted to a frontline squadron as 'supernumerary', which is to say as an extra pilot, after a break from active operations, to gain experience of current operational circumstances and conditions. This was usually preparatory to taking command of a squadron themselves.

On the wider stage, on this date Winston Churchill authorised a resumption of the RAF's offensive daylight operations over France.

At this time, the Spitfire Mk VB was still Britain's frontline fighter, whereas the enemy had largely replaced the comparable Me 109F with the superior FW190 – able to beat all comers. Another issue facing Fighter Command was that the fighting in both the Middle and Far East had absorbed experienced fighter leaders and pilots, men like Billy Burton and 'Nip' Heppell for example, meaning that the overall level of combat experience throughout the Command was much less than the previous year.

Conversely, 1941 had provided the Germans great experience of how best to react to the RAF's massed formations – and the 'Abbeville Boys' and 'St Omer Kids' were ready for a fight. Indeed, German combat experience and confidence on the Channel coast had never been higher. In 12 Group, nonetheless, 616 Squadron patiently awaited the call to enter the fray.

Wednesday, 4th
Melton Mowbray. Sold my .25 Automatic (via Ross) for £6 and £1 the ammo – restored the finances a trifle. Steady day at home – in bed most of the time.

Back at King's Cliffe, low fog prevented any flying.

Thursday, 5th
Melton Mowbray and King's Cliffe. Back from Melton – weather – low cloud snow and ice, the Governor met me at Stamford – Flight released – pushed off to Peterborough in the Commer – Derek, Bob, Sandy, Tess and I met Pat – to the flicks and saw Colin afterwards in the Bull. All joined the rest of the boys at a hop in the Grand. Ran various females home in the truck, must start a taxi service.

Again, fog had prevented all flying from King's Cliffe, as it would for the next two days.

Friday, 6th
King's Cliffe. No flying today, weather u/s, ice, snow and low cloud. In the evening, the CO, Colin Gray, and a few of us beetled off to the Wheatsheaf for a few beers – no 'fripp' about.

'Fripp' is, of course, girls/women/ladies.

Saturday, 7th

King's Cliffe. Weather still u/s. To Duxford for a talk on Australian Army Service Corps by an army type – rather a waste of time as he told us so little. Saw Cocky – the overseas business looks grim at the moment as Group want to keep me in the Squadron for two or three months. Letter arrived today from Nip, he is approaching Gibraltar and very pleased with life – says how good it is to have a decent CO!

Colin stooged off to Preston today. Derek's posting to Middle East though, the prick has mislaid his log-book however and had to get a chit with all his times and claims signed by the CO. A few gallons of beer at the Stilton Cheese on the way home from Duxford. Humber Brake packed up and we had to be towed home.

Sunday, 8th

King's Cliffe. To Lakenheath several times today in Squadron formation for practice attacks on dummy troops, Ken Holden on the ground, controlling and giving the chaps a spot of advice. Sgt Smithson to Cawley to collect T and Sgt Welch to Bircham Newton.

Meet Pat in the Haycock, and to the Mermaid, and eventually took her home to Peterborough – it's about! Back to Wittering to collect Squadron Leader Brown from the Mess, a few hours with Squadron Leader Gilroy (just back from a Channel sweep with three FW190s destroyed), and so to bed.

Squadron Leader George Gilroy owed his nickname, 'Sheep', to his pre-war profession as a Scottish sheep farmer. A pre-war auxiliary with 603 'City of Edinburgh' Squadron, on 28 October 1939 Gilroy was credited with a share in bringing down the first German aircraft to crash on British soil during the Second World War. The squadron would be heavily engaged during the Battle of Britain, flying from Hornchurch, by the end of which 'Sheep' was an ace decorated with the DFC.

Further success followed during the offensive operations over France during 1941, leading to him being given command of 609 'West Riding' Squadron at Gravesend. Having destroyed yet more enemy aircraft, on the day in question Gilroy had damaged a FW190. The following month he would leave for North Africa, commanding 324 Wing, a further string of victories seeing him made a companion of the DSO and awarded a Bar to his DFC.

Returning to England as a group captain in November 1943, the remainder of the war was spent as a station commander. Leaving the

RAF in 1945, like Ken Holden, who re-joined the RAAF in 1946 and commanded his old auxiliary squadron, 'Sheep' did likewise with 603. He died in 1995

Monday, 9th

King's Cliffe. My Birthday – 'like as the waves make towards the pebbled shore, so do our minutes hasten towards their end.' Lots of air firing today, cannon and m/g, attacked a shoal of seals basking in the wash.

Sgt Brownhall posted to the Middle East. Took the flight down to the Fitzwilliam at Castor for a few beers and whiskies.

With improved weather, low flying attacks, cine gun and formation practice flights took place. Johnnie flew on two such training exercises (AA932 and BL345).

Tuesday, 10th

King's Cliffe. Letter from Jeff West today, he is now in Malta and in Stan Turner's squadron – Woody also there, must answer as soon as possible.

Early morning readiness: Took Joe, Winter and Welch about 80 miles out to sea in the hope that we might see something – nothing about. On the return locate the seals and attacked with full war load – cannon and m/g – two or three destroyed and a lot of blood.

Convoy patrol at dusk with the Trapper, Joe and Sandy – relieved by 151 Squadron. Sandy's flying and his keenness seems to have fallen off – I don't think he has ever recovered from the day we lost Scott and he was thrashed up by the 190s. Must get him posted to an OTU or CFS.

Strouts ran off the runway when taxying 'B' to 'A' Flight and nosed-in – clapped him under open arrest.

(Meet Pat in Angel at 9 pm).

Johnnie's log book records four flights this day: cine gun, squadron attacks, then to Docking from where Convoy 'Parallel' was patrolled (all in AAA932).

Wednesday, 11th

King's Cliffe. Bad weather today again today – weather test only, slipped down to Peterborough on Tommy's motor cycle and nearly froze to death.

Johnnie's only flight was a twenty-five minute 'Air Test' (AB266).

Thursday, 12th

King's Cliffe. Sandy posted to Merchant Ship Fighter Unit at Speke, as he thinks he will be able to get home on the convoys and he seems quite keen on the idea. Large flew him up in the Maggie and had to put down in a field on the way back – short of petrol. When taking off on Saturday he confirmed a bullock ("it did a hand spring") and wrote the Maggie off – the prick.

28.40 hours flying today – weather test, guns and cannon test, squadron formation, convoy patrol "Evidence" from Docking.

The squadron undertake various training flights and four convoy patrols. Johnnie flew four training flights and patrolled convoy 'Evidence' (AB266). According to the 616 Squadron ORB, Pilot Officer Sanderson's MSFU posting and Flying Officer Large's accident in the Magister occurred the following day.

Friday, 13th

King's Cliffe. Johnnie Townsend over from Melton Mowbray to insure the MC which belonged to the late Jess Sutherland. One of the old instructors from Marshall's (Sullivan) also over for lunch and to fly a Spitfire for the first time. Peter Clapham here for a yarn and tea.

Flight experience, squadron formation and cannons.

Johnnie flew once, a 'Flight experience and cannon test' (AB266).

Saturday, 14th

King's Cliffe. Mist and fog about today – no flying before lunch. Pushed off with Tess, Joe and Berny to play rugger at Upwood; game started late and was buggered after the first ten minutes, scored the only points with a dropped goal – nine tries against. Shot down to the Haycock with the CO, the Pusher and a few of the chaps.

A foggy morning cleared by mid-day, enabling cine gun practice, line astern attack practice and air to ground firing at Sutton Bridge. Johnnie did not fly this day.

Sunday 15th

King's Cliffe. Convoy patrol 'Attempt' off the Norfolk coast – convoy in a hell of a mess as it has been attacked by E-Boats during the night – one destroyer and one merchant ship sunk – we arrived there in time to see another destroyer picking up the survivors.

Flight exercise in the afternoon with the CO leading and Smithson and I jumping the weaving section of four – got my sights on several times.

Welch hit a tree when making a very bad approach on No. 3 runway and his Spitty fell vertically downwards and disintegrated rapidly – only hurt a cut eye.

Cocky over this afternoon in his Typhoon.

Winter, May and Smithson – dusk landings.

Tess, Strands, Bob and I – night flying.

Unlike previous days, this was a good flying day. Johnnie patrolled the convoy, practised 'surprise attacks' and night-flying (AB266).

Monday, 16th

King's Cliffe. Bob, Tess, Strouts and I climbed out at 0430 hours for a spot of searchlight co-op but the Army said they wanted more notice, so carried out a normal patrol. Cloud at 300' over WB2 when we landed. Tess landed immediately after me and I had to run on to the grass to avoid him. Strouts came in immediately afterwards without a good look and hit Tess's starboard wing with his starboard wing – two machines out of the line at one crack.

Squadron formation to Docking and then we split up into pairs and carried out a long recco over the North Sea, the Trapper and I made landfall at Spurn Head!

To the Fitzwilliam for a few beers and a couple of dozen eggs.

Johnnie's early morning sortie was recorded as 'night flying' (AB266), followed by flying with the squadron to Docking before participating with seven other Spitfires in a low-level sweep over the North Sea (AA932).

Tuesday, 17th

King's Cliffe. (Two pilots to Leconfield to talk to 86 MU on the 18th. Cancelled).

Party at Wittering – Cocky coming over. The 22.40 hours on convoy patrols today – some pilots did 7 hours. Tess and I went with the rugger team to a school and enjoyed an excellent game although we lost by a big margin – 27-3. Picked up Pat and Dorothy from Castor, and on to Wittering via the Haycock. At the dance and party Ken Holden, Cocky, Dingle Wren, Peter C., Mrs Johnnie W., and a gaggle of others including 'Sailor' Malan with whom we had a big talk. Lots of hooch and good food and a bloody fine time enjoyed by all. Ditched the car several times on the journey home but eventually made the grade. Cocky and I tackled Air Vice Marshal Saul and told him what a bloody awful Group we thought it – any time now! To bed at 6 am.

As far as flying was concerned, Johnnie was airborne three times (AA932), there was an aileron test, then down to Docking from where Convoy 'Radio' was patrolled. On this day, several Free French pilots joined the squadron, which now comprised personnel of various nationalities and in no way resembled the pre-war auxiliary 616 Squadron.

Group Captain Adolph Gysbert Malan was another Fighter Command legend – and certainly the most influential so far as improving air-fighting tactics were concerned. Born in Wellington, South Africa, on 3 October 1910, when aged 14 Malan became a cadet in the merchant marine, later being commissioned in the Royal Naval Reserve – hence his nickname 'Sailor'. In 1935, like many other young men across the Commonwealth, Malan was given a Short Service Commission in the RAF, this being another initiative to increase the establishment of pilots, who served for four years before joining the reserve – thus providing a trained reserve which could be mobilised in an emergency.

After training, Pilot Officer Malan joined 74 Squadron at Hornchurch, flying biplane fighters before converting to the Spitfire, by which time he was a flight lieutenant and commander of 'A' Flight. Over Dunkirk he rapidly demonstrated his exceptional ability as an aggressive and successful fighter pilot, destroying three German aircraft, probably destroying and damaging various others, leading to him being awarded the DFC. On the night of 19 June 1940 he made the Spitfire's first nocturnal kill, no mean feat in an aircraft not intended for night-fighting. Throughout the Battle of Britain he led 74 Squadron with great distinction, increasing his own score substantially and being awarded a Bar to his DFC and appointed to the DSO.

In March 1941, Malan, like Bader, was amongst the first wing leaders appointed and went to Biggin Hill. In the forefront of the action over northern France that season, between 17 May and 24 July 1941 alone Malan destroyed twelve Me 109s, receiving a Bar to his DSO. Unlike Bader, however, after so much action, Malan recognised in himself the signs of combat fatigue. In air combat, fractions of seconds in sighting or reacting to threats can make the difference between life and death. Malan knew that the time had come for a new, fresher, wing leader to replace him, and so took the eminently responsible step of having himself stood-down from operations.

This is what Bader should have done, in whom similar signs were well apparent, causing concern to friends. Bader's press-on spirit, however, prevented him ever taking such a course of action, instead continuing on operations until, on 9 August 1941, he lost precious seconds in sighting enemy aircraft, as a result of which the Tangmere Wing was bounced by a superior force and the great man ended up a prisoner of war. On the same day, Malan became Chief Flying Instructor at Grangemouth, more concerned with passing on his hard-won experience than personal glory. Later Malan commanded the Central and in due course Advanced Gunnery Schools, passing on his 'Nine Rules of Air Fighting' and helping countless young fighter pilots.

Wednesday, 18th
King's Cliffe. Talk by Adolph Malan on his squadron and wing tactics, he certainly talks a lot of sound common sense and has the experience to back up his theories - but I didn't like to hear him say that the Tangmere Wing and Douglas Bader were ropey and our results not comparable with his.

Felt bloody awful today so slipped down to the Mermaid with the CO for three quick drinks which didn't improve me one iota. Flew for an hour in the afternoon with hood well open and got three or four seals confirmed with my cannon.

Everyone doing a lot of readiness these days as we have so few pilots, if we have to post any more pilots I shall put in a report to the CO – the chaps are becoming very tired.

Another foggy day, so overall little flying took place. Johnnie's 'cannon test' flight was his only flight this day (AA932).

Thursday, 19th
King's Cliffe. Weather u/s Fog and rain, although we had to get out of bed at 0530 for dawn readiness. Rang up Group and had the Flight released from 1300 hours until dawn tomorrow. Fixed up the Commer and jogged off to Leicester with Bob, Tess, Smithy, Mac and 'Red' Winter, quite a jolly evening with a few noggins and the London Fire Fighters' dance at the Munford Hall.

Smithson: 'The Eagle shits tomorrow' meaning that tomorrow is pay day!
Johnny Townsend over with my (and Joe's) repaired flying boots.

Again, low-lying fog prevented any flying.

Pilot Officer Johnnie Johnson at Kirton-in-Lindsey whilst serving with 616 Squadron during the winter of 1941.

Above left and right: Douglas Bader, the legendary legless fighter pilot and leader, was a huge influence on Johnnie Johnson and the pair became lifelong friends. The 'Great Man', as Johnnie called 'DB' is seen here when leading the Tangmere Wing in 1941.

Above left: Johnnie flew with 616 Squadron during Tangmere Wing days, commanded by the highly respected and popular Squadron Leader HF 'Billy' Burton DFC, seen here at Westhampnett in 1941.

Above right: Another lifelong friend of Johnnie's was Hugh Spencer Lisle Dundas – commonly known as 'Cocky', on account of his taste for cocktails, and who later became a highly decorated Group Captain and was knighted post-war.

Flight Lieutenant Ken 'The Bull' Holden DFC, Johnnie's Flight Commander in 616 Squadron during Tangmere Wing days.

Wing Commander Bader (second right) at 616 Squadron's Westhampnett dispersal, summer 1941, with, from left, Squadron Leader Billy Burton, Pilot Officer Johnnie Johnson, Flying Officer Cocky Dundas and Sergeant Alan Smith. Burton, who is wearing a captured German lifejacket, did not survive the war.

Another great friend of Johnnie's was 'Nip' Hepple, also seen here as a Pilot Officer at Kirton.

Billy Burton was succeeded in command of 616 Squadron by the New Zealander Squadron Leader Colin Gray DFC (centre), pictured at King's Cliffe in 1942 with Flight Lieutenant Johnnie Johnson DFC (third from left), the commander of 'B' Flight.

At King's Cliffe, 616 Squadron was part of the Wittering Wing, commanded by another fighter ace from New Zealand, Wing Commander Pat 'Jamie' Jameson DFC.

Flight Lieutenant Johnnie Johnson DFC, in cockpit, with pilots of 616 Squadron at King's Cliffe in 1942. The Spitfire Mk VB is a presentation aircraft, 'Manchester Civil Defender', AA879.

Johnnie had great respect for the groundcrews, and was lifelong friends with his Rigger, Arthur Radcliffe (left) and Fitter, Fred Burton, pictured at King's Cliffe in 1942.

Above and left: Whilst at King's Cliffe, Johnnie was filmed by the Army Film Unit, the film being shown in cinemas nationwide.

Johnnie with the 'Pusher' – sadly killed in an accident at Ludham in 1942.

Squadron Leader Johnnie Johnson DFC & Bar with his first command: 610 'County of Chester' Squadron at Ludham in 1942.

Another lifelong friend of Johnnie's was Denis Crowley-Milling, later knighted and retired from the service an Air Marshal.

Above: Johnnie with 'Sally'.

Left: In August 1942, Johnnie met and fell in love with Pauline Ingate from Norwich.

On 14 November 1942, Johnnie married 'Paula' at Norwich Registrar's Office, his Best Man being Squadron Leader Cocky Dundas DFC, later Godfather to the couple's first born, Christopher.

Friday, 20th
King's Cliffe. Weather u/s again, low fog and slight drizzle.

There was no flying again, nor for the next two days.

Saturday, 21st
King's Cliffe. Weather again u/s with thick mist and low cloud.
Vs Upwood at rugger and surprisingly won 9-8 after a good game. Squadron Leader Brown playing scrum half for King's Cliffe.
Two beers in the Haycock with Dorothy, her sister and Pat.

Sunday, 22nd
King's Cliffe. Weather u/s.
Inoculations today together with Winter, Ware and Strands – completely u/s after a few hours and following the CO's advice knocked back a few whiskeys, which knocked me completely out – had to be put to bed by Joe.

Monday, 23rd
King's Cliffe. Most of the day spent in bed as a result of the Doc's inoculation. Weather better today and we put in a couple of Squadron Balbos, flying in the new formation.

Johnnie's logbook, however, records no flight. A 'Balbo' was the name given to wing or multiple squadron formations, on account of the Italian general of that name who, pre-war, had advocated use of mass formations.

Tuesday, 24th
King's Cliffe. McDermid posted to a delivery flight for one month. Squadron Balbo with Hurricanes from Digby attacking. 12 Group Wing Show – hope to be on one pretty soon. Plenty of cine gun - have only done 411 feet up to date.

Johnnie flew three times on what the ORB describes as a 'busy day': a weather test, the Balbo, and cine gun practice (AA932).

Wednesday, 25th
London. Borrowed the Station Commander's Tiger Moth and with Smithson in the back pushed off to Wilmington to collect the MG belonging to

the late Jesus Sutherland. Landed at White Waltham for refuel and then into Wilmington, but when we arrived there found nothing but a bloody ploughed field with Wilmington painted on it. Flew back to Shoreham and got out there.

Collected the car from Ringmere and despite the fact that £17 had first been spent on it, it looked in a decidedly ropey condition – however I couldn't argue the point as I had never seen the thing before. Charged up to London and spent the night at Waltham Abbey with T/R.

Back at King's Cliffe, 616 Squadron again flew a Balbo practice with the Wittering Wing, during which the Spitfires were 'intercepted' by a squadron of Typhoons. In the mêlée following the break, Sergeant Baxter's Spitfire was 'struck by another aircraft and he was forced to bale out at 16,000 feet', fortunately only suffering a 'cut leg'.

Thursday, 26th
King's Cliffe. On to King's Cliffe at 0715, but ran a big end this side of Royston and limped home in very dreary style. Saw Roe, the MT officer and his chaps are going to fix the big ends up for me.

Convoy patrol 'Plum' and a spot of party? flying just before dusk.

Johnnie flew three times, aileron test and convoy patrol from Docking (recording the Spitfire as 'BE-E' for both flights, which is puzzling as 616 Squadron's code letters were 'YQ' at this time, and all other entries record the aircraft serial number, as opposed to code letters), and 'Flight Formation' (AA932).

Friday, 27th
King's Cliffe. Practice Wing show with 609 Squadron and 56 Squadron (Typhoons).

1. Sgt Baxter ('A' flight) collided with pilot of 609 Squadron and both pilots baled out.
2. Piece of the wreckage hit Sgt Winter ('B' Flight) and knocked off half his wing, but he managed to get back safely and land at Wittering - which was an excellent effort on his part.
3. P/O Linton ('A' Flight) tipped up on his nose after landing at Peterborough.
4. Self pranged the CO's car into a Stamford bus at the Haycock cross road.

Dusk patrol with Ware and Strands, landed at Wittering in the dark with 9/10 cloud at 1000 feet. Ollivier claims a smack at a Do 217 when patrolling the convoy at dusk.

Larporak Dance at King's Cliffe.

Johnnie flew three times, cine gun practice followed by a trip to Docking, from where Convoy 'Ocean' was patrolled (AA932).

Saturday, 28th
King's Cliffe. Party at Kirton. Rugger game versus an Army XV, lost heavily with the poor team we turned out.

Took off for Kirton at 1800 hours, Bob Bowen and Peter Clapham having gone on ahead with the Tiger Moth; excellent party with Group Captain Hardy, Johnnie W, Ken Holden, Robbie and a few odd pieces of fripp. A session with Teddy St Aubyn.

Johnnie's only flight this day was to Kirton for the party (AA932). 'Teddy' St Aubyn was an Old Etonian and a pre-war Grenadier Guards officer, who resigned his commission in the Army Reserve, having completed his Colour Service, when he joined 503 Squadron of the AAF in 1937, from which 616 Squadron was formed in 1938. Shot down and wounded during the Battle of Britain, sadly St Aubyn was lost over the North Sea in 1943.

Sunday, 29th
King's Cliffe. Returned from Kirton in my best suit and greatcoat with the hood well open; C.O at a party at Digby last night, and he came back feeling pretty ropey too. Squadron Balbo – jumped 609 Squadron, but a bloody shambles coming home.

Dusk patrol with Bob Bowen and Joe Crofts, latter pranged when landing at Docking owing to u/c not being fully retracted - his own fault entirely. Sgt Winter – Night Patrol – 1.00.

In spite of feeling 'ropey', Johnnie flew four times, back from Kirton, then on the Squadron Balbo exercise, climbing to 30,000 feet, before flying down to Docking for the dusk patrol (AA932).

Monday, 30th
King's Cliffe. P/O Brown posted to Flight from 253 Squadron. Night flying – Davidson and Miller Liberator cooperation flight. Flew with Lepel Cointet and Brown – both promising well.

Johnnie first flew to Polebrook, from where a cine gun exercise was flown with B-24 Liberator four-engine bombers. Afterwards a cannon firing exercise and finally 'Formation and aerobatics' (AB266).

Tuesday, 31st

King's Cliffe. Weather u/s. Link and squash at Wittering. Released from 1300 hours until dawn, except for those on Fighter Nights.

Combat films and lecture on escaping.

To Peterborough in the Ford Brake with Bob, Tess, Joe, Marc. Vassie Brown and Welch to Boscombe Down for experience on Spitfire Mk VI.

Johnnie did not fly on this last day of March 1942, during which he had flown a total of 44.10 hours, 5.10 of them operational, increasing his personal total of operational hours to 110.

The Supermarine Spitfire Mk VI was an interesting development. The Ju 86P was a high-flying reconnaissance aircraft able to largely evade interception owing to its exceptional maximum ceiling. To negate this, the Spitfire Mk VI was produced using the more powerful Rolls-Royce Merlin 47 engine driving a four-bladed propeller (as opposed to the Mk V's three blades). The new Spitfire's wingtips were also extended and pointed, intended to increase manoeuvrability at high altitude.

Owing to the heights achieved, up to 40,000 feet, and as previously mentioned, the cockpit had to be pressurised and the canopy bolted on – which was understandably unpopular with pilots. Only ninety-seven of these aircraft were built, with some of which 616 Squadron would soon become acquainted.

April

Wednesday, 1st

King's Cliffe. Good start for a new month with 27 hours flying, including Squadron formation, cannon tests and a Flight exercise.

There was no operational flying, only training flights, Johnnie flying his first two sorties as described above in Spitfire Mk VB BL574, and the Balbo exercise in AA932.

Thursday, 2nd

King's Cliffe. 23.30 hours flying today.

F/O Ollivier posted back home to Australia.

Wing Commanders Jameson and Churchill over for tea and a chin-wag.

Flight party at the Fitzwilliam at Castor including all pilots, NCOs and most of the ground crews.

Strouts and Crofts unconscious. Unfortunately on the way home a dispatch rider struck the off-side of the brake which threw them into the ditch and broke his leg. Carried him down to Sick Quarters and shoved him back to Wittering where Doc Christie attended to him.

Vaissier ('A' Flight) pranged night flying.

Johnnie flew down to Docking with 'B' Flight (AA932), remaining at readiness there, but no operational flights were ordered and so various training sorties were undertaken, Johnnie leading a 'flight exercise' (AA932).

Flight Lieutenant J.G. Vaissier was a Free French pilot who mistook Sibson airfield for Wittering when night-flying at 2200 hours, overshooting the field, wrecking his Spitfire and suffering a cut nose and lip in the process. More pilots were sent to Boscombe Down to learn about the new Spitfire Mk VI, and in particular the 'new pressure cabin'.

The 'Wing Commander Churchill' referred to was Walter Myers Churchill, a Cambridge graduate and pre-war member of 605 'County of Warwick' Squadron. During the Battle of France he had been made commander of 3 Squadron's 'A' Flight, then commanded the unit after the CO was killed in action. During ten days of fighting during that fateful month of May 1940, Churchill destroyed a number of enemy aircraft, for which he was awarded the DFC, and appointed to the DSO for his inspirational leadership. The following month he returned to 605 Squadron, taking over command, at Drem. Slightly wounded during the Battle of Britain, at the end of September he was posted to command and form 71 Squadron, the first such unit of all-American volunteers. In early 1941 however, Churchill was forced to relinquish command and stop flying owing to sinus trouble, subsequently commanding RAF Valley and employed in other ground roles.

By July 1942, promoted to group captain, Churchill was fit for operations again, and went out to Malta, flying a Spitfire off HMS *Furious* and commanding RAF Ta Kali. From there Churchill devised and led the first RAF offensive sweeps over Sicily, leading the first on 23 August 1942. He was shot down by flak and killed while leading the second sweep four days later. So perished a 35-year-old very accomplished and decorated officer – but one whose name is little known: yet another forgotten hero.

Friday, 3rd
King's Cliffe. Cine Gun - Flight Exercise and a Squadron rehearsal of the Lakenheath show.

Had lunch with Holgate from Melton Mowbray who is the surveyor in his Squadron for Mars Bros, the contractor Loughborough. Said he couldn't obtain any decent assistant surveyors so I suggested that he saw Ross, who has now done over a couple of years with Jarvis. He rang up his Director, and I rang up Rodd and arranged for him to meet Holgate tomorrow. Be a good thing if he gets the job as it will be a few quid in his pocket and furthermore he will be in a semi-reserved occupation.

Johnnie flew three times, an aileron test, 'flight exercise and cannons', and on the squadron demonstration at Lakenheath (AA932). Other pilots provided escort for 'a captured German plane'.

Saturday, 4th
Snailwell. PARTY AT SNAILWELL

Ollivier posted back to Australia. Peter Clapham and WAAF Waisom over for a little liaison. Persuaded him to come with me to Cocky's party at

Snailwell near Newmarket. Tess and he in the Maggie and self in (Spitfire) YQ-U, set off at 1800 hours, and after a little difficulty found the place. Good stag party, beer and whisky with Cocky, Ken, Denys Gillam and a few others. Slept in a single bunker with Tess.

Eleven Fighters lost over Northern France.

By this time, Fighter Command's offensive operations were well underway, the brunt of these sweeps and escort sorties being borne by 11 Group. On this day, 'Circus 119' comprising twelve Boston medium bombers, escorted by fourteen Spitfire squadrons, was despatched to attack the railway marshalling yards at St Omer. The FW190s of I/JG26 attacked the escorts of the Polish Northolt Wing as the bombers turned for home – shooting down four Spitfires. Then the 190s of II and III/JG26 pounced from the sun as the 'Beehive' withdrew over Calais through a cloudless sky. Four Spitfires from Kenley, two from Biggin Hill and another from Hornchurch were rapidly despatched. In total JG26 claimed fourteen Spitfires destroyed during this operation, with two more being hit later while on a search and rescue sortie, one crashing in the sea, the other crash-landing back in England. It was a disastrous result for Fighter Command – and an early indication that April would be little different to the previous month, during which 32 Spitfires and 27 pilots had been lost.

At King's Cliffe, Johnnie flew a firing practice sortie before flying 'To Snailwell for 56's party' (AA932). From there he flew with Assistant Section Officer Debenham as his passenger in Magister L8090, a 'pleasure trip for a WAAF of thirty minutes'.

Sunday, 5th (Easter Day)
King's Cliffe. Convoy patrols, Air Firing and Air to Air. Went over to Wittering and had the boys cracking at the MG. A Rhodesian had it down in very short time and found a con rod completely gone. Convoy Patrol 'Ocean'.

Numerous convoy patrols and training flights were made by 616 Squadron this day, Johnnie returning from Snailwell before flying aerobatic practice and then patrolling the convoy.

Monday, 6th
King's Cliffe. Air Firing at the Drogue all day long, convoy patrols and swept channel patrols for the Groupy. Ops getting bloody (Edmondson); when they can't get what they want he promptly rings up the Wing Co. Flying.

Over 100 hours flying to date this month, but I don't think we can hold the pace.

More convoy and 'swept Channel patrols' were made along with the usual round of practice flights. Johnnie's first sortie was 'air to ground firing' (AA932), the second 'air to air firing' (AB266). Flying Officer J.N. Ollivier, an Australian, was posted home, 'much to his delight'. Those servicemen and women were a long way from home; many, sadly, would forever remain far away from their homelands and loved ones; Ollivier was one of the lucky ones.

Tuesday, 7th
King's Cliffe. Air Firing and Air to Ground Practices. Balbo in the afternoon with Hurricanes of 253 trying to jump the formation, saw them each time but on the journey home 'B' Flight was detached and sent forward to Docking.

There was no operational flying for 616 Squadron on this day, only training flights. Johnnie flew on the 'Squadron Balbo', landing at Docking before returning to base (AA932).

Wednesday, 8th
King's Cliffe. Cine Gun, Squadron and Wing formations, shooting seals in the Wash.
    24.10 flying hours today.

Again, no operational flying took place, only wing, cine-gun practice and 'machine-gun tests in the Wash'. Johnnie flew twice, on 'Squadron Formation' and the firing exercise (AA932).

Thursday, 9th
King's Cliffe. No flying at all today owing to bad weather and the state of the aircraft. Played squash at Wittering.
    CO v Wing Co.
    Keynes v Padre
    Jeff v Groupy
    And were all soundly beaten.
    Malta heavily raided all this week – wonder how the old Nip and Jeff West are faring – wish to goodness I was with them.

Johnnie's friends were faring well on the beleaguered little island, where both took further toll of the Luftwaffe. There, many miles away, in his own diary Jeff West wrote: 'After lunch, borrowed a bicycle and went to Mtarfa. Saw Nip and watched a big air raid – dozens of 109s over island. Cheeky buggers with no opposition.'

Friday, 10th

King's Cliffe. Lakenheath show - cancelled.

Flight released from 1300 hours until dawn tomorrow. Scratched a rugger team together and played the Groupy's Station Medical Quarter's team – lost 6-3.

Ops informed us of the probable Wing show, so nipped up to flights and carried out a few cannon and air tests.

	'B' Flight	
	F/LT JOHNSON	GB
Posted May 1942	P/O BOWEN	CANADA
Killed May 26/42	P/O WARE	NZ
	P/O CROFTS	NZ
Missing 12/4/42	P/O STROUTS	CANADA
Wounded in action 25/5/42	P/O BROWN	GB
Missing 12/4/42	P/O LEPEL COINTET	FRANCE
Killed. 13/4/42	SGT DAVIDSON	NZ
	SGT SMITHSON	AUSTRALIA
	SGT WINTER	RHODESIA
Posted Africa/42	F/SGT McDERMID	CANADA
	SGT WELCH	GB
Shot down in ? Africa/42	SGT MILLER	AUSTRALIA

Johnnie's pilots certainly emphasised the Commonwealth's contribution, 616 Squadron now being multi-national and far removed from its pre-war auxiliary incarnation.

Saturday, 11th

King's Cliffe. Lakenheath Show – cancelled.

Party at Duxford.

Readiness at 0800 for Circus operation from West Malling. Took off at 0810 and were on the ground at West Malling before 0900 hours. To join up with 609 and 412 Squadrons and be withdrawal cover for 12 Bostons returning from HAZEBROUCK. At 1030 hours we were recalled to King's Cliffe so that the AOC can inspect the Squadron.

However, the Wing did not operate from West Malling owing to poor weather conditions, so we did not miss a show. In the afternoon slipped over to Travellers Hill with the CO for a recco.

Had to patrol 'Booty' out of our Sector as Coltishall were u/s.

Over 200 hours to date.

Early in the morning, Wing Commander Jameson had led eleven 616 Squadron Spitfires off from King's Cliffe to West Malling, close to the Kentish coast. At that 11 Group Station, the aircraft were to refuel and carry out a sweep over northern France. This, at long last, was to be the squadron's first 'Wing show' but the pilots were naturally disappointed to be recalled.

Back at base, before lunch there were high-ranking visitors: Air Chief Marshal Sir Sholto Douglas, Fighter Command's Commander-in-Chief, and the 12 Group Commander, Air Vice-Marshal 'Birdy' Saul, who inspected the squadron. During the afternoon, convoy patrols were flown, and six aircraft made 'low flying attacks at Lakenheath' – but this was no recompense for a scrubbed offensive operation. That chance would come the following day, and for two of these keen young pilots, the night ahead would be their last alive.

Johnnie flew four times, to and from West Malling, then to Traveller's Hill (BL574) before patrolling a convoy and returning to King's Cliffe (AB266).

Sunday, 12th

King's Cliffe and West Malling

Strouts and Lepel Cointet missing

Called to readiness and left WB2 for West Malling at 1800 hours.

	+W/C	
SELF+	+C/O+	KEYNES
DAVIDSON+	+STROUTS+	MOORE
BOWEN+	+LEPEL COINTET+	M/C
SMITHSON+	BLANCHARD	

Took off from West Malling at 1245 with 412 and 609 Squadrons to cover the withdrawal of 12 Bostons returning from bombing HAZEBROUK MARSHALLING YARDS. Rendezvoused with the Kenley Wing over West Malling and set course for Gris Nez, crossing the French coast in brilliant sunshine at 18,000 feet! When about 10-15 miles inside France I saw a few 109s up-sun of Yellow Section and warned them; a few seconds later they broke and I saw two 109s dive past their Section. Two 109s dived over the CO's Section and they broke, the CO getting in a squirt. Shortly afterwards I saw a FW190 a few thousand feet below and Keynes instructed his 3 and 4 to attack, but they did not hear him and it seems very probable that Strouts and Leppel mistook the order and dived after the e/a, as several pilots saw two Spitfires diving after a FW190, and Blanchard saw this, and four or five FW190s diving after the two Spitfires. The old story – probably they were both bounced and shot down if they did follow the decoy any distance down.

This sounds very feasible as if they had remained at their height they would have been OK, as no pilot from the 12 Group Wing found himself in a difficult situation.

Everyone noticed absence of flak over the usually well defended French Coast.

And thus the 1942 air-fighting season started in earnest for Flight Lieutenant Johnnie Johnson DFC and 616 Squadron.

The operation concerned was *Circus* 122, a raid by twelve Bostons on the Hazebrouck marshalling yards. The Wittering Wing, comprising 616, 609 and 412 Squadrons, was 12 Group's 'Duty Wing' that day, so flew down to and refuelled at West Malling before heading to France as Rear Support Wing. Johnnie's diary well details the action, in which the Canadian Pilot Officer Harley Strouts, of Saskatchewan, and the French Pilot Officer Lepel Cointet, failed to return, both of whom remain missing. A pilot of 412 Squadron was also lost.

Having flown on the operation and returned to King's Cliffe (AB266), Johnnie flew a ten minute 'air test' (W3370).

Monday, 13th
King's Cliffe and West Malling. Called to readiness at 1100 hours and just had time for our photos to be taken by the Yorkshire press before we steamed down to West Malling to form the 12 Group Wing again, with 609 and 412 Squadrons. Took off at 1345 and joined up with several other Squadrons to patrol LE TOUQUET – DESURES – GRIZ-NEZ at heights from 15,000-30,000 – practically the whole of Fighter Command there.

+SELF	+W/C	+KEYNES
+SMITHY	+C/O	+MOORE
+BOB	+TESS	+M/C
+WINTER	+PARES	+BLANCHARD

Returned to West Malling safely and unmolested, and after tea returned to base. The CO managed to take us almost into the balloons this morning and landed up in Melton Mowbray this evening!

Paddy Davidson killed in YQ-X when carrying out a low roll over the aerodrome. Did not recover high enough and was killed instantly.

During this fighter sweep the RAF fighters remained over the Channel and French coast, only Kenley's 602 Squadron engaged the enemy, destroying a 1/JG26 FW190, and all Spitfires returned safely. Johnnie flew Spitfire Mk V BM121 on this operation. Sergeant G.L. Davidson, a married 26-year-old New Zealander from Taranaki, was on a practice flight when he tried to roll his Spitfire at just 100 feet – and killed instantly when the aircraft crashed in a field near the aerodrome. As the 616 Squadron diarist recorded, 'It was an awkward situation for the press to be there and all personnel were warned not to mention the accident.'

Tuesday, 14th

West Malling. Today as we climbed steadily up from West Malling to Dungeness I could see Selsey Bill and the Isle of Wight to the West - and what recollections of the Tangmere days it brought back; I am the only pilot of the Squadron that remains (from Tangmere Wing days) and I couldn't help thinking of the chaps with me a year ago – Nipple and Jeff West fighting like hell in Malta; Billy Burton not then a grounded Wingco, the Bull at 12 Group, Cocky the CO of the first Typhoon Squadron; Mac, Bink, McCount, Morton and one or two others prisoners of war with Douglas Bader; good old Mabbett, Jenks, Brewer, Brown and Fellows honourably dead and buried in French soil.

No Wing show today. Saw Ross in the evening and fixed up drinks for him at the 'Fitzwilliam'.

The weather was poor on this day, as a result of which only one convoy patrol was carried out by 616 Squadron. Johnnie's diary entry is inconsistent with his log book, which details that he returned from West Malling the previous day and on 14 April 1942 flew a single air test from King's Cliffe (BM314).

Wednesday, 15th

King's Cliffe and West Malling. Squadron called to readiness and took off to West Malling at 1035. Joined up there with the 609 and 411 Squadrons and after lunch took off to provide escort cover to Hurribombers attacking DESVRES.

+KEYNES	+W/C	+SELF
+MOORE	+W/C HANKS	+SMITHSON
+MAC	+C/O	+BOB
+BAXTER	+MILLER	+TESS

APRIL

Crossed the French coast at Le Touquet at 14,000' with 609 and 411 above and stepped into the sun. We saw some a/c ahead and shortly afterwards saw Me 109s and FW190s glinting in the sun, waiting for an opportunity to pounce. Saw one come down on my Section's tail and broke them round to port in time, and when straightening out saw a 190 and a 109 passing by – I turned after the 190 and gave him a burst from the quarter with cannon only and saw strikes on his port wing root and also glycol (this also seen by Bob Bowen). I didn't follow him down, however, as there were more e/a about, so Smithson and I made our way up to GRIS NEZ and eventually back to West Malling without incident. Heard that Miller had landed in the sea with engine trouble but had been picked up by ASR.

Before the offensive operation, Johnnie first completed a cannon test (BM314), then flew down to West Malling for the operation over France, later returning to King's Cliffe (BM212). 'Hurribombers' were Mk II Hurricanes employed as fighter-bombers, usually attacking targets such as airfields and shipping from low level. The FW190 Johnnie attacked was credited as damaged, his personal combat report describing the action in more detail: -

'When about five – seven miles inside the French coast, near Le Touquet, I saw several FW190s and Me 109s 4,000 feet above the Squadron and manoeuvring for position in the sun. One FW190 broke away and came down to attack Number Four of my Section so I ordered them to break to port. The 190 fired and pulled away in a fast climb. When straightening the Section out I saw two E/A – a FW190 and a 109 diving ahead of me. I followed the 190, closing in from the quarter, and gave him a one – two second burst with cannon at 200 yards range, and observed strikes on the port wing root. He emitted glycol immediately and a piece of fuselage fell away. This was also observed by Pilot Officer Bowen (Blue Three). I broke off the engagement, as I had lost 4,000 feet and there were many E/A about, and climbed back to re-join the Squadron at 19,000 feet.'

Thursday, 16th
King's Cliffe. YQ-U u/s.
Paddy Davidson buried today at Wittering Village Church – quite the wrong sort of day with lovely warm April sunshine and the chestnut and elm trees just in bud.

Returned to flights and made preparations to take the chaps to Traveller's Hill, but after getting airborne in U I could not get the wheels up and nor could I get them fully down; had to use the CO_2 bottle as the glycol was getting very hot and on landing found that the induction and suction pipes had been connected arse about face. Saw Hally who put the Fitter responsible (Maintenance) on a charge.

On this day the squadron flew numerous convoy patrols, bomber affiliation and various practice flights, in addition to low flying attacks at Traveller's Hill. Johnnie flew four times, firstly acting as 'target aircraft' for other pilots on a cine gun exercise, then to Traveller's Hill, but was forced to land at Snailwell before returning to King's Cliffe (W3370); his fourth flight was testing cannons (AD932).

Friday, 17th

King's Cliffe and West Malling. Sweeps.

+SELF	+C.O
+BOB	+MOORE
+WINTER	+JOE

Went down to West Malling in a hell of a rush, the CO leading and followed the usual route – Greenhouses and balloons, one of these days someone is going to get hurt. Scrambled a bit of lunch and then took off on a fighter sweep only, with 411 and 609 Squadrons – W/C 'Cowboy' Blatchford leading. Went well inland of Le Touquet but my No 2 (Smithson) had to return to West Malling with a/c trouble.

Patrolled inland of Le Touquet in poor weather, turned East and almost up to Dunkirk, then orbited and back to Boulogne and Calais. Plenty of accurate flak from Boulogne and Calais but we didn't see any e/a, although 609 were bounced and squirted at. Returned to Base for 1900 hours.

Bob and I took the Ford Brake and slipped into Peterborough via the Fitzwilliam – ended up at a Dance at the Grand – half boozed, picked up a couple of farmers daughters and spent an enjoyable evening.

That morning Johnnie first tested cannons (AA932) then flew an exercise 'jumping Typhoons' from Duxford (BM121) before flying to West Malling for the sweep and returning to King's Cliffe (BM212).

Saturday, 18th

King's Cliffe. Typhoons. Cooperation today with the Duxford Wing of Typhoons, the CO led us badly but I managed to make a bit of height at the last moment and jumped a section of four Typhoons. We were all absolutely amazed as we had no difficulty in keeping them in our sights, although once or twice I had well over 450 on the clock when diving down on a 'Tiffy' and following it to the deck.

Two sections released in the evening so Joe, Bob, Rowe and I shot off to the Fitzwilliam where we were rebuffed by a couple of ATS! And then on to Peterborough to the Town Hall for a bit of a jig.

Not a very successful evening as I couldn't make a good contact, but the Trapper was there with his farmer's lass.

The squadron flew many training flights this day, including more low flying attacks at Traveller's Hill, and another cooperation sortie with Duxford's Typhoons. Johnnie participated in the latter, which was his only flight this day (BM121).

Sunday, 19th
King's Cliffe. To West Malling. Recalled from Typhoon co-op to come to readiness and proceed to West Malling. What a bloody shambles – 'A' Flight didn't join up over base and we set off with five a/c only, CO, Joe, Bob, Smithson, Winter and self. The CO flew down the Great North Road and once again we steamed to the West of London, this time skating merrily over Hatfield and nearly confirmed a Tiger Moth! Turned sharp left and came out over Hornchurch, but here I lost the CO owing to poor visibility and other a/c fluttering around. Called Moleskin and was ordered to return to base, which I promptly executed.

Jumped the Typhoons again in the afternoon. No trouble at all.

Self – over 50 hours this month!

The squadron made the typical range of flights, Johnnie again participating in the Typhoon cooperation exercise before being recalled en route to West Malling owing to the proposed sweep being cancelled due to bad weather (BM121).

Monday, 20th
King's Cliffe and Melton Mowbray. Weather rather u/s so spent all morning spraying FARQUHAR and making him operational, and after lunch belted off to Melton Mowbray. Had tea at home, then onto Nottingham to meet Valerie and to see a flick. Stayed at Melton the evening.

Johnnie did not fly this day. The meaning of the reference to FARQUHAR is unclear.

Tuesday, 21st
King's Cliffe and Melton Mowbray. PARTY IN THE MESS.

Returned to King's Cliffe after a few quick sherries at lunch time with Archie Tyers (now a corporal at Cottesmore), Johnny Townsend, and Bob Goodacre. Returned to WB2 in Farquhar in time for a bath and change, and settled down to a little steady drinking with Cocky, his Squadron Doc, Ken Holden and a few others, no one from Kenton present. Had a cock fight with the Dundas and lost again as usual.

Was almost seduced by the ginger job in the Squadron brake, she co-opted the help of Laurie Pleger – the rat.

There was no flying this day.

Wednesday, 22nd
King's Cliffe. To the Fitzwilliam for a yarn and a pint of beer with Ross.

Johnnie flew twice, to Traveller's Hill, then back from Snailwell (BM121). 616 Squadron's first two Spitfire Mk VIs arrived.

Thursday, 23rd
King's Cliffe. Good Poker game in the mess with Joe and Bob – won £5 from Joe – rather keen,

Lucky Leigh down for tea.

Johnnie flew low flying attacks at Traveller's Hill twice (BM121). The squadron also practised line astern aerobatics and formation practice.

The reference to 'Lucky' Leigh concerned Wing Commander Rupert Leigh, a pre-war Cranwell graduate and close friend of Douglas Bader's. Indeed, when the legless pilot undertook his flying test, which he had to pass to be readmitted to the service in a flying capacity, it was Leigh, then on the CFS staff, who flew with him – operating the Harvard's foot brakes, which Bader was unable to do, and passing his friend fit to fly. This has often been cited as an example of the 'Old Boys' Club' helping out a chum, which it may well have been, but in fairness, British aircraft, unlike the American-built Harvard trainer, which Bader would fly operationally, did have hand-operated brakes.

The pair would meet again at Duxford during 1940, where Bader first served with 19 Squadron on re-joining the RAF, before becoming a flight commander in 222 Squadron, which, coincidentally or otherwise, was commanded by another Old Cranwellian, namely Squadron Leader 'Tubby'

Mermagen. At Duxford, Leigh took command of 66 Squadron, which he led throughout the Dunkirk fighting and most of the Battle of Britain, during which he personally destroyed two enemy aircraft, and shared in probably destroying another and damaging one more.

After a spell as a staff officer, Leigh commanded the Havoc-equipped 23 Squadron in 1941, thereafter resuming a staff role. He did return to operations, survived the war, during which he was five times Mentioned in Despatches, retiring in 1954; he died in 1991.

Friday, 24th

King's Cliffe. Squadron to Snailwell, briefed for Traveller's Hill by Squadron Leader Holden, refuelled then on to Travellers Hill.

My Flight put up an excellent show and were complemented by Squadron Leader Holden and Wing Commander Jameson. 'A' Flight – led by the CO – not so hot. Returned to base and after tea took the chaps over to the target again, and then on to the Wash to practice on a few seals. Returned to base and after supper carried out a Swept Channel Patrol ("Ocean") with Tess, Joe and Bowen. Landed at Wittering at 2230 after a very steady day's work.

36.45 hours today.

After parking up at Wittering we went round to Wing Commander Jameson's place for a pint of beer and a pickled onion.

Typhoon crashed and made a nasty mess just North of Stamford.

Johnnie flew four times, to Snailwell, then a 'dress rehearsal' for a low flying and firing demonstration at Traveller's Hill, followed by air to ground firing (AA932). His final flight of the day was a dusk patrol (BM121).

Saturday, 25th

King's Cliffe. Flight and Squadron to Traveller's Hill for Squadron rehearsal of Sunday's show – my attack well buttoned up.

Valerie over at the Haycock for the evening – went down to the Fitzwilliam with Valerie and Turner and was very boozed at 2230 on beer and whisky.

Johnnie flew twice, on a cine gun practice at Traveller's Hill, followed by the squadron sortie to same (BM121).

Sunday, 26th

King's Cliffe. To Snailwell for lunch and the Squadron took off at 1345 hours for the big show at Traveller's Hill. My Flight was magnificent. The tactical approach was timed to a second and it had everyone foxed – complimented by the Bull and one or two others. All the Squadron hit their targets and I am told that we were the feature of the day.

Took Valerie back to Melton Mowbray in the Brake (Joe coming along too) and on the journey met young Ross on a bicycle – upped him into the Brake and all spent the evening at Melton – few beers in the George with Bob Goodbeer.

According to the squadron diarist, it was 'The real thing at last. Twelve Spitfires fired machine guns and cannons at dummy troops and armoured vehicles in front of an audience of about 5,000 men, mainly army. It was a very impressive display. Thy were followed by Beaufighters, Bostons, Gliders, smoke screen laying and bomb dropping. This demonstration was the climax to a great deal of hard work on the part of the pilots and they were congratulated for their efforts'.

The 'Big show at Traveller's Hill' lasted an hour and ten minutes, and was Johnnie's only flight of the day (BM121) – and what a sight the demonstration must have been! It was certainly a portent of things to come, with single-engine fighters in due course to play a vital role on the continent as fighter-bombers, supporting the advancing army.

Monday, 27th

Readiness at 1100 hours Debden. Squadron took off for Snailwell shortly after 1100 hours and after lunch we took off providing Escort Cover Wing to six Bostons attacking the docks at OSTEND. I must say 'Jamie' (Wing Commander Jameson) led nicely and we met the Bostons with their attendant escort north of the Thames Estuary. Proceeded steadily across the North Sea and after about half and hour's sea journey saw the Dutch coastline. The Bostons didn't waste any time but waded straight in and bombed the docks – but the flak, although isolated, was accurate and two Bostons were accounted for. I saw 133 Squadron, above us on the starboard side, engaged on the turn and we couldn't do anything to help as we were two or three thousand feet below – one Spitfire shot down and another had his mirror shot off – they claim two enemy aircraft probably destroyed. Later we carried out a fighter sweep over Northern France and although we were shadowed when inland we were not engaged. Two pilots of 403 Squadron collided and are missing. Returned to base tired after a steady day's work.

Together with 133 (Eagle) and 412 Squadrons, 616 Squadron had operated from West Malling as Rear Support Wing for the Boston attack on Ostend docks. Some fifty FW190s were seen by 616 Squadron but not engaged; one pilot of 133 Squadron and two Bostons failed to return. In the early evening, the same three squadrons swept over the French coast together but did not encounter the enemy. The two 403 Squadron pilots, from another wing, were seen to collide and crash in France. Johnnie flew four times, to West Malling for both operations and return to King's Cliffe (BM121).

Tuesday, 28th
Quiet day – a late breakfast and then down to Flight. We have done over 500 hours flying this month so I am not pushing the boys.

In the night we were called out of bed (at 2 am) as the enemy bombers were dribbling in, but we didn't go off as they steamed North up the coast then turned inland and bombed the ancient city of York.

Understand that 253 Squadron put up a good show and shot a couple down.

During the day there had been no operational flying, only practice flights, although one interesting sortie, according to the ORB, involved cooperation with a squadron of new four-engine Avro Lancaster heavy bombers. Johnnie flew on this sortie, describing the bombers as 'Manchesters' (BM121).

Wednesday, 29th
To West Malling, lunch and then CIRCUS 145 – Target Support to six Bostons attacking DUNKIRK. We met the Kenley Wing over Hornchurch but they bogged off and we had to orbit Herne Bay for fifteen minutes while they caught up with us – then the positions were changed and we steamed over as Top cover and met the bombers off Dunkirk – no engagements.

Fighter Night pilots called out to repel a raid on NORWICH – Crofts, Ware, Brown, Smithson and Winter – Norwich burning brightly when they arrived (sent off too late – AOC controlling) consequently they saw FA and all returned to Wittering safely. I think they all did bloody well. 'A' Flight didn't get off as they were all in Stamford on the beer and I believe Keynes has dropped a large one. If I were the CO I'd Court Martial the bugger 'absent from his post in the face of the enemy.'

At the time of this Circus operation, King George VI was visiting Biggin Hill, so that the bombing was successful was well-timed. Although the Wittering Wing saw no enemy fighters, the Polish Northolt Wing was engaged over Le Tréport, losing both its Wing Leader and

317 Squadron's CO. Johnnie flew down to West Malling, completed the operation and returned to King's Cliffe (BM121).

At night, Britain was once more under German bombs, these being the so-called 'Baedecker Raids', named after the German tourist guidebooks of that name which Luftwaffe planners used for target selection – this revolving around a location's cultural and historic, rather than military, significance. The offensive arose in response to the increasing damage being wrought against German cities, including such ancient centres as Rostock and Lübeck, by Bomber Command.

Thursday, 30th
Took the Spitfire VI up this morning (pressure cabin) and reached 41,000'. Flew over the observer camps at Melton at 500 feet and should imagine I foxed them. Took up Lee and Rowe in formation – Lee OK but Rowe can do with some more practice. Afterwards sent Rowe and Neville (a new USA pilot) up with Joe, and Rowe had engine trouble with V (my old YQ-U) and had to force land in a ploughed field.

Fighter Nights – Bob, Joe and myself called to readiness at 2 am but did not go off.

41,000 feet was very high for a Spitfire. Johnnie's first flight in the new type took place in BR174. Of the high-flying Spitfire, many years later Johnnie commented: 'So there we were at King's Cliffe with these high altitude aircraft, designed to operate in the desert and shoot down those high flying Ju 88s etc, and what do they do? Put us on convoy patrols at 500 feet! So that was really a waste of a good aeroplane and not very pleasant because, as they were pressurised to some extent, the hood was locked down and had to be unlocked by the groundcrew, although you could blow it off if there was an emergency. It wasn't such a nice feeling as the old hood, which slid back, so I often took to flying with no hood at all, especially on comparatively low-level convoy patrols over the sea. You still suffered though, as it was so noisy without the hood that you couldn't hear the R/T very well.'

April 1942 had been a much busier month for 616 Squadron. Seven fighter sweeps or bomber escorts had been flown over France, during which a FW190 was damaged but both Pilot Officers Strouts and Lepel Cointet had failed to return from Circus 122, their first operational flight, and Sergeant Davidson was killed in a blameworthy flying accident. During this month, Johnnie had flown 80.05 hours on Spitfires, 13.40 of them operational, bringing his total of operational hours to 123.

May

Friday, 1st

Melton Mowbray. Four days leave commencing today. Steamed off to Melton Mowbray after the boys had left for West Malling; they carried out a couple of operations over Northern France, Brown got in a good squirt at a 190 which was on Welch's tail – range up to 25 yards – shot the hood and other pieces off the Hun but he is only allocated a 'probable' although Gibby is trying to step it up to a Destroyed – unfortunately his cine film was not switched on – that will cost the prick 2/6d for Johnson's fund.

Arrived home at 4 pm and saw Valerie shortly afterwards, took her for a run in the model together with Pusher.

616 Squadron had swept the French coast that afternoon with 411 Squadron, engaging twelve JG26 FW190s over Cap Gris Nez, one of which Pilot Officer Brown claimed as a 'probable'. The reference to 'Gibby' concerns Flying Officer C.R. Gibbs, the Squadron Intelligence Officer, who had been with 616 since before Tangmere Wing days. A second sortie was flown later this afternoon when the same two squadrons provided close escort to six Bostons attacking Calais; enemy fighters were seen but not engaged.

Saturday, 2nd

Melton Mowbray. To Leicester with Valerie on a shirt hunting expedition – managed to get three reasonable garments from various shops. As we couldn't get in to see a flick returned home and in the evening Dad, Val, the Pusher and I slipped off to Holwell Mouth for a look round in the lovely spring sunshine.

Holwell Mouth is a Site of Special Scientific Interest, a marsh bisected by the river Smite, south-east of Nether Broughton in Leicestershire. Back at King's Cliffe it was a busy day of convoy patrols and training flights.

Sunday, 3rd

Melton Mowbray. A few quick sherries with Johnnie T., Bob G., Val and Ross in the George before lunch. In the afternoon took Mother for a run over to Shepsted which she seemed to enjoy.

On Thursday we heard that Sgt McCairns, who was wounded and shot down on July 6 last, has now arrived at Gibraltar having escaped from Germany. What an incredible journey he must have had.

On this day, 616 and 411 Squadrons flew as Target Support Wing for Bostons attacking Dunkirk; no enemy aircraft were seen.

Monday, 4th

Melton Mowbray. A lovely morning so Val, the Pusher and I set out fairly early and drifted through Loughborough, Kegworth and Castle Donington to Donington Park where I used to camp when a boy. Parked the car and ambled through the woods by the Trent to Kings Mills and then on to the bogland. A sleep in the warm sunshine and then we walked by the Hall back to the car.

Cruised leisurely down to Nottingham, where we visited Audrey and after a feed took her along to the Ritz to see an amusing flick. Valerie drove the model home to Melton Mowbray.

At King's Cliffe it was an uneventful day of routine training sorties.

Tuesday, 5th

King's Cliffe. Leave up lunchtime today, so after farewells drove slowly back in convoy with Johnnie T. to find the boys on a sweep. Gave Johnnie some lunch and then belted off to West Malling and arrived here as the Wing (19 and 616) were orbiting base. Landed and met the old Bull and had a long chat on the veranda of the Watch Office with him – he knows that I have been recommended for a Squadron and I think if he gets a Wing he would like me with him – I should like that too – the old 'A' Flight days all over again. The boys all arrived back eventually not having seen any enemy aircraft.

Returned to Wittering leading Ken – enjoying a little formation practice.

Johnnie flew to and from West Malling in two different Spitfire Mk Vs (W3370 and AA928), 616 Squadron not yet having a full complement of the high-flying Mk VI. This is the first mention of Johnnie anticipating receiving command of his own squadron. As a decorated pilot with substantial operational experience, it was the next natural step after commanding a flight – and just a question of time.

Wednesday, 6th
King's Cliffe. Wing Show cancelled today.
Squadron practice with myself jumping them in a Spitfire 6.

There was no operational flying on this day of training flights, including practice interceptions in the new Mk VIs, Johnnie flying BR178 'Jumping Squadron'.

Thursday, 7th
King's Cliffe. The sixes are arriving steadily and I soon hope to have a section of four to operate in the Wing Shows from West Malling. I hold the height record so far with 41,000 feet.

More practice flying took place, Johnnie flying once on a cannon test (BR186).

Friday, 8th
King's Cliffe. Cocky arrived here this morning to see about a Wing show but unfortunately it has been cancelled. Instead, after lunch, we take a couple of sixes up to Snailwell and before landing there I have a beat up with a Mustang. I can hold and maintain the American aircraft quite easily.
Cocky takes up a Typhoon and at 7,000 feet he leaves me; at 15,000 feet I can barely hold him but above that I simply walk away. We return and after tea set off for Tangmere, park at our old dispersal to find a Free French Squadron here. A few beers in the mess with Baxter, and two or three others, and then on to the Old Ship for rum cocktails, claret and brandy. Awfully pissed, fell in the creek and returned to Tangmere to meet the Wing Co – Johnnie Walker.

Another day of training, including intercepting Typhoons. Johnnie flew four times, testing a Mk VI against a V, Johnnie flying the new VI (AR286), then to Snailwell (BR256) with Squadron Leader Dundas flying his Typhoon, followed by the pair climbing to height and comparing aircraft performance, and finally to Tangmere, where the two fighter aces stayed overnight at their old station.

Saturday, 9th

King's Cliffe. Took off from Tangmere at 0715, myself leading and on Cocky's advice steered 070° for West Malling. Eventually hit the balloons at Dover so whipped round and followed the railway to Maidstone. Breakfast at West Malling.

The Squadron didn't turn up, so returned to base only to leave for West Malling again a few minutes later. After lunch took off on a Rodeo – fighter sweep only and in my opinion bloody useless. In at Dunkirk, St Anne's and out at Le Touquet without seeing a bloody thing, but later in the day when escorting six Bostons a 10 Group squadron were bounced badly and lost seven pilots.

At King's Cliffe found Val at Stamford, so put her up at the Haycock for the evening.

On this day, 616 Squadron flew the new Spitfire Mk VI operationally for the first time. Johnnie flew five times, Tangmere to West Malling, then to King's Cliffe (BR286), the uneventful fighter sweep (AR178) and return to King's Cliffe (BR178).

On Circus 168, and attack on the Hazebrouck marshalling yards, the 10 Group Wing was bounced by II/JG26 during the withdrawal. 118 Squadron lost four Spitfires in the attack with another crash-landing in England; 501 Squadron lost a pilot. III/JG26 then pounced on the Spitfires over the coast, destroying another. The FW190 was the undisputed master of the air – and nine Spitfires were being lost for every two FW190s and Me 109s. How long Fighter Command could sustain this high rate of attrition was questionable.

Sunday, 10th

King's Cliffe. Took off after breakfast for West Malling and bet the CO a bob that we should not go off as the weather looked grim. Won my bob and returned to King's Cliffe, although a show was scheduled.

Later, Wing Co Jameson, the CO, Smithson and I flew to Martlesham, refueled and took off for a look round the Dutch and Belgian coasts. Climbed steadily to 15,000' at Walcheren, but the weather looked pretty u/s and as my engine almost dropped out we turned west for England. (Saw twenty E-Boats).

Bob and I had dinner with the Doc and Jean in the charming cottage in Apethorpe.

Later the AOC balled out Jamey for not having attacked the E-Boats.

The squadron had first flown to West Malling but the weather was unsuitable for an offensive operation over France. Instead it was intended to use cloud cover 'to attack train targets in southern Holland', but when the Spitfires were fifty miles over the North Sea, the weather cleared, forcing them to return. Johnnie flew to and from West Malling, then to Martlesham, returning to King's Cliffe after the aborted Dutch sortie (BR286). That offensive patrol was flown by a section of four, Wing Commander Jameson, Squadron Leader Brown, Sergeant Smithson and Johnnie. In his log book, Johnnie wrote, 'The weather gradually lifted until we reached the Dutch coast at 15,000 feet. My engine very rough – boost capsule sticking. No e/a seen but about fifteen – twenty E-Boats sighted approaching Zeebrugge harbour (reported).'

Monday, 11th
Weather u/s. No flying.

Instead the pilots attended ground lectures and reviewed cine gun camera footage.

Tuesday, 12th
King's Cliffe. Took off in the Maggie with Steadman, destination – Snailwell, object – 2000 Guineas. Landed OK and Basil Hudson and Cocky whipped us up to the course in his car. Got off to a good start by backing the winner of the first race and making 8/- for 20/-. Then backed the winner and No 3 of the second race, and Jeepers Creepers, trained by Chubb Leach in the 4th, yielding a nice dividend.

The King's horse, Big Game (and a very lovely animal too), won the 2000 in grand style – Gordon Richards up but I did not back this owing to the very poor price. Last in the next couple of races but nevertheless enjoyed a grand day meeting Ken, Teddy and one or two others.

Ken returned to King's Cliffe and we spent a very enjoyable evening at the Fitzwilliam.

Again, there was no flying owing to continued bad weather. Johnnie's day at the races was at Newmarket.

Wednesday, 13th
King's Cliffe. Very little flying today – weather hazy. The CO shot off on 48 hours (may be 4 days) in YQ-M. (the anti G model).

To the Fitzwilliam with Bob.

The weather improved sufficiently for training flights, although Johnnie did not fly on this day.

Thursday, 14th

King's Cliffe. Bob posted today. Tried my utmost to alter this but absolutely no good.

To Ludham re Wing show. cancelled. Led the flight up to 37,000 feet in seven Spit sixes – all fired our cannon.

MacClairn's back in England after escaping from Germany – it took him about four months to reach Gibraltar.

Cocky dropped in by Master about 630 with one of his pilots, so we have a couple of beers in the Mess and then on to the Haycock. After supper we tried unsuccessfully to start the Master and so shot the obvious cause and whipped down to the Fitzwilliam - and I am afraid I returned to the Mess once more in a drunken condition.

Johnnie's only flights were to Ludham and return (BM121). There was no operational flying.

Friday, 15th

Saw Cocky off to Snailwell, then proceeded to organise the Squadron to go to Coltishall for a practice Wing show with 610. Took off at 1345 (self leading) and flew in a straight line to C. Met by Wing Commander Hanks (Champ) and took off to lead 610 – the object being to play with four Bostons. Rather a back-up with a lot of RT natter (browned off) and eventually after Rossy called out "OK chaps, let's call it a day" we all drifted discontentedly back to Base 2.

After tea Joe and I were scrambled for a Dornier off the East coast but Group sent us off too late and we missed it, although one section of 610 got in a good squirt and claim a probable. Neville here when I arrived back so took him down to the Fitz and Haycock for a couple.

Johnnie flew four times today, practising aerobatics (BM121), to Coltishall for the Wing practice (BR286), and on the scramble (BM121).

From York, Wing Commander Peter Prosser Hanks had joined the RAF in 1935, was a pre-war member of 1 Squadron at Tangmere, flying biplane fighters, and a noted aerobatic pilot. Having converted to the new Hawker Hurricane on 31 January 1938, when war broke out his log book recorded 767.45 flying hours – an experienced pilot. 1 Squadron famously fought throughout the Battle of France, during which Prosser, as he was commonly known, became an ace and was awarded the DFC. Afterwards he was posted as an instructor to 5 OTU at Aston Down, missing the Battle of Britain, but nonetheless seeing action when a lone Ju 88 was intercepted and shot down over the Cotswolds.

In December 1940 he was posted to 257 Squadron as a flight commander, increasing his score by two more German bombers, one at night, then commanded 56 Squadron – introducing the new and initially problematic Typhoon. In December 1941, Hanks became Wing Leader at Duxford, and took over the Coltishall Wing in February 1942. Like others mentioned in this diary, Wing Commander Hanks would soon find himself in Malta, in the thick of it, surviving the intense air-fighting and, indeed, the war.

Saturday, 16th

Very little flying – had to send four Spitfires to Biggin Hill yesterday evening and that has left me rather short. Three unsuccessful attempts to take off a drogue for PP after which we scrambled out for air firing. Flight released (two sections) from 1800 hours, so pushed off in the CO's car to Leicester with Neville, Bob, Joe, Tess & Bowen. Good evening with plenty of liquor.

Only routine flying took place from King's Cliffe, Johnnie flying twice, a cine gun practice, landing at Wittering and return (in a Spitfire Mk V, serial unrecorded).

Sunday, 17th

King's Cliffe. Squadron formation complimented by W/C. One of Neville's pals from 15 Squadron came over for lunch (name Francis Doyle) and afterwards I sat in No 2 pilot seat and took over the controls when airborne. Passengers included Sagar, Doc, Bob, Smithson and half a dozen ground crew. The Neville took a Spit down to Wyton and I went down in the Stirling, returning in the Spit.

Neville stayed behind to go on a mine laying raid off Copenhagen in the Baltic Sea. He is second pilot to a squadron leader pal of his and they are flying F for Freddie – 'MacRoberts Reply'.

CO back from four days leave today, Stan Turner up at Snailwell for lunch.

For some reason Johnnie had reverted to flying a Spitfire Mk V, participating in the squadron formation practice (BM121). Then, Johnnie and ten others flew twice in the 15 Squadron Short Stirling (W7515), a massive four-engine bomber, a complete contrast to the tiny Spitfire. Afterwards Johnnie flew back from Wyton to King's Cliffe (BM314).

Monday, 18th

Neville missing.

Doyle rang up form Wyton this evening and said that Neville was missing from his Copenhagen raid – but there is a chance they may have force landed and if so may make Sweden.

This was sad news indeed. 'MacRobert's Reply' was the second Stirling so named, in memory of the three sons of Lord and Lady MacRobert, all killed flying, one in 1938 and two on operations with the RAF during the war. On the night of 17/18 May 1942, the Stirling was shot down over Denmark, only the mid-upper gunner, Sergeant Jeffs, surviving the crash.

At King's Cliffe, only one convoy patrol and training flights took place. Johnnie flew an air test, then to and from Wittering (Spitfire Mk V, serial unrecorded).

Tuesday, 19th

King's Cliffe. Fly down to Wyton to collect Neville's kit – Francis Doyle seems to think they were hit by a flak ship when off Copenhagen as he was on the same show and was attacked himself when only a few hundred feet up. Bloody bad show as this was Neville's first operational trip after almost three years flying at FCS's and of US.

Wrote to his old Dad at Manchester.

Wednesday, 20th

King's Cliffe. Sanderson came down today from Speke in a Tiger Moth. He has made one Atlantic crossing in (MSFU) but wasn't sent off. Took advantage of his stay in Canada to become married.

News today from Malta via Wing Commander Stan Turner. Nipple was shot down by our own ack-ack (typical) when chasing a J88 at 500 feet across Malta. He was blown right out of the cockpit, doesn't remember opening his parachute and is now in hospital with leg and back injuries.

616 Squadron flew a practice Wing flight, but Johnnie took a Spitfire Mk VI (BR181) to Hamble, near Southampton, where specialists attended to an aileron issue. Two test flights later the matter was resolved, and Johnnie returned to King's Cliffe.

Freepost Plus RTKE-RGRJ-KTTX
Pen & Sword Books Ltd
47 Church Street
BARNSLEY
S70 2AS

✂ DISCOVER MORE ABOUT PEN & SWORD BOOKS

Pen & Sword Books have over 4000 books currently available, our imprints include: Aviation, Naval, Military, Archaeology, Transport, Frontline, Seaforth and the Battleground series, and we cover all periods of history on land, sea and air.

Can we stay in touch? From time to time we'd like to send you our latest catalogues, promotions and special offers by post. If you would prefer not to receive these, please tick this box. ❑

We also think you'd enjoy some of the latest products and offers by post from our trusted partners: companies operating in the clothing, collectables, food & wine, gardening, gadgets & entertainment, health & beauty, household goods, and home interiors categories. If you would like to receive these by post, please tick this box. ❑

We respect your privacy. We use personal information you provide us with to send you information about our products, maintain records and for marketing purposes. For more information explaining how we use your information please see our privacy policy at www.pen-and-sword.co.uk/privacy. You can opt out of our mailing list at any time via our website or by calling 01226 734222.

Mr/Mrs/Ms ....

Address. ....

Postcode. .... Email address. ....

Website: www.pen-and-sword.co.uk Email: enquiries@pen-and-sword.co.uk
Telephone: 01226 734555 Fax: 01226 734438
Stay in touch: facebook.com/penandswordbooks or follow us on Twitter @penswordbooks

Thursday, 21st
To Grantham with CO, Bob Large and Parks ('A' Flight) for a visit to the MARCO cannon factory. Interesting but rather tiring, lots of fripp about – arranged a date for tomorrow evening – Blue Ram 0830.

Left the factory at 4 pm and onto Nottingham, quite a pleasant evening but rather expensive.

There was another Wing practice, but Johnnie did not fly today. The factory visited was that of Hispano Suiza, near Grantham, which produced the Spitfire's 20mm cannon.

Friday, 22nd
Bob posted today – Middle East – saw him off on the train at King's Cliffe and gave him my Yeomanry cigarette case – the best Canadian I have ever met, in fact about the smartest man I have come across. Weather u/s no flying. Squash with CO.

To Grantham again but the Blue Ram closed so spent a very average evening here and there mooching around.

There was no flying on this day of heavy rain, on which 'Pilot Officer R.D. Bowen regretfully leaves us for overseas posting, probably getting a flight commander post. We are all very sorry to lose "Bob" (otherwise known as "Trapper" due to his activities in Arctic Canada) Bowen for he had been with us since Tangmere Wing days and had shown his worth as a cool fighter who used his head.'

Saturday, 23rd
Whitsuntide
What is Operation *Lancing*?
We shall know pretty soon.

Weather still pretty duff and just possible to carry out a little flying.

Smithy and I with the dog Pursher lurking after a few rabbits – two confirmed.

Letter today from Neville's father. I am to keep his kit until I go to Manchester.

Rowe, Latimer and Baxter posted to Malta.

There was no operational flying. Johnnie flew on a 'flight exercise' and a formation practice sortie (BR181).

Sunday, 24th

King's Cliffe. PP firing, Joe towing Drogue, self and Smithy shooting at it.

Self – 11 hits – not too bad, Smithy – f.a.

Squadron exercise with W/C Jameson and self pumping the boys – good fun. Colin Gray dropped in for a cup of tea and a chat and after flying a bit pushed off to Preston.

Joe and I took the evening off and pushed off to Melton Mowbray expecting to meet Valerie there but was disappointed. Met Mairie and David and took a few Gills at the George.

Again no operational flying. Johnnie flew on a cooperation flight with Typhoons, then firing practice and 'Jumping Squadron' (BR181). 'Pumping' meant dummy firing, the Wing Commander and Johnnie being the 'attacking' aircraft.

Monday, 25th

Brown wounded in the eye.

Blue Section (P/O Brown and Sgt Welch) and Green Section (self and Sgt Smithson) scrambled shortly before 9 pm for a raid near Leicester. Afterwards Smithy and I intercepted it at 4000 feet about four miles NW of base – dived down to investigate and saw large British type on the mainplane – could not identify type so closed in to identify when the rear gunner opened fire on me – broke away and Smithy attacked from behind me – e/a dived into cloud and blue section engaged it below cloud; Brown closed right in but his Perspex was hit and a piece struck his eye – carried out a beautiful landing at North Luffenham – (unfortunately he has lost his eye – operated on at Rauceby) – Welch then attacked but does not seem to have hit the Dornier 217.

It was last seen flying over Luffenham with white smoke burning from one engine and is therefore claimed as damaged, shared between Brown, Welch and Smithson.

This was 616 Squadron's first engagement with the Spitfire Mk VI. Having been hit in the right eye, Pilot Officer Brown nonetheless pressed home his attack, firing at his assailant. After landing safely, he was rushed to hospital where his eye was removed. In spite of all the drinking and high jinks off duty, the measure of these men is personified by Brown's actions this day, and this ORB entry: 'He made a rapid recovery and appears none the worse for his experience.' These were fit, spirited and extremely courageous young men, make no mistake. The Dornier was claimed as damaged, shared with 411 Squadron: someone had 'had a crack at it before we encountered it'. The enemy reconnaissance aircraft appears to have returned home safely, and was probably from KG2 *Holzhammer*, based in the Netherlands, which supplied most of the aircraft used in the Baedecker Raids.

Johnnie's log book page for this and the subsequent few days of May 1942 is unavailable, so exactly what flights he made, and in which aircraft, is unknown (the 616 Squadron ORB only records operational flights, so those can be identified, but is scant in detail, not recording aircraft serials or codes).

Tuesday, 26th
Tess killed and Welch force-landed.

This afternoon while leading Blue Section in cloud, Tess suddenly turned to the right at 16000 feet and began to dive, his speed increasing to 280. His No 2 (Sgt Featherstone) broke away and went onto his own instruments eventually returning to base – Tess was seen by people on the ground to break cloud – (without wings and on fire) and dive straight in. Welch had broken away a few minutes earlier with a dud engine and executed a perfect forced-landing in a Lincolnshire field with wheels and flaps down and hood on – a bloody good show but what a prick! Found poor old Tess – a good chap and had the making of an excellent flight commander – just reached a useful number of hours too – between five and six hundred. We shall never know what happened to him.

To the Fitzwilliam with the Flight.

The reference to 'Tess' concerns Pilot Officer Leicester Bond Ware, who, on this 'tragic day', 'lost his life in a practice interception with 303 Polish fighter Squadron. The circumstances of his death are not known, except he was seen to dive down at great speed, the wings of his aircraft fell off and the aircraft burnt out, crashing near RAF Station Scampton. He was a most popular fellow and his loss is keenly felt by the Squadron.' The 26-year-old was buried in Scampton churchyard, a long way from his home in Canterbury, New Zealand.

Johnnie's derogatory remark concerning Smithson's forced-landing was because, being made on an unprepared surface, it was safer to land wheels up, rather than risk tipping the aircraft up on uneven ground, possibly with fatal consequences. Landing wheels-down saved the aircraft but put the irreplaceable pilot at risk.

After such a day, it is hardly surprising that 'B' Flight went for a drink.

Wednesday, 27th
King's Cliffe. This afternoon I took Welch and Featherstone to Hamble to have smooth ailerons and new hoods fitted to a couple of sixes. Took off from Hamble in a rainstorm and into cloud at 500 feet – out at 1800 feet, a very shaky do.

There was no operational flying, only another cooperation flight with Typhoons and the usual training sorties.

Thursday, 28th
King's Cliffe. Party at the Tompkins' and a very good evening too with lots of good food and drink – present the Grumpy Jamey and wife, Tubby Clayton, Ted Edwards and one or two others.
Mick Murray up for a few beers.

Three 616 Squadron Spitfires operated from Martlesham, again intending to use cloud cover to their advantage on an offensive patrol over southern Holland, but half way across the North Sea this cleared, so once more the Spitfires returned to base, the lack of cloud to hide in making them too vulnerable to visual detection.

Friday, 29th

Johnnie made no entry this day, on which only training flights were carried out.

Saturday, 30th
Valerie over for the weekend, staying at the Haycock, setting down for a few Pyans in the Glassey when the CO rings up and says it's about tomorrow – an early morning show. The Gen is that the biggest concentration of bombers ever is attacking Cologne this evening – about 1500 of them. This rather upset the evening and naturally we had to take it fairly steady.
    Ken Gough down with the latest Group news: -
    Ken Holden (W/C) to Hutton Cranswick.
    Stephen Hardy to Middle Wallop.
    John Barraclough to Command.
    John Johens still in 616 and nearing the completion of his second year (makes you think!).

Dawn and convoy patrols were flown from King's Cliffe, and 616 Squadron was represented at Pilot Officer Ware's funeral, who was buried with full military honours. The squadron was also visited by the Army Film Unit, which took 'numerous pictures of our pilots and aircraft'.

Sunday, 31st

King's Cliffe. Rose from a warm comfortable bed at 0300 and were airborne shortly after 0430. Morning with low cloud and heavy driving rain. The idea was for the fighter squadrons to patrol off the North West to escort our bombers returning from Germany, but we were rather late and didn't see 'em, but Smithson and I did see and report a submarine, so swept Channel a few miles off Spurn Head. Tony Gaze down from Hawarden – he is slowly going to take over 'A' Flight. Took Valerie home to Melton – a miserable journey in the brake as it kept continually conking.

At 0515 hours, eleven 616 Squadron Spitfires had taken off to cover the last aircraft returning from the first thousand bomber raid, made against Cologne. The submarine sighted by Johnnie submerged, but its position was reported.

At this stage of the war it was hoped that strategic bombing alone could destroy Germany's ability to continue fighting, and fatally undermine the German people's morale. Such a high-profile raid was also a means for Bomber Command's chief, Air Marshal Arthur Harris, to show the War Cabinet what his night-bombers could do. 1,047 bombers participated, including the new four-engine Lancaster and Halifax, although twin-engine aircraft, mainly the ubiquitous Vickers Wellington, made up most of the attacking force – and to make up the numbers, aircraft and crews were drawn from training units, and 113 night-fighters supported the raid through flying intruder operations. On the night, 868 aircraft hit Cologne, with fifteen more visiting alternative targets. In total, forty-three RAF aircraft were lost, just 3.9 per cent of the attacking force. 1,455 tons of bombs were dropped, nearly half of which tonnage was incendiary – which caused 1,700 large fires. Ninety per cent of the city centre was flattened, 3,300 homes were destroyed, and 45,000 made homeless. 474 German civilians died that night, with 5,000 injured, a surprisingly low figure owing to well-constructed shelters and deep underground cellars. As Harris said, 'They sowed the wind and now they are going to reap the whirlwind.'

Frederick Anthony Owen 'Tony' Gaze was an Australian, a colourful and exceptional character who Johnnie had known in the Tangmere Wing when Gaze flew with 610 Squadron. A former Cambridge scholar, Gaze destroyed eleven enemy aircraft during the war, including shooting down an Me 262 jet while flying a Spitfire in 1945. Decorated with the DFC and two Bars, he survived the war Australia's tenth-ranking ace, thereafter enjoying a successful career as a racing driver.

Indeed it was Gaze who in 1946 suggested to Lord March that the former Westhampnett airfield, from which he had flown with the Tangmere Wing in 1941, would make a great race track – his Lordship agreed, and today the result, Goodwood, is world famous. Squadron Leader Gaze died in 2013.

June

Monday, 1st

Returned from Melton early today with Ross and the Pusher but the MG finally gave up the ghost (plugs I suspect) at Langham, so I cycled into Oakham and rang up for the Brake from the Police Station. Doc Barney is now at an MO just outside Newmarket and was down today for lunch and a yarn. Keynes and I have only six or seven aeroplanes between us. I managed a release and Mac, Smithy, Winter, Parry, Moore and I set off for Rauceby to see young Brown. We found him remarkably cheerful and hopping about like a young sparrow, we must get him back to the Squadron somehow. Hit Nottingham at 6 and settled down to a little steady drinking – Flying House, Black Boy and later the Victoria. Met a WAAF captain by the name of Mary Walker. In all a very good evening, although I pranged the brake slightly on a keep left standard.

The squadron made two convoy patrols, completed an army cooperation exercise and other training flights; Johnnie did not fly.

Tuesday, 2nd

Arrived back from Nottingham at 4 am in a very shaken condition just in time to change and to climb into our cockpits for a dawn patrol – Smithson groping his way about Dispersal quite boozed and Winter, Parry, Mac and I little better. However, we flew with hoods off and got plenty of fresh air, and all arrived back at base safely. Dear old Cocky rang up this evening and said that he had heard I was badly wounded and off my rocker in some hospital!

Party at Group tomorrow night – Ken is pushing a boat out on the strength of his promotion to Wing Commander, Hutton Cranswick.

The dawn patrol was made by eleven 616 Squadron Spitfires, including Johnnie (BR250) and friends somewhat the worse for wear, patrolling the

North Sea to cover aircraft returning from the latest thousand-bomber raid on the industrial Ruhr valley. Johnnie later flew a test flight in the same Spitfire, on another day of training exercises.

Wednesday, 3rd
King's Cliffe and West Malling
Tony Moore missing

Took off just after 1100 for West Malling and there met 610, Scruffy Heywood and the crew – the Wing being led by 'Champ' – Wing Commander Hanks. Took off at 1555 with four other 11 Group squadrons, the rendezvous being over West Malling at less than 900 feet – a very keen show but by the grace of God we made it and then on to Boulogne – west to the Somme and then east again towards Germany. On this last turn (down-sun) I noticed a squadron of a/c [aircraft] climbing up on our port side and sure enough they turned in behind us so as to attack from the sun. I broke blue section smartly round and found myself mixed up in a squadron of 109s but could not get a squirt as I had a bit of a job to get away. Tony Moore 'A' Flight missing. Came home early and after a bath and a change, bunked on to Hucknall for the Buck's (Ken Holden) farewell party – now Wing Commander at Hutton Cranswick. Present – The Baron, Pete, Gough, Welch and one or two other Groupites.

This was a busy day for Johnnie, first flying an air test, then to West Malling for the operation and returning to King's Cliffe, and finally to Watnall for the party (AB543).

The offensive patrol was a diversionary sweep by eleven 616 Squadron Spitfires, while other RAF formations operated further south, attacking targets in Le Havre and Cherbourg. It is possible that Pilot Officer P.J. Moore, an Australian who was taken prisoner, had fallen victim to *Oberfeldwebel* Leibold of *Stab* I/JG26, who made the unit's only combat claim that day. The laurels that day belonged to JG2 Richthofen's pilots, who, in response to the main RAF effort, claimed twenty-three Spitfires for no loss.

Thursday, 4th

Johnnie made no entry today, on which he flew three times: back from Watnall, 'Jumping Squadron' and a climb to 35,000 feet (AB543). On this day, Flight Lieutenant Gaze DFC replaced Flight Lieutenant Keynes as 'A' Flight Commander.

Friday, 5th

King's Cliffe and King's Cliffe to West Malling. Another low rendezvous show again. There were two other bombing operations at the same time – OSTENDE and LE HAVRE and ours was le DIVERSION show. Rendezvoused off Dungeness at 500 feet - ten squadrons again – a trifle keen – then climbing out to the Somme where we orbited for a quarter of an hour. The Wing Co saw some e/a but lost them in the haze and although Smithy and I stayed for a long time we didn't see any e/a.

Johnnie flew down to West Malling, on the sweep and back to King's Cliffe (BR181). The sweep was flown over the Somme–Le Touquet area, returning via Dunkirk.

Saturday, 6th

King's Cliffe and Kirton-in-Lindsey To Kirton in Lindsey with 'B' Flight as the Poles are carrying out a wing show from West Malling, and we have to cover them.

Saw the friendly old faces again and enjoyed a delightful lunch. Returned to King's Cliffe shortly after tea.

616 Squadron flew a number of convoy patrols and training flights while Johnnie took 'B' Flight to Kirton, providing cover there for squadrons taking part in a cooperation exercise with the army and Stirling bombers.

Sunday, 7th

2100 hours flying today but everyone getting rather tired owing to the heat of the cockpits. Smithy and I commenced to take the MG right down, as the bloody thing has never run properly since I brought her up from Ringmer.

It was a busy day of training flights and inconclusive scrambles for 616 Squadron, Johnnie flying four times: air-to-air firing twice (BR186), a climb to 35,000 feet (AB543) and 'jumping Typhoons' (BR1186).

Monday, 8th

Featherstone passed out today when flying, and he had only been airborne for a few minutes. He had omitted to turn on his oxygen, the prick, but nevertheless there is still something very wrong with these cockpits.

Cocky drifted along about sixish – he always smells out a party as the sergeants are coming into ours' this evening.

The squadron flew convoy patrols and training flights; Johnnie did not fly today.

Tuesday, 9th

To Nottingham in Clume's car with Smithson and Joe. Made a good start in the Flying House and then went to the Black Boy with a couple of damsels whom we soon dropped. On to the Palais in a shaky condition and then I was foolish enough to ring up Val who was rather browned off when she saw me lurching about.

Johnnie made no flights today, another of routine flying.

Wednesday, 10th

At 3 pm today, Holly rang up and passed the amazing news about my being awarded a bar to the DFC - which came as a distinct shock. Bob Bowen also awarded the DFC, which he thoroughly deserved - and he will be bloody delighted as I know it was one of his ambitions. A Party in the Fitz and then we brought Ross up to the Mess, and the CO and I were almost on our knees.

The citation to what was effectively Johnnie's second DFC, gazetted the previous day, reads as follows: 'Since being awarded the DFC in September 1941, this officer has participated in many sweeps over enemy territory, during which he destroyed two Me 109Fs and damaged a FW190. He has also carried out a large number of convoy patrols. Flight Lieutenant Johnson is an exceptional leader and the magnificent example he sets is an inspiration to other pilots.'

Johnnie flew once on this day, practising aerobatics (AB523), while 616 Squadron's other pilots likewise largely engaged in training flights.

Thursday, 11th

Johnnie made no entry today, another of training flights, Johnnie climbing to 30,000 feet (AB543).

Friday, 12th

'B' Flight these days: -

F/LT Johnson	England
P/O Crofts	NZ
P/O Winter	Rhodesia
P/O Smithson	Australia

P/O Neville	USA
P/O Wright	USA
P/O Cleland	NZ
Sgt Welch	England
Sgt Lee	England
Sgt Featherstone	England
Sgt Miller	NZ

Johnnie did not fly today, and would not do so until 16 June 1942; he was on leave.

Saturday, 13th
48 hours
Drew 'Working Street' and 'Big Game' in the Derby and won £14.
To Nottingham after lunch-time session with the Groupy.

Joe, Smithy, Winter and self had tea at Group, then pushed on the Black Boy with Ken Gough and Hanken. After a while met up with the CO and I regret to say that we were all found on our knees. We are all putting a fair amount back these days and taking no exercise.

Back at King's Cliffe there was no flying, the pilots instead visiting Wittering to review cine gun film and intelligence.

Sunday, 14th
Melton Mowbray
Murlass Range all day in ? of 151.
Quiet day at home with Valerie. To Leicester in the evening to see a flick.

Low cloud and mist decreased flying at King's Cliffe, which was again training only.

Monday, 15th
Johnnie T over.
Finished off at the Red Lion at 3 am.

To [illegible] on the 16, and after a little flying a few of us pushed off to Leamington to the Clarendon where the whiskey flowed thick and fast. Back to the mess where the very decent Station Commander kept the bar open until about 2 am.

Persistent low cloud prevented all but two cannon tests at King's Cliffe.

Tuesday, 16th

To Honiley. Lecture by F/Sgt McCairns, who was shot down last July, turned up today to give us a lecture on escaping. He was shot down at ground level when returning from a show and hit by light flak. He crash-landed on Dunkirk beach and had to be assisted out by a couple of Huns as his sliding hood had jammed. He was given first aid and then introduced to a 'phony' RAF flying officer, who was undoubtedly bogus. And Mac wasn't taken in! He was removed to St Omer Hospital and then taken to a *Dulag Luft* in the heart of Germany (an aircrew prisoner reception camp). He escaped once but was recaptured and taken to the prison camp where Douglas Bader is kept, but the German authorities would not allow him to see Douglas. He was eventually sent back to his original camp and given twenty-one days solitary confinement. He laid his plans and escaped a second time, and after four days of extreme hardship, skill and courage crossed the German frontier (in a blizzard) into Holland. He was then so cold and wretched that he climbed into a pigsty and snuggled up to a porker for warmth and heat!

He got in touch with the farmer's son the next morning and he put Mac in touch with the right people, and he had a very comfortable time travelling through Holland, France and Spain. A very stout effort indeed and it will live long in the annals of the Squadron.

Johnnie flew a formation and cine gun sortie, then to Honiley with the thirteen other 616 Squadron Spitfires, from where formation and cine gun practice flights took place (AB543). Groundcrews were moved to Honiley by road, this being an exercise to assess the difficulties of a fast move. Experience in North Africa had given a clear indication of the vital importance of RAF fighter-bombers flying in support of ground troops, keeping on the move, and such would be the case when enemy occupied Europe was eventually liberated.

Wednesday, 17th

Johnnie made no entry today, flying two affiliation exercises with Typhoons from Honiley, landing back at base on conclusion of the second (AB543), the moving exercise having gone smoothly. Back at King's Cliffe, Johnnie then took an army visitor, Lieutenant Tompkins, 'local' flying in the squadron Magister (L8090). Other pilots patrolled a convoy; an approaching enemy aircraft thought better of it and turned about for France.

Thursday, 18th

Towed the MG to Melton Mowbray and exchanged it smartly (with Geo. Hayston) for a 1933 Morris S. Sandy and I had tea at home and then back under our own steam to King's Cliffe. She doesn't pull too well on hills and so we commenced the decoke today.

A telegram from the Bull and a very charming letter from the Marquis of Titchfield about my Bar.

Johnnie did not fly today, low cloud lifting in the afternoon to permit other pilots to fly a formation exercise.

Friday, 19th

Pushed off down to Snailwell to buy Cocky a drink and eventually tracked him down at Duxford. Over a pink gin he told me that Heywood is leaving and that Prosser Hanks had told him (Cocky) that I might get the Squadron (610). Made my way up to Coltishall and joined up with the remainder of the boys, 610 and 411, for a practice Wing show. Before taking off, Prosser pulled me aside and said that Heywood is definitely on his way and he had asked for me as Squadron Commander. "It is not official", he said "but it's up to me and you'll be hearing about it this week!" Well, everything would be rosy were it not for the fact that 610 are re-equipping with Typhoons…

Dance at Wittering. Ken Holden down, Mary Walton again and a very pleasant evening.

Well, what news – tempered only by the prospect of 610 Squadron exchanging Spitfires for the Typhoon fighter-bomber. Johnnie now had to patiently await official confirmation. He flew five times that day, to Snailwell, then to Duxford, back to Snailwell, from there to Coltishall for the Wing practice, landing back at King's Cliffe (AB543).

Saturday, 20th

Squadron moved to West Malling for one week's operational flying with 11 Group. This operation again cancelled, the reason I do not know. The CO and Wing CO left to attend a Fighter Command conference at London, leaving me to hold the fort. Smithy, Mac and I changed and made a rush for Leicester after tea, where we spent a very enjoyable and rowdy evening. Mac missed us on the return journey but miraculously turned up for breakfast at King's Cliffe.

Sunday, 21st

Took the Squadron over to Coltishall for a practice Wing Balbo with 610, 411 and 616, led by the Champ (Wing Commander Prosser Hanks). Landed at Coltishall and took off about 1100. A good show and I managed to keep the Squadron in a fairly steady position – the Prosser was quite pleased about it.

We intercepted a wing of Tiffies [Typhoons] and then returned to Coltishall for lunch. Met Cpt Fish (ex-Kirton) and had a couple of beers with the Station Commander – Group Captain Lees. Took off again after lunch but we could not make the Wing show as the bloody ground crews had not changed the oxygen bottles, so I brought the Squadron back to King's Cliffe.

Johnnie flew three times, to Coltishall for a Wing practice and return to King's Cliffe (BR543). Four aircraft swept over the Channel uneventfully, and practice flights were undertaken.

Monday, 22nd

A little more flying today. I took some of the ground crew up in the Maggie. Stoker made a balls of a sticky u/c and only just managed to land at Wittering. Featherstone ran into [illegible] when taxying YQ-Y and managed to damage the mainplane.

Borrowed Gibbo's car and meet Betty in Stamford at 8. The Pusher with me. Sauntered along to the Wheatsheaf where we had a few beers and gin, and then on to see Ross and the Fitz.

This was another day of training flights, although Johnnie's only flight was a jolly in the Magister.

Tuesday, 23rd

Squadron formation today, myself leading, 'A' Flight with restrictors in, ourselves with them out. The whole of 'A' flight except Tony Gaze, who has a pressure tank fitted, cut out around 26,000 feet and the remainder climbed steadily up to 35,000 feet, which is about the height a squadron can operate in these sixes. Heard from the CO today that very probably we shall soon be moving down to Kenley in 11 Group, which will no doubt liven the proceedings a trifle. The Flight released from 4 o'clock so I dashed into Stamford to meet Betty at six. Took her into Peterborough in the Morris, the flicks, a beer with Ross at the Fitzwilliam and home to Kelton via the well-known Colly Weston Woods, ya-ya! Put in the preliminary work for a weekend in Leicester.

Again Johnnie flew but once today, a 'Squadron climb in line abreast' (BR523), on what was another day of routine training for 616 Squadron.

Wednesday, 24th
No news about the 610 job yet but the Prosser said it would take about a week, so there's hope yet. Took Stokes up this morning for some live astern aerobatics and he startled me by putting up a really good show and sticking close. Led the squadron in a steady climb to 36,000 feet where we opened up into line abreast and everyone thought it a bloody good easy formation!

Johnnie flew four times, formation practice, the squadron climb, then to and from Kirton (BR178). It was another unremarkable day of training flights at King's Cliffe.

Thursday, 25th
To Kirton to have lunch with Cocky, at 56 Squadron, and Ken Holden. After at least a dozen Worthingtons, Cocky and his boys strapped me gleefully into a bloody great Typhoon and before you could say 'Bob's yer Uncle' I was hurtling along at a steady 300. Went for a trip via Melton and King's Cliffe and then back to Kirton where after the fourth bounce we slipped her down much to the relief of the 56 Squadron onlookers.

According to Johnnie's log book, he only flew once this day, a cannon test (AB543), the Typhoon flight being recorded the following day, so there may be some confusion if one or other of the records was completed historically.
Another day of routine flying for 616 Squadron, although Pilot Officer Smithson burst a tyre on landing, but no other damage was sustained.

Friday, 26th
Today we heard that a German flight lieutenant, after mistaking the Bristol Channel for the English Channel, landed at an aerodrome in South Wales and taxied up to the Watch Office for petrol. The poor bugger switched off his engine before he realised his mistake and was of course captured. When he saw the Station Commander he said 'Give me 60 gallons of petrol, put a squadron of Spitfires over the aerodrome and I'll guarantee to get back to France.' Some of the boys have been down to see the 190 (which he was flying) and they say it is really a delightful machine with four cannons firing through the air screw.
Sally born.

Oberleutnant Armin Faber of *Stab* III/JG 2 landed by mistake at Pembrey in South Wales on 22 June 1942 – presenting the RAF with an intact FW190 – and negating the desperate need for a proposed commando raid to capture one from a German airfield in France. The feared enemy fighter was rapidly evaluated at Farnborough, and the essential data discovered immediately fed into the Spitfire development programme.

Fighter Command's need to get the Spitfire back on top was urgent, and the engineers responded to the call. That month the first Spitfire Mk IXs began reaching the squadrons. Production output increased slowly however, and while eventually the improved Spitfire, with its two-stage supercharger, would eventually redress the balance for Fighter Command, in the meantime most squadrons continued operating the obsolete Mk V.

According to Johnnie' log book, he flew three times today, to Kirton where he went up in the 56 Squadron Typhoon (US-A) for an hour, then back to King's Cliffe where the squadron experienced 'a very full practice day'. Johnnie's reference to Sally concerned another black Labrador who would accompany him on many adventures.

Saturday, 27th
King's Cliffe. To Leicester with Smithy, Joe and Betty Green of Kelton. Kicked off at the Grand, where we soon met Wigston Winnie, Jill and Teresa (the bloody Russian!), Judy Dent looking rather attractive, Phil Russell, now a flight lieutenant on Mosquitoes whom I have not seen since Marshall's days. Steady evening on Pyms and then Betty and I slipped away to the Palais where we danced a little and then back to the car in the Grand garage. As usual Joe missed the bloody van and he had to stay at the Grand – he turned up at Stamford the following morning.

Johnnie flew once, an aerobatic practice flight (BR181), on another day of training for 616 Squadron.

Sunday, 28th
King's Cliffe. Did a little readiness with my Flight by way of a change.

Johnnie flew a single cloud flying practice this day (BR181), while other pilots patrolled Wells and 'beat up' the Home Guard during an exercise at Wellingborough.

Monday, 29th
LEAVE.

Beadle pranged. Ken Gough came down from Group for a bit of a chat and we had a talk about the 610 job, he told me not to worry, everything was under control. After lunch and a bath, the Pusher and I drifted along to Melton where we had tea, and then on to Nottingham where I meet Valerie in the American bar of the Black Boy. On to the flicks and then on again via 240 to Melton Mowbray.

Johnnie flew once, an uneventful scramble responding to an unidentified X-Raid, (AG543), while other pilots flew an exercise with Typhoons. Pilot Officer Neville taxied into another Spitfire while preparing to take off, severely damaging both aircraft – attributed to 'gross carelessness'.

Tuesday, 30th
LEAVE

So ended a largely uneventful month for 616 Squadron, with less operational flying than usual, but sadly Pilot Officer P.J. Moore had been lost on the first of the two sweeps flown. Also, on 20 June 1942, Sergeant Clouston had been killed while performing aerobatics below 1,000 feet. The squadron had now fully converted to the Spitfire Mk VI, problems with which explained the lack of operational flying: excessive heating of cockpits below 20,000 feet prevented 616 Squadron flying operations below that height. During the month Johnnie had flown 41 hours on the Spitfire Mk VI, only three of them operational, with other flights in a Typhoon and the Magister increasing his total flying hours to 848.10. For Johnnie personally, the month had been significant, owing to receiving a Bar to his DFC and the prospect of getting his own squadron.

July

Wednesday, 1st
LEAVE

At King's Cliffe, yet more routine practice flights took place.

Thursday, 2nd
Returned to King's Cliffe after a good lazy three days spent at Melton Mowbray. Took up the four that will be flying with me in the big scale operation that is planned and which depends on the moon, tide and wind.

No copy of Johnnie's log book exists between 1 and 12 July inclusive, so only details of operational flights can be identified in the 616 Squadron ORB. On this day the squadron flew the usual round of training and a Typhoon affiliation.

Friday, 3rd
Squadron moves to West Malling. Cocky turned up just before lunch and as usual we established ourselves in the bar and were soon joined by the CO, Laurie Lagan and Group Captain 'Lucky' Leigh. About a dozen excellent beers and then a cola lunch followed by a couple of quick vintage ports. Funny how every time Cocky turns up we always seem to have a bloody good drinking session. He staggered off for Snailwell just before tea and afterwards the Squadron took off for the South being cheered on our way by S/Ldr Clayton and Peter Clapham. Brownie brought us down in a very nice straight line and we were soon at West Malling where Joe had done an excellent job of organising dispersal, rooms etc.

To Maidstone in the evening with young Merry, Joe, Smithy, Red and Wright. Finished up at the Stow Dance Hall and promptly snatched a woman and lurked off into the country.

Pilots and groundcrews moved to West Malling, reinforcing 11 Group, according to the Squadron ORB, on a 'special operation. Everybody looking forward very much to some action. Arrived in time for strawberries, which were in abundance. Food excellent.'

Saturday, 4th

West Malling All our nice clean aeroplanes have been camouflaged in the most amazing manner with 4/9" bands of white painted between the spinner and the cockpit and 2 on each tail plane – they look like a gang of wasps buzzing around.

I can't find out any gen about the 'do' we are on, the two Wing COs know all about it but they are not talking. Prosser says that there will definitely be some fighting if the show takes place and that we shall be operating in sections (of four probably) and not as a wing or as squadrons. No flying today, with the exception of the Readiness Section, so about 3 pm the Crow, Smith, Joe, Mac and I wandered off to Maidstone to see a flick, then on to Stow Cocktail Bar where we started on Rye and Dry and finished up on beer, and then into the dance.

During the forthcoming invasion, still two years away, the volume of Allied aircraft required that they were uniquely marked for ease of identification, so black and white stripes were painted on their wings and fuselage. The reference to 616 Squadron's Spitfires being painted in a similar pattern at this time provides a clue as to the type of operation being planned.

There was no flying from West Malling owing to heavy rain.

The reference to 'Crow' concerns Air Marshal Sir Denis Crowley-Milling (as he much later became), an Old Malvernian and pre-war Rolls-Royce apprentice at Derby who learned to fly with the RAF Volunteer Reserve. During the Battle of Britain, 'Crow', as he was universally known (or 'DCM'), was a very young and impressionable pilot flying Hurricanes under Douglas Bader's command in 242 Squadron. Immensely inspired by the swashbuckling Bader, Crow became an ace, and later served in the Tangmere Wing as a flight commander on 610 Squadron, a post he still occupied at this time.

Sunday, 5th

West Malling. The 'do' again not on today so I took up Smithy, Red and Gill Wright for a recco round the South East of England (invasion corner).

After lunch and a few quick ales we took the road for Hindon Manor, which possesses an excellent swimming pool, a couple of bars, a dance and dining hall – just the place for tired fighter pilots. We returned for tea, learnt that the 'do' had again been cancelled for another 24 hours, and so returned for a swim and then commenced the drinking at 7 prompt. At one stage the Prosser and I had six whiskeys each in a half pint tumbler, a very shaky do indeed, and we had the good sense to move on around 9 pm. Whisked out to the dance hall, pinched the Brown Job's girlfriends and generally made a hell of a noise.

Only cannon tests and formation practice sorties were flown by 616 Squadron.

The reference to 'Brown Jobs' concerns army personnel, owing to the khaki colour of their uniforms.

Monday, 6th

West Malling A further 24-hour postponement, the bloody tide will soon be wrong for the Brown Jobs and if the weather is not suitable before the 9th, the operation will be scrubbed out. Prosser took the Wing up for a practice Balbo this morning and after lunch we all made our way to Hindon Manor for a bathe. Recalled to meet Leigh-Mallory, and then after tea returned to Hindon. This was the shakiest evening of the whole bloody lot and the boys were almost on the knees at closing time. The 610 crowd seem to be a rather good bunch of fellows especially their IO – an excellent type. Gough came down from Watnall today and the 610 news is not encouraging from my point of view – apparently Heywood got a Hun a few evenings ago and the AOC seems to think the guy's OK and should stay on with his Squadron. But Prosser and the Station Commander are doing their best to kick him out, so the only thing is to wait and see.

Mention of 'Brown Jobs' in this operational context provides another clue as to the nature of this mysterious operation. Clearly, whatever it was involved many aeroplanes and soldiers. This could only mean one thing, especially with mentions of the importance of moon and tide: a joint service operation and a landing of some sort on the French coast. Time would tell, as it also would regarding Johnnie's promotion prospects.

Tuesday, 7th

The operation definitely cancelled today so we can all return home. Cocky rang up from Ludham and said that he wanted to see me this evening, and that this was an order, so I flew over to Snailwell in a Mk V after tea. Just before leaving I learnt that 485 Squadron (at Kenley) are arriving up at King's Cliffe tomorrow so it seems likely that we shall be there pretty soon. Cocky, Lyle, Finch, Pat Pollock and self got off to a pretty quick start with a few rum cocktails and then a few more at a club in Newmarket, dinner at the White Lion and then on to the Black House for a few quick pints of ale and then back to the Mess where we locked ourselves in the bar and declared a guest night! I fell down in the bog, banged my head and passed out, coming round at 4 am feeling awful.

The 'special operation' had been cancelled due to bad weather, much to the disappointment of 616 Squadron, who were ordered back to the monotony of King's Cliffe. This, however, was tempered with much more welcome news: 616 Squadron were to replace 485 Squadron in 11 Group's Kenley Wing.

Wednesday, 8th
KENLEY Took off from Snailwell in a Typhoon flying No 2 to Cocky for a practice Typhoon wing led by Wing Commander Denys Gillam DSO, DFC and Bar, AFC. Eventually broke away and landed my Typhoon at King's Cliffe to find that the Squadron was leaving for 11 Group and Kenley after lunch. Cocky soon trickled into King's Cliffe in my Spitfire and we commenced a lunchtime session in the bar eventually locking ourselves in, which rather shook the CO! Took off about 3 pm and flew in a straight line to Kenley making quite the worst landing of my life.

Talk by Wing Commander Wells, and Group Captain Atcherley ('Batch') and then I saw Bob Pavelow (602 Sqd) in the Mess and we drifted up and spent a rather poor evening in town.

It was a busy day for 616 Squadron, eagerly packing for the impending move south. The 'air party arrived for lunch and rail party by 9 pm. Excellent accommodation and good food'.

Wing Commander Denys Gillam, to whom Johnnie refers, was himself a former member of 616 Squadron, who had personally accounted for most of the unit's combat victories during' its ill-fated stay at Kenley during the Battle of Britain – earning himself the nickname 'Kill'em Gillam'.

Thursday, 9th
Kenley. Squadron released after tea, so Tony, Mac, Joe and I set course for the Channel and French coast to have a look round and to see if there was

anything about. Found 10/10 light thin cloud over the channel so we nipped under it and patrolled at 4,000 – 5,000 feet but didn't see a thing, not even a little flak.

According to the 616 Squadron ORB, 'Flight Lieutenant J.E. Johnson DFC & Bar is posted and promoted to Squadron Leader, to take command of 610 Squadron at Ludham. He joined us at the end of 1940 and has done excellent work with us, having destroyed six enemy aircraft'.

Friday, 10th
KENLEY. LEAVE 616. At breakfast this morning the CO told me that I had been posted supernumary to 610 Sqd as a Flight Lieutenant, which shook me a little, and he advised me not to go until I had been made up to squadron leader.

A great farewell party in the GREYHOUND at Croydon with the CO, all 'B' Flight pilots and all the ground crews, Sanderson, Turner, Gledhill, Varley, Jackman, Fred Burton (my Fitter), Randy, Walty, Windy, in fact the whole bloody Flight. A good evening but a little pathetic and touching at times as I have been in the Squadron almost two years and have seen a great many changes amongst the pilots - but the ground crews and I have remained constant and naturally have become attached to each other. We all had a great singsong on the train.

The squadron was released all day, which, given the level of alcohol abuse likely to be involved with celebrating Johnnie's well-deserved and long-awaited promotion, was no bad thing.

Saturday, 11th
KENLEY, SNAILWELL, WITTERING With the help of Gledhill and Varley I left Kenley at 8.30 in the Morris very much overladen and complete with the Pusher. Said goodbye to everybody with a break in my voice and felt an awful clot but we were soon underway and after a couple of hours I dropped in at Loughton to see my old colleagues there. A few beers with Freer and Cole, a handshake with Sydney Manfield, a chat with the Trevallions and on to Newmarket where Cocky soon turned up from a couple of days in Yorkshire.

After tea, he, Lyle, Finch and I set course for Wittering for the big party, calling en route at the Bridge, Huntingdon and the Haycock at Wanford. A good party with lots of ale and spirits, lobster and crab, and Ken Holden, Jamie, Basil Embry, Peter Clap, Mac from Kirton, Bill Tomkins and a dozen others.

Sunday, 12th

WITTERING AND SNAILWELL Before leaving Wittering, Ken said he would ring Group, obtain all the form and ring me back at Snailwell at 1200 hours. This he did in his usual efficient manner and I am taking over 610 w.ef [week effective as of] tomorrow, 13 July. This afternoon Cocky fetched Diana over from Cambridge and the three of us went for a swim in a delightful privately owned pool in Newmarket.

In the evening, 56 gave a party, and a very good one too, in their own mess there being present Group Captain Grandy (Duxford) Wing Commander Gillam DSO DFC (Bar) AFC, and Squadron Leader Paul Ritchey DFC (bar) author of 'Fighter Pilot.'

A good drunken evening.

Johnnie: 'On the way to 610 Squadron at Ludham in Norfolk, I spent the night with Cocky Dundas at Newmarket, he was at a place called Snailwell, commanding the first Typhoon squadron, 56, which was having a lot of teething troubles and killing a lot of pilots. He kept the morale up; he was a very good leader, Cocky. We then set course for the big Wittering summer party, calling in at "The Bridge" at Huntingdon, and "The Haycock" at Wansford. We had lots of beer and spirits, and, oh yes, lobster and crab - we certainly lived well in those days! The following evening, Cocky organised a party to celebrate my promotion with his pilots, and this was attended by, amongst others, John Grandy, who went on to become Chief of the Air Staff, and Paul Richey, author of *Fighter Pilot*. We had a right old session, but the following day it was off to Ludham and 610.'

Monday, 13th

Ludham

Promoted Acting Squadron Leader

610 F Squadron (County of Chester) AAF

Sqd Leader JE Johnson DFC. (Bar)

'A' Flight	'B' Flight
P/O Collinge (i/c)	F/Lt Crowley-Milling DFC
P/O Wright	P/O Smith
P/O Hokan (Canada)	P/O Pearson
P/O De Patoul (Belg)	2/Lt HVINDEN (Norway)
LT Pabiot (France)	P/O Maisgrove
Sgt Fallon	Adj Geudand (France)

Sgt Creagh (Australia)	W/O Jackson (Canada)
Sgt Brown	Sgt Turner
Sgt Peart	Sgt Leech
Sgt Edwards	Sgt Roberts
Sgt Harris	Sgt Hawkins
	Sgt Warley

Travelled up to Cottesmore by road. The old Morris almost on its last legs. A chat with Group Captain Lees and the Prosser, some lunch and then on to Ludham to meet the chaps of 610 who seem to be a pretty fair bunch. This Squadron was of course commanded by the Bull (Ken Holden) during their stay at Tangmere and it seems strange that I, at one time in his Flight, should eventually take over his old Squadron.

Johnnie (from interview in person):

> First, I went to the Sector Station, Coltishall, where I had an interview with the Station Commander, Group Captain Lees, and met the Wing Commander (Flying), a chap called Prosser Hanks who had flown during the Battle of France with Paul Richey. Ronnie Lees told me that I would be taking over 610 Squadron from a chap called "Scruffy" Haywood, a regular chap, but he said "I don't know whether you'll see him or not because I haven't even seen him for several weeks. So far as I can make out he is shacked up with some society woman in a caravan just outside the airfield!"
>
> The "society woman" was Lady Margaret Strickland, who had been a bit of a beauty in her day, and still was, and achieved a certain amount of fame for anti-blood-sports and that sort of thing. Then it was off to Ludham, hard by Hickling Broad, to meet the people of 610 who seemed to be a pretty good bunch. The Squadron had been commanded by Ken Holden when in the Tangmere Wing, so I knew a bit about it. We had eleven pilots in "A" Flight, and the same in "B". These included people from Canada, France, Belgium, Norway, and even a Rhodesian, people from all over the place. That was a big change from pre-and early war days.

That Johnnie, the policeman's son and former grammar schoolboy from Melton Mowbray should be promoted to command an AAF unit was an equally 'big change': he had achieved this through merit, not the connections of a privileged socio-educational background.

610 'County of Chester' Squadron had been formed in 1936 at Hooton Park, Wirral, and was initially equipped as a light-bomber squadron with first Hawker Hart, then Hind, biplanes. As war with Germany became increasingly likely, on New Year's Day 1939, 610 became a fighter squadron but did not receive its first fighters, Hurricanes, until the month war broke out. By the end of September 1939, however, the unit had been re-equipped and converted to the Spitfire, with which it would have a long association. During the Battle of Britain, 610 Squadron was based at Biggin Hill during August 1940 and heavily engaged, also losing a number of ground personnel when that famous RAF fighter station was bombed several times. Having rested at RAF Acklington, the squadron returned south in 1941, to Tangmere, where from March onwards it was a part of Wing Commander Bader's Tangmere Wing, along with 145 and 616 Squadrons. It was, therefore, another squadron with a proud history, and as Johnnie's first command, this was a landmark moment in his distinguished career.

At Ludham, Johnnie lost no time in flying a local familiarisation flight in one of his new Squadron's Spitfire Mk Vs (ED245).

Johnnie: 'When I got to Ludham, Denis Crowley-Milling, or "Crow" as we called him, was a flight commander on 610, with whom he had flown during Tangmere Wing days. He was really senior to me, having been commissioned before me and won a DFC before me, and it put me in a bit of an invidious position to suddenly become his Boss. I told the Group Captain, who lived at Coltishall, this when I took over the Squadron, but he told me not to worry as Crow would be getting his own squadron any moment now. In fact he very soon got one of the very first Typhoon squadrons.'

Tuesday, 14th
Ludham. Settling down at Ludham, writing letters and getting to know the Squadron pilots and personnel. They include Englishmen, Canadians, New Zealanders, Australians, a Rhodesian, fighting French and Norwegians.

To Wittering to see Jamie, but, unfortunately, he was on the well-known Wing practice.

It is worth mentioning here that the compilation of squadron ORBs was of an inconsistent style and standard. While, for example, the 616 Squadron diary only recorded operational flights in its Form 541, being the daily record, its Form 540, a monthly summary, was completed on a daily basis, describing events. 610 Squadron's diarist, however, did things differently, instead only keeping a record of largely personnel postings in the 540, but going into more detail in the 541 regarding operational flights.

Wednesday, 15th
Ludham. Squadron formation in five abreast for an hour which went quite well and after tea the Crow and I took off for Texel to Ijmuiden, 'Jim Crow' recco flight. Long range tanks fitted and we needed them, as it is 44 mins flying time to Texel. We saw quite a reasonable convoy off the coast, near Ijmuiden consisting of eight cargo vessels and two escort ships – either flat or E-Boats.

610 SQUADRON WHEN I TOOK OVER – 13 JULY 1942
F/LT COURTNEY ENGLAND. Posted India Aug.
P/O COLLINGE   ENGLAND. Promoted F/LT Aug 1942, Awarded DFC Nov/42
P/O HOKAN   CANADA. Posted to a Canadian Squadron Aug and killed in action immediately
P/O WRIGHT   ENGLAND Recommended for DFC with Doug and Smithy in Oct but turned down by AOC
P/O PABIOT   FRANCE
P/O DE PATOUL   BELGIUM Posted to a Belgian Sqd in Sept.
SGT CREAGH   AUSTRALIA Commissioned in Sept. shot down over Dieppe, bailed out and home with Navy
SGT FALLON   ENGLAND Posted away once but came back to Sqd in September
SGT BROWN   ENGLAND Posted to Malta October '42
SGT EDWARDS   ENGLAND Posted September
SGT PEART   ENGLAND Posted to Malta October '42
SGT HARRIS   NEW ZEALAND Posted to Malta October '42

On this day, Johnnie flew twice, a 'Squadron Balbo' and the 'Jim Crow' (a coastal reconnaissance patrol) with Flight Lieutenant Crowley-Milling to Texel and Ijmuiden on the Dutch coast (JEJ: DW-B, EP245, DCM: DW-X, EP361). Ludham, situated near Norfolk's east coast, was being used for such offensive operations over the Dutch coastal areas, although this was a long flight in a Spitfire across the North Sea, and hence the use of auxiliary fuel tanks to extend range. On this occasion, Johnnie and Crow, White Section, took off from Ludham at 1900 hours, thirty-five minutes later sighting Texel and a 1,000 ton cargo ship steaming north. The two Spitfires continued along the coast at 240 Indicated Air Speed, noting a convoy and flak ships a mile north of IJmuiden, returning to Ludham with that intelligence at 2030 hours, after a forty-minute flight home.

Thursday, 16th
Ludham. Group Captain Lees over for a chat and to see the Crow, who I understand is to get the first available squadron in 12 Group. Took Coffin, Doug, Guy, Aunt and Pierre along to the Ferry at Wroxham for a beer or two and ran into the Prosser and his wife.

Johnnie's flights today were just to Coltishall and return (EP245, DW-B). Flying Officer Coffin was 610 Squadron's Intelligence Officer, who would feature heavily in Johnnie's equally relentless pursuit of good times.

Friday, 17th
Ludham. Poor day with low cloud and rain, took off for Wittering to collect my suit and see Jamie but had to turn back owing to bad weather. Getting all the 'gen' about *Rhubarbs* on the Dutch Coast – there are several likely looking places and it should interest the boys especially if we can seek out a few places with little or no flak.

There is LAIDEN, where we should find some goods trains and/or a gasometer, and/or some German troops, and there is also a likely looking wireless station right on the coast near IJMUIDEN.

To the Ferry with Doc and HVINDEN and Poggi where we met Prosser and No 2, and also Valentine and No 2. A very good steady evening's work and then onto a dance at Wroxham, where I picked up with rather a charming little WAAF by the name of Judy.

Johnnie's aborted trip was in his now usual Mk V, EP245, and recorded in his log as 'Aerobatics'.

As already mentioned, a *Rhubarb* was the codename for an offensive operation seeking targets of opportunity. They were flown very low so as to approach undetected by the enemy's radar: the pilots flew so low they were 'down amongst the *Rhubarb*' – it was decided that no German listening in would ever understand what this meant! They were highly dangerous, however, owing to flak in particular, and many experienced pilots were lost on such sorties. Offset against the collateral damage to the Germans achieved by *Rhubarbs* however, these losses were not commensurate with the outcome.

Saturday, 18th

Ludham. Coltishall Party } 'Fraid I can't make them both
Hayton Cranswick Party }

This morning I sat listening to the 8 o'clock news in bed when they announced that Paddy Finucane had been killed in action. Apparently, he had been beating up a German post in occupied France and his Spitty was hit. He tried to get back to England but when over the Channel his motor cut and he went straight in. Some of his boys circled the spot for some time but all they saw was a patch of oil on the surface – what a bloody end. Although he had shot a line at one time I think that since he had had the Wing he had improved tremendously, at least that is what recent combat films prove. How the ranks of the old stagers are thinning – I was looking at the photograph of 610 and 616 yesterday and there are truly 'only a few of us left.'

Johnnie did not fly today, while 610 Squadron completed a number of convoy patrols and uneventful scrambles.

The loss of a fighter leader of Wing Commander Finucane's calibre on an ad hoc ground-attack sortie is very much a case in point emphasising the futility of these operations and calibre of pilots being lost.

Brendan Eamon Fergus Finucane – known as 'Paddy' – was born in Dublin on 16 October 1920, the eldest of five children. Before the Second World War the family migrated to Richmond, Surrey, Paddy achieving a short service commission in the RAF during 1938. His elementary flying training was completed at Sywell – a course he nearly failed. Eventually his Service Flying Training was completed at Montrose, Evanton, and South Cerney before reporting to 7 Operational Training Unit at Hawarden on 28 June 1940 to fly Spitfires. On 13 July 1940, three days after the Battle of Britain officially began, Pilot Officer Finucane arrived at Hornchurch and 65 Squadron. Paddy joined 'B' Flight, commanded by Flight Lieutenant G.A.W. 'Sammy' Saunders (later to become squadron commander), whose pilots included the 'ace' Bill Franklin DFM, Ken Hart and Tommy Smart (later killed over Malta).

During the Battle of Britain, 65 Squadron operated from Hornchurch and Rochford. Between 1 and 18 August 1940, Paddy flew fifty-two sorties, and continued flying operationally until the squadron moved north to Turnhouse in Scotland, on the 28th. During that critical period in 11 Group, Paddy had destroyed two Me 109s, probably destroyed two more and damaged another.

A year after war was declared, Paddy was promoted to flying officer – and was remembered by a comrade, the Polish 'Gandy' Drobinski, as 'a very quiet sort of man, totally dedicated to being a fighter pilot; he spent little time in the bar'. Gandy even engaged Paddy in dogfight practice – which ended far below the specified minimum height, such was the pair's enthusiasm. On 28 November 1940, 65 returned south, to Tangmere, flying from where Paddy destroyed more enemy aircraft before again heading north, to Kirton, on 26 February 1941.

There a new Australian fighter squadron, 452, was being formed, on which Paddy, promoted to flight lieutenant, became a flight commander on 14 April 1941. Soon afterwards, while providing a display of air drill over Scunthorpe, he collided with his commanding officer, Squadron Leader R.G. Dutton. Paddy's airscrew nearly severed Dutton's tail, but the Squadron Leader miraculously managed to crash-land in a turnip field, smashing through a dry-stone wall, and survived. A month later Paddy was awarded the DFC, and on 21 July 1941, 452 Squadron moved to Kenley, the famous Surrey sector station.

Almost immediately Paddy's score of aerial victories increased, recognised with not one but two bars to his DFC. By this time, his exploits had captured the public's imagination to the extent that the press, having previously described him as an anonymous Irish flight lieutenant, could withhold his name no longer. Three weeks before Paddy's twenty-first birthday an Air Ministry bulletin declared that as his score stood at twenty, he required one more victory before his birthday. He got it. On 9 August 1941, RAF legend Wing Commander Douglas Bader was captured – leading to the press dubbing Paddy 'Bader's successor'. The propaganda machine had lost one hero but found another.

Paddy was wounded only once during operations, when a German bullet hit his leg on an anti-shipping sortie. After a perfect landing he was found unconscious in the cockpit and duly hospitalised until January 1942. On 21 October 1941 he received the DSO, and in February 1942 was promoted to squadron leader and given command of 602 Squadron at Redhill. More combat successes followed. On 21 June 1942, Paddy was promoted to wing commander and became 'Wing Commander (Flying)' at Hornchurch. Sadly this well-deserved appointment, the pinnacle of a fighter pilot's career, would be short-lived.

On 15 July 1942, Finucane had briefed his pilots for a 'Ramrod' operation against a German army camp near Le Touquet. The Hornchurch Wing flew east, across the Thames, then over the Channel at zero feet, avoiding detection by German radar. The attack was timed for the Spitfires to arrive over their target while enemy soldiers queued for lunch. At 1222 hours they crossed the French coast at Le Touquet – when a German machine-gunner opened fire from the dunes below. A single bullet damaged Paddy's radiator – of which he was unaware. His wingman, Pilot Officer Aikman, informed his leader of the damage, causing Paddy to turn hard right, taking a course that would take him back over the coast and home. As the two Spitfires re-crossed the coast, Aikman let fly, destroying a German machine gun position.

Streaming white glycol fumes, Paddy had no choice but to ditch in the sea. The Spitfire gently alighted on the waves, but instead of momentarily remaining afloat, giving Paddy time to get out, it plunged vertically into the depths. Aikman circled the spot, directing RAF Air Sea Rescue launches to the spot, but only an oil slick marked the watery grave of the great Paddy Finucane – one of Fighter Command's greatest fighter pilots.

The free world mourned, three thousand people attending Winchester Cathedral for his Requiem Mass. In his adoptive home town of Richmond, the Mayor launched an appeal for a 'Finucane Memorial'. The Finucane family received a plethora of sympathetic messages, including telegrams from officers of air rank and even two Soviet aces.

Wing Commander Finucane remains missing.

Sunday, 19th
Ludham. What a bloody party, yesterday we meet up with Cocky, Paul, Peter and one or two others at Coltishall, and all were soon absolutely stinking, we all came home in my car, eleven-up, and Coffin driving. This morning, after a couple of eggs for breakfast and a prairie oyster, Lyle, Cocky, the Commandant and myself shot down to the Ferry for a steady three-hour lunchtime session, returning for a chicken and vintage port at 1330. Cocky should have been on a wing show over France and after the port he shot off in my aircraft – I believe he is in for a bollocking! [illegible] and I went to bed for couple of hours, and after another chicken we slipped down to the Ferry and met up with a couple of jobs from London. We rowed across to their house boat, hid the oars and so of course had to spend the night with them. Returned to Ludham for a bath and an egg in the small hours.

Johnnie did not fly today and only routine patrols took place.

Monday, 20th
Ludham. Squadron formation very good, went to bed at 8 pm.

Johnnie flew twice, practising air-to-air firing and on the 'Squadron Balbo' (EP245). Other pilots again flew routine patrols.

Tuesday, 21st
Ludham. To Wittering to collect my suit and to have a yarn with Jamie, Groupie Eubane, Tubby, Groupie Lee and Peter Clapham.

Grouse shooting. Knipton 23.

Jamie is going to come over during the moon period and talk to the Squadron on Intruder work.

Squadron beating up the army all day long with cine films.

Johnnie flew twice, to Wittering and return (EP245).

Wednesday, 22nd
Ludham. Poor weather, flew over to Coltishall to do a *Rhubarb* but the Groupie postponed this until the morning as the weather was really becoming "duff".

To the Ferry with Aunt and Coffin but I think we shall have to park up the lane as our seniors are always there to observe our misdeeds.

Johnnie flew four times, two army cooperation exercises, and to and from Wittering (EP245).

Thursday, 23rd
Ludham. Fighter night commences.

Took off at 0500 hours with Doug, Collinge (Red Section) for *Rhubarb* operations in Holland. Yellow Section (Group Cpt Lees and P/O Wright) turned back as the Groupy's a/c developed tank trouble. We hit the Dutch Coast a little to the north of our target and crossed it in cloud. When about five miles inland we came out 6/10 at 600 feet and looked for a target. I soon saw Alkmaar and noticed a lot of barges and an attractive looking lock gate on the canal there. Doug and I came round and attacked the gates away from the town, and saw cannon and machine gun strikes on the target, at the same time some light flak opened up on us from the tower.

We carried on and seriously damaged a couple of large barges on the canal and then we were split up so I had a bang at a dredger on the way home. Both returned safely to base and were met by the Group Captain who seemed fairly pleased.

Party in the Sergeants' Mess. Coffin and I had to put Poggi to bed again – drunk as a coot.

Johnnie flew five times today (EP245). On the first, early, trip, the Spitfires crossed the North Sea at 200 feet before climbing to 4,000 feet over the

Dutch coast and jettisoning their long-range tanks. After shooting up various targets, as Johnnie described, the Spitfires returned safely to Ludham at 0650 hours after a flight of one hour forty minutes. Johnnie's other flights were transit flights, in formation with the squadron, to Warton, Westhampnett, Kenley and return.

Friday, 24th
Ludham 21491

Group Capt 'Lucky' Leigh down from 12 Group HQ to talk about Intruder work.

Air Commodore HRH The Duke of Kent (Welfare) came for a look-see with his P/A and Group Cpt Lees. 'How long have you been in the RAF my man?'

Plenty of night flying including a trip myself.

To Tangmere (Shades of 1941) to see Mac about Intruder work but unfortunately his Squadron has moved to Acklington and he himself has gone to Crosby OTU. Had lunch with S/Ldr Thomas (12G), S/Ldr Spraight and 'Uncle Bert', who has recently returned from Malta. He said that the old Nipple was shaken when he took off from the a/c carrier and he also told me how well Jeff West did out there, winning the DFC, so that he now has both – the cross and the medal (DFM). Uncle Bert tells me that "Jeff" is back in this country – I must try and locate him.

Johnnie flew once, an aerobatic practice (EP245).

Saturday, 25th
Rang up Bernard Abbot re Grouse shooting in Scotland.
July 31st – August 9th
Mars Fenom Private Hotel
Broughton
By Biggan, Peeblesshire
Broughton 25.
30 miles South of Edinburgh
Turnhouse 25 miles away.

Dingy in Wrexham Broad with Doug, Guy, Sgt Brown and Jamie. Arranged for a Squadron boat and dingy for the boys which should be good fun. Located the Wing Commander's dog (he is away on leave) at the Ferry and there met Max Aitken, who was celebrating with his boys. I joined them with Poggi and invited them all back to the Mess at Ludham where we drank a few gallons of ale and a couple of bottles of whiskey. Max disappeared eventually up the road on his motorcycle combination at 0300 hours.

Johnnie flew once, an uneventful night patrol of thirty-five minutes (EP245).

Squadron Leader Max Aitken DSO DFC was the CO of 68 Squadron, a Coltishall-based Beaufighter-equipped night-fighter unit. The son of the press baron and Minister for Aircraft Production, Lord Beaverbrook, Aitken had been a pre-war auxiliary, flying with the socially elite 601 'City of London' Squadron – the celebrated 'Millionaires' Mob' – which he was promoted to command in June 1940. Having already been decorated, Aitken was rested as a staff officer between the following month and February 1941, when he took over 68 Squadron, with which he recorded four nocturnal victories – including the Ju 88 and Do 217 destroyed the night before celebrating at the Ferry.

Later, Aitken commanded Coastal Command's Banff Strike Wing, survived the war and became a Tory MP, succeeding his father as Chairman of Beaverbrook newspapers. When his father died in 1964, Aitken inherited the title Baron Beaverbrook, immediately renouncing it on the grounds that there would only be one such in his lifetime – his father. Knighted in 1965, Sir Max died in 1985.

Sunday, 26th
Squadron formation very good indeed in five abreast, five astern. Dropped in at Coltishall for lunch and who should lob in but Cocky in his bloody great Typhoon. A good lunch time session, very steady.

Johnnie flew twice, on the 'Squadron Balbo', landing at and returning from Coltishall (EP245).

Monday, 27th
Ludham. Max [Aitken] awarded the DSO.
Saw group Grp Cpt Lees about Collinge and Crow. A couple of postings to Malta and one or two other jobs. Fighter Nights called out over Norwich, eight of us took off but we were soon recalled as a ground mist was creeping across the aerodrome. Hvinden gave me a few grey hairs but eventually I managed to talk him in and he just made it before the weather closed completely down.

Johnnie's only flights today were to and from Coltishall (EP245). Second Lieutenant Arnt Hvinden, mentioned by Johnnie, was a Norwegian pilot.

Tuesday, 28th
Ludham
Dinner with the Suttons at Wroxham? No – too bloody busy.

Johnnie's Fighter Night patrol over Norwich was followed by a flight to Coltishall, then cloud flying (EP245). That evening he also flew a 'Night Flying Test' (EP250, DW-G).

Wednesday, 29th
Ludham. The 'Adj' [Adjutant] posted to Public Relations Branch, Air ministry, probably to fill Flight Leut post. Smith and Hvinden had a bang at a couple of 217s well out to sea – no claims. When on a Jim Crow later on in the day off the Dutch coast, Doug, Collinge and Brown (our new Sgt) had a bang at a Ju 88 - range about 800 yards.

No results seen. Wroxham ATC over with Mr Sutton. Army security police over for a dekko.

Johnnie's first flight was a local sortie in a Miles Master with Corporal Hitchen, followed by an air test (EP245).

Thursday, 30th
Ludham. The cine films which Doug and I took on our *Rhubarb* a week ago came back today and were very disappointing, as nothing whatsoever was to be seen on the negative. Squadron formation very good except for Blue 4 - Musgrove. Took off at 1845 and flew up to Kirton to see if Mr Smith had obtained my Bolton [illegible]. Found the aerodrome full of Yanks with their Lightnings. A few quick sherries with Herdy, Mac, and one or two others, followed by an excellent meal and a couple of vintage ports. Took off at 2200 and carried out a shaky landing in the gloaming to find a bit of a party in the Mess.

Johnnie flew three times, the squadron formation practice followed by his trip to and from Kirton (EP245).

The reference to 'Yanks' and 'Lightnings' is significant. Still haunted by the spectre of the First World War, having pursued a policy of Isolationism from events in Europe, on 7 December 1941 the United States fleet at Pearl Harbor was subjected to a major surprise air attack in what was an undeclared act of war by Japan. Subsequently Germany declared war on America, bringing the sleeping giant into the war against the Axis.

In February 1942 the Americans had sent staff officers, under the command of Brigadier General Ira Eaker, to England where they prepared for the arrival of US combat units. These men and machines of the Eighth Air Force were to be based in England for participation in operations against Hitler's *Festung Europa*. Eaker believed in the concept of strategic bombardment as a war-winning use of air power, and had already spent two years in England studying RAF operations. Although the Eighth Air Force and the RAF were to work alongside each other, there would be a major difference in their respective operations: while RAF Bomber Command continued to pound the Third Reich by night, the Americans intended to do so by day, when they could do so more accurately – thus generating 'round-the-clock' bombing.

Having already suffered heavy losses very early on in the war during daylight bombing operations, the RAF was sceptical of the Americans' intention to attack without the protective cloak of darkness. Nevertheless, at the Casablanca Conference on 21 January 1943 the Combined Chiefs of Staff would agree that a combined RAF Bomber Command–Eighth Air Force strategic bomber offensive should indeed be mounted, beginning in 1943, and immediately the weather sufficiently improved. The 'Combined Bomber Offensive Directive' (CBOD) was therefore intended to be a strategic preparation for Operation *Overlord*, as the proposed invasion of enemy occupied France was codenamed.

The Directive to Allied air force chiefs was: 'Your primary objective will be the progressive destruction and dislocation of the German military, industrial and economic system and the undermining of the morale of the German people to a point where their capacity for armed resistance is fatally weakened.' Targets were listed in order of priority: U-boat construction yards, the German aircraft industry, enemy transportation networks, oil installations, and 'other targets' connected with the German war industry.

On 17 April 1942, General Eaker had flown in the lead aircraft of the second wave of B-17 Flying Fortresses attacking the railway marshalling yards at Rouen-Sotteville. Visibility was excellent, and from 23,000 feet Eaker's bombardiers dropped 36,900 pounds of general-purpose bombs. The bombing was reportedly 'reasonably accurate', with half of the bombs falling within the target area. The mission's success confirmed the Eighth Air Force's faith in high level precision daylight bombing.

What was lacking was the availability of a long-range single-engine escort fighter. The Spitfire was a short-range interceptor and lacked the airframe and fuel capacity to fulfil this role. The addition of auxiliary, jettisonable, fuel tanks helped extend range, but it was insufficient to take the Americans all the way to Germany and back. The ubiquitous twin-engine Lockheed P-38 Lightning, however, with its distinctive twin-boomed tail and cockpit contained in a central nacelle, had greater range, 1,200 miles, which could be increased with drop tanks. It was the first American fighter to arrive in theatre. Towards the end of 1942 the massive single-engine P-47 Thunderbolt appeared in Britain, with 800 miles range without drop tanks, but the P-51 Mustang would emerge as the escort fighter par excellence, with a 1,650 range without auxiliary measures.

Friday, 31st
Ludham. Coffin and I had a scrounge round Wroxham and district after a boat and we finally located Herbert Woods of Potter Heigham who is going to supply us with a couple of house boats and two sailing dinghies free! In the afternoon we collected Walter (brother of Herbert) and journeyed down to Wroxham Broad where we spent the afternoon choosing a couple of house boats and generally obtaining the 'gen' - a quick whiskey with the 'resident' - Doc Morris.

Wroxham should prove well worthwhile to the boys as they are flying hard these days and it will be a bloody good rest to spend a couple of hours in the sunshine whenever they have a day off.

This is another example of leadership.

Johnnie only flew to and from Coltishall (EP245). By the end of the month, since 13 July 1942, Johnnie had added a further 25.40 flying hours to his total number, 3.20 operational by day, 1.15 by night. Ludham, in 12 Group, was not best-placed for air-fighting action – but that time would soon come.

August

Saturday, 1st

Ludham. 137 Squadron going to Drem for a week commencing today, so that we shall have to do the whole Readiness with 266 Squadron (Typhoons) coming up from Duxford. This evening Coff, Doug and I tooled into Norwich via The Globe at Blofield and although an excellent pub we found it rather deserted. On to Norwich and to the Castle where we were absolutely outnumbered by fripp - amazing. A funny thing because the last time I was in N was almost two years ago when I joined the 616 Squadron at Coltishall. Doug and I picked up a couple and wandered down to the Samson & D, where we spent quite an enjoyable hour – the band from Tangmere were there and my girl (Dixie) was the singer (not crooner).

We took them home and then drank beer in the Bell until 3 am and there, in strange coincidence, I met Neville Broth's girlfriend from Duxford, a large buxom WAAF, name of Tanya. Back to Ludham for a beer at 4 am. A good evening.

Johnnie flew twice, an 'Army Co-operation', landing at and then returning from Coltishall (EP215). Otherwise it was another day of routine, uneventful, scrambles and convoy patrols off the east coast for 610 Squadron.

Sunday, 2nd

Johnnie made no diary entry but flew three times, a weather test, landing at Snailwell, returning therefrom followed by a *Rhubarb* over the Dutch coast, but no enemy aircraft or shipping were seen.

Monday, 3rd

Again, unusually, no diary entry. Johnnie flew once, another *Rhubarb* to the Dutch coast (EP215). This operation was structured so that Green Section, Pilot Officer Gaudard and Warrant Officer Jackson, took off at 1210 hours,

Blue Section, Pilot Officers Smith and Hvinden, at 1215 hours, with Red Section, Pilot Officers Collinge and Wright, following five minutes later. At 1225 hours Johnnie led Yellow Section off, comprising Pilot Officers Pabiot and de Patoul, Flight Sergeant Creagh and Sergeant Harris.

While Green, Blue and Red Sections streaked low across the North Sea towards the enemy occupied coast, Squadron Leader Johnson climbed Yellow Section above cloud, orbiting the Dutch coast at 10,000 feet, between Zanvoort and IJmuiden hoping that any intercepting German aircraft would be silhouetted against the cloud. After orbiting for ten minutes, nothing had been seen, so, with the low-level element having attacked shipping and barges before turning about, Johnnie withdrew back to Ludham.

Tuesday, 4th

The Crow due back from his ten days (leave). Shall probably travel to Scotland today if weather permits for some Grouse shooting with Messrs Wair and Abbott.

Party at Kenley.

616 now at Saffron Walden. The Crow reported back today so just before 6 am I clambered into a heavily laden spitfire and set course for Turnhouse, eventually arriving there at 7.30 am after a pleasant trip. Scrounged a lift into Edinburgh, a bus to Peebles and a motorcycle to Brampton where I met Jack, Bernard and Lance Newton.

While Johnnie flew to Scotland for four days leave (EP215), 610 Squadron flew more convoy patrols and reported on German shipping movements.

Wednesday, 5th

Scotland

First day.

Jack and I shooting all day long with Ken, the ghillie, as Bernard and Lance were in Edinburgh. Walked at least twenty-five miles and the pair of us shot 15 brace of grouse and a few hares.

Back at Ludham, 610 Squadron flew the usual sorties, including another *Rhubarb*, shooting up barges, and a 'shipping recce'.

Thursday, 6th

Scotland

Second Day.

Shooting all day, fourteen brace Grouse, two Woodcock, two Snipe, rabbits and hares – an exceptionally fine day.

610 Squadron flew more patrols and *Rhubarbs*, Flight Lieutenant Crowley-Milling leading Blue and Red Sections to attack a military camp, strafing a camouflaged area, huts and a machine gun post.

Friday, 7th
Scotland
Third Day.
All day again with Bernard, Lance (and Mrs L) and Jack, nine brace of grouse and a few hares – I shot very well today.

Only routine patrols were flown from Ludham.

Saturday, 8th
Fourth day.
Party at Kirton-in-Lindsey.
Ken Mitchell, BLENDEWING, BROUGHTON BY BIGGAR Peebbleshire.
Jim Pear, COUNTY HOTEL, Peebles.
Bernard ran me up to Turnhouse and I cracked off at 1730, but had to put down at Acklington owing to bad weather. There met old Wilky (now CO 1 Sqd) who had first walked here from France where he was shot down when bombing Abbeville in his Hurricane. On to Ludham in poor weather to find Johnnie Loudham Wing Co (Flying).

Johnnie's transit flights to Acklington and Ludham were in his usual Spitfire, EP215. Only routine flights were undertaken by 610 Squadron.

Sunday, 9th
Fifth and last day.

Johnnie flew twice, aerobatics followed by 'Wing Practice' (EP215). One shipping recce was flown but there was little to report.

Monday, 10th
Ludham. Three sections took off at 1130 for offensive operations in Holland - ground targets but the weather was 4/10 cloud and good visibility so I instructed all sections to withdraw immediately which they did – all

returning to base without firing. One flight released from 1600 hours so that Crow, Reg Pearson and I slipped into Norwich and drank steadily from 7-10 pm and then on to the Lido where I met Paula!

Johnnie's sole flight was the *Rhubarb* (EP215), which he called off owing to unfavourable weather conditions. This was, however, a landmark day in Johnnie's personal life, which, having met Paula Ingate, would never be the same again.

Tuesday, 11th

A signal from Group posting Peter Poole as Flight Commander 'A' Flight. Max (Aitken) rang up and invited two or three of my boys to a "do" at the Samson and Hercules at Norwich. So Poggi, the Doc, Coff and I slipped over to have dinner with Rodger Frankland, Max, Johnnie London and one or two other types. After the meal and a couple of bottles of red ink we shot off to the Samson where we were entertained by Brother Bush. Met Paula and went to sleep with her in the back of the car. Poggi came out boozed, drove home and nearly had a fit when Paula came into the mess for a gin at 3 am. Paula and I had a few words, as a result of which I drove her home at 7 am in the morning.

Johnnie flew twice, to and from Snailwell (EP215). That evening, twenty miles east of Yarmouth, Black Section, Warrant Officer W.M. Jackson and Sergeant E.S. Roberts, were patrolling at 1,000 feet when they sighted and engaged a Ju 88 at sea-level. Using full boost, the 'bandit' escaped but was claimed as damaged.

Wednesday, 12th

Met Janice and Hilda in the Ferry.
Arranged to meet Paula in the Ferry but she did me wrong and didn't turn up. I had quite an enjoyable evening with Janice and Hilda who are staying on a house boat in Wroxham Broad. Poggi and I left the ferry quite pickled and made an unsteady way back to Ludham.

There was comparatively little flying, only Red Section flying a shipping recce to the Dutch coast, reporting nothing of interest. Johnnie's only flights were to and from Coltishall (EP215).

Thursday, 13th

Snailwell. To Snailwell for a party with Cocky.

Apparently, it is 56's last night at Snailwell, so they are pushing out a bit of a boat in the form of a dinner party. A good evening with G/C Grandy, Denys Gillam, Paul Richey etc. But to bed fairly early and reasonably sober as 56 have a wing show at crack of dawn tomorrow.

Johnnie had first completed a 'Range Test' before flying to Snailwell (EP215). Green Section flew a shipping recce, but only saw a fleet of eighty fishing boats, with canvas sails.

Friday, 14th

The Tiffie Wing show was cancelled early this morning, so Cocky flew with me to Ludham and we had an egg for breakfast before he returned to Snailwell.

Johnnie flew three times, back from Snailwell (EP215), remarking in his log book 'very ropey', then to and from Coltishall (AR509). An interesting incident occurred that evening, when Blue Section, Flight Lieutenant Crowley-Milling (Blue 1) and Pilot Officer Gaudard (Blue 2), scrambled at 1833 hours to intercept a 'bogey' (unidentified radar plot, possibly hostile). Fifteen miles north-east of Yarmouth, flying at 1,000 feet, Blue 1 sighted a Boulton Paul Defiant, which was a mile ahead and at sea level, making a left-hand turn. Blue 1 dived and turned inside the Defiant which let fly, tracer passing Blue 1's port wing. Breaking away, the Spitfire pilot alerted Operations, 'Friendly aircraft firing at me'. Blue 2 fired a short burst, to miss, following which the Defiant sent up colours of the day. Blue 1 then signalled the Defiant, which was from 277 Squadron at Martlesham Heath, and all three aircraft landed together at Ludham at 1930 hours. Considering the mauling Defiant squadrons had by daylight during the Fall of France and Battle of Britain, it was unsurprising that the two-man crew were perhaps a little 'twitchy' at the appearance of two fast-moving fighters.

Saturday, 15th

Ludham. Party in our Mess – men only and present, The G/C, Johnnie L, Rodger, Fish and Humphrey C (the CO of 137). An excellent lobster supper, plenty of wine and beer but unfortunately it was cut short as the G/C told me at midnight that certain modifications had to be carried out on the A/C and that we were due to leave for West Malling at dawn tomorrow. So we called out the Squadron, packed the pilots off to bed at 12 am and then sat down to entertain our guests – they eventually left about at 4 am.

Johnnie flew once today, aerobatics (EP250, DW-G), and only one uneventful patrol was undertaken, by Black Section, Pilot Officer R.W. Pearson and Sergeant J.G. Leech.

Sunday, 16th

Took off at 1200, sixteen a/c, and flew down to West Malling but overshot slightly and had to turn back. Shortly afterwards the other two squadrons arrived (485 and 411) and with them Jamie. We were quickly released and most of us pushed on to the swimming pool at Hildon Manor where we swam for a few minutes and then drank steadily from 1910. About 2130 the fun started, Peter Poole as drunk as an owl breaking glasses, Jamie, self and the 485 (NZ) boys singing feisty songs. Then we tried to get on the dance floor but were refused admission, so I forced a breach which was quickly enlarged by 485 Squadron and a bicycle, who came to grief on the dance floor – to round off the shambles the Pusher pinched a steak off someone's plate and hey ho! We're all banned from the dump!

Johnnie's only flight was to West Malling (EP215).

Monday, 17th

West Malling

Practice Wing show in the morning and then a shaky 'do' over Cayeux and the Abbeville area in the afternoon. We closed the French coast staggering up to 6000 feet and I thought the whole bloody Wing would be shot down by flak, but we didn't see either a burst or any tracers. Granty, leading the NZ boys, saw a few 190s taking off from Abbeville but he lost them when they flew low over the woods near the aerodrome.

Wing released again. To the Stow at Maidstone with Jamie, Grant and his lads, Bill Newton and 411, and Jim Johnson and 610. The Pusher is down here with me and enjoying himself – Coffin brought him down in the V8.

Johnnie flew twice, on the practice sortie followed by the Wing sweep to Berck-sur-Mer (EP215). 610 Squadron had rendezvoused with two Hornchurch squadrons over West Malling, then proceeded to the French coast at 500 feet, climbing to 7,000. The wing orbited in a wide semi-circle but, apart from the brief sighting of the 'Abbeville Boys', nothing of interest appeared and so the Spitfires returned home.

Tuesday, 18th

West Malling

A practice Wing show in the morning with Grant leading as Jamie has gone to Group for a conflab. He returned at lunchtime and at 1430 we took off for a quickie in the Dunkirk area but no e/a were seen. Peter Poole flying well in both shows. After tea Jamie shot off to Group again and we knew that the big show was nigh.

Again, Johnnie flew twice, the practice and the sweep (EP215). The 'big show' was indeed 'nigh'…

Wednesday, 19th

West Malling.

The Wing took off at 0740 to provide cover for Army & Navy operations at Dieppe. Jamie leading with 485 Sqd, 411 next and ourselves top cover. We saw a lot of aircraft returning and when halfway across saw a heavy smoke fall over the town. When about five miles off the coast we were heavily engaged by over 100 190s and 109s.

> Self 1 FW190 Destroyed.
> Self, F/Sgt Creagh & P/O Smith. 1 Me 109 Destroyed.
> Self & P/O Smith. 1 FW190 Damaged.
> P/O Hokan. 1 FW190 Damaged.
> F/Lt Crowley-Milling. 1 Me 109 Destroyed
> Our Casualties.
> F/LT Poole & Sgt Leech Missing.
> F/Sgt Creagh – Bailed out & picked up by Navy
> 2nd Patrol, 3rd Patrol & 4th Patrol

This was the 'big show': Operation *Jubilee*. By this time the Wehrmacht was rolling ever onwards to the Russian Caucasus, having annihilated 300,000 Soviet troops at Kharkov and Kiev. The Japanese were overrunning the Far East and even threatening to link up with advancing German forces in Russia. In North Africa things were also going badly: the British Eighth Army was in headlong retreat. In spite of demands made by Stalin for the Allies to invade France, such an enormous undertaking was still impossible at this time. Yielding to pressure from Stalin, and because ultimately the Allies' intended to liberate enemy-occupied Europe, it was agreed to probe the enemy's coastal defences on 19 August 1942. Operation *Jubilee*, the proposed amphibious landing at Dieppe, represented the largest combined service operation of the war so far.

Dieppe, a thriving French coastal town, was protected by high cliffs, on which were situated heavy coastal batteries. Overlooking the town, it was necessary for commandos to destroy these guns prior to a seaborne assault by two brigades of the Canadian 2nd Army and a Canadian Tank Regiment. Of the 6,000 men involved, 5,000 were Canadian. The operation's intention was to ascertain whether the harbour town could be seized and held for a day. While on French soil, Allied troops would also destroy installations and any naval vessels moored in the harbour.

Air Vice-Marshal Leigh-Mallory, still AOC of 11 Group, which would bear the brunt of the Dieppe aerial fighting, saw the operation as an opportunity to lure the Luftwaffe into action on a scale not seen since the Battle of Britain. The fighter force at his disposal comprised fifty-six squadrons, forty-eight of which were Spitfire-equipped. For Johnnie's 610 Squadron, according to the ORB, 'Dieppe Day' started early with 'a breakfast of egg and chips in the wee sma' hours'. By 0300 hours the squadron was at readiness: 'Pilots were very early astir, but ground crews were before them – busy as bees through this night, fitting long range jettisonable tanks to the Spitfires.'

At 0740 hours, Squadron Leader Johnson led 610 off from West Malling in Spitfire VB EP254, DW-B. As a part of the 12 Group Wing, with 411 and 485 Squadrons, 610's brief was to patrol Dieppe as top cover at 10,000 feet. Some three miles off the French coast, Johnnie and his pilots found about fifty enemy fighters, both Me 109Fs and FW190s, flying singly, in pairs, or in fours. From Dieppe the Spitfire pilots could see a heavy pall of black smoke rising. 610 Squadron reported that the German fighters 'fought persistently'. A large-scale dogfight was already in progress ahead of 610 Squadron, into which Johnnie and his boys sallied forth, engaging the enemy at 7,000 feet. Not surprisingly, during the ensuing scrap the wing's squadrons were split up. 610 Squadron's CO reported:

> I saw thirty-forty Me 109s and FW190s 2,000 – 3,000 feet above the Squadron and manoeuvring to attack us. I climbed the Squadron fast and when the attacks commenced I broke in towards them. I climbed after a 190 and opened fire from astern, closing from 250-150 yards. The E/A turned to port and I closed in and attacked from the beam with both cannon and machine gun. The E/A commenced smoking, its wheels dropped and it dived steeply to crash into the sea, as seen by Flight Lieutenant Crowley-Milling DFC, Pilot Officer Hokan

and several others. We were then attacked three or four times and had to take violent evasive action.

I then chased an Me 109F and opened fire from astern, closing from some 250-200 yards with cannon and machine-gun. Two other pilots of my Section also fired at this E/A. Pieces flew off as he started to smoke heavily. I closed right in and the E/A half-rolled and dived vertically out of control. Pilot Officer Wright and I saw him crash into the sea. After we attacked, I saw one of my Squadron with glycol pouring from the aircraft but under control and heading for the emergency landing ground east of Dieppe.

This FW190 was Johnnie's eighth kill and his first of that feared type. The Spitfire seen streaming glycol was flown by the Australian Flight Sergeant 'South' Creagh, who later reported:

At approximately 4,000 feet, while doing a climbing turn to port I was then attacked from below and behind, receiving hits in the engine and fuselage behind the cockpit. The cockpit became filled with liquid glycol and smoke. I was temporarily blinded and on recovering found that I was diving at 280 mph. I wiped the windscreen and pulled up, then seeing white smoke issuing from the starboard exhausts I decided to bale out. I eased the stick back to 200 mph, at the same time trying to contact Red One on the R/T. I was then facing Dieppe and with the glycol temperature at 130° I slid back the hood, opened the side cockpit door, took off my helmet, released the Sutton harness and rolled aircraft onto its side. I fell out with ease and after a few seconds pulled the ripcord. I jumped at about 4,000 feet and immediately lost sight of the aircraft. On nearing the water I was trying to blow up my Mae West using CO_2, but this did not function so I concentrated on the landing but could not release the 'chute till I struck the water. Once in the water there was no difficulty so I then blew up the Mae West by mouth. My dinghy came away from the pack and was still attached to the Mae West but I did not bother to blow it up as an MGB was heading my way and just visible. I was picked up six miles to the NE of Dieppe by MGB 317. I was told that my Spitfire had gone in about three miles south of that position.

Meanwhile, Johnnie had regrouped 610 Squadron and turned inland at 20,000 feet. 'Heavy reinforcements' could be seen approaching Dieppe from the south-east. Having informed the Wing Leader, Wing Commander Jameson, Johnnie turned to outflank a 190 flying on his port beam at the same height. With only machine-gun ammunition remaining, Johnnie closed from the starboard beam and let fly. He saw strikes around the cockpit and small pieces flew off. The 190 then began streaming white smoke (which was not glycol, the 190's BMW 801 radial engine being air-cooled). At just fifty yards range, the Spitfire broke off and re-joined Red 3, Pilot Officer Smith. The latter had also attacked the same 190 before tagging onto four Spitfires of 411 Squadron.

An Me 109F then pounced out of the sun, but Smith managed to get on his tail and fire a long shot from 500 yards. The 109 then pulled away back into the sun, too fast for the Spitfire pilot to follow.

Flight Lieutenant Crowley-Milling also reported a success:

> On climbing up into sun on the left of Colon Leader (Squadron Leader Johnson DFC), I saw an Me 109F and an FW 190 coming up behind my Number 4, Pilot Officer St Remy. I turned hard to starboard over the top of Colon Leader and got on the tail of the Me 109F. I gave it a short burst of cannon and machine-gun fire, followed by three bursts of machine-gun fire only. As it turned over onto its back, I saw a small stream of glycol coming from underneath the E/A. I then had to break hard to port as an FW 190 came up on portside and behind. On doing two complete turns to evade the 190, I saw a pilot bale out of a 109 about 8,000 feet below me. I also saw two Spitfires going down pouring glycol about three minutes later.

Pilot Officer 'Hokey' Hokan:

> I saw one FW 190 go down belching white smoke and hit the sea after a short burst by Red 1. I attacked an FW 190 flying at 8,000 feet, firing a two-second burst from port quarter, closing from 350-300 yards. I saw strikes on the tail and claim this aircraft as damaged. While carrying out this attack, shells from another 190 hit my Spitfire, severely damaging it. Having lost sight of my Number Two and being without radio contact I returned to base alone at sea level.

Alone over Dieppe, Squadron Leader Johnson singled out a 190. As Johnnie bore down on the German, he yawed his Spitfire to check the blind spot before attacking. As he did so the enemy pilot saw him, turned and came hurtling at the Spitfire. Both pilots broke left into a tight turn, each trying to bring their guns to bear. Despite the Spitfire Mk Vs reputation at being able to out-turn the lethal 190, in this case the 190 was gaining. The two fighters had descended to virtually nought feet and it appeared to Johnnie that they were 'street fighting in Dieppe itself!'

The Spitfire swung out to sea, roaring over the promenade and beach. Sighting a RN destroyer, despite the danger from 'friendly' flak, Johnnie pushed his throttle through the gate and, with an extra 16 pounds of boost, skimmed above the waves, hurtling towards the British ship. Inevitably the destroyer's gunners opened fire, and tracer flashed dangerously close to Johnnie's cockpit. Hauling back on the stick to pull up over the destroyer, once clear he broke left, searching for the 190, of which he was relieved to see no sign. Either the German had broken the chase off over the coast or had been hit by the destroyer.

At 0920 hours, 610 Squadron landed back at West Malling. Three pilots were posted missing: Flight Sergeant Creagh, Flight Lieutenant Pool and Sergeant Leech.

Two hours later, 'Colon Leader' led 610 off to Dieppe once again. Little opposition was encountered on this sortie, although four 190s were chased inland beyond Dieppe. Unable to catch up, in frustration Johnnie loosed off a burst at 800 yards. Flight Lieutenant Crowley-Milling, however, was able to damage a 109 from 300 yards. At 1256 hours, 610 Squadron returned, intact, to West Malling. At 1400 hours, 610 was off again, but once more there was little incident. Johnnie fired ineffectively at two 190s from extreme range, but both half-rolled out of sight. Four other 190s approached but were attacked by Hawker Typhoons. The squadron was safely home at 1525 hours. 610 Squadron's last sortie of 'Dieppe Day' was flown between 1735 and 1905 hours, when the Spitfires orbited mid-Channel. Four 190s approached but were driven off and headed back towards Dieppe. Johnnie led his Spitfires in hot pursuit, only closing within range when at zero feet over the French coast. Opening fire at 400 yards without result, Colon Leader broke off the chase. The Spitfires then gave cover to a British rescue vessel patrolling about five miles off Dieppe, before heading home.

The 610 Squadron ORB concluded:

> Not the least memorable activity of the day was the take-off in rapid succession in the early afternoon of six fighter squadrons – three

of Spitfires and three of Typhoons. How eagerly was news lapped up when the Squadron's first aircraft returned from the first patrol; as it happened, Squadron Leader Johnson was able to report quick successes for 610 and an altogether terrific party. What hearty congratulations there were when "Hokey" safely landed his Spitfire with the tail almost shot away; what relief when it was learned in the evening that Flight Sergeant Creagh, who had to bale out during the first patrol, had been picked up safely from the sea. Altogether a stirring day, but one which left among the exaltations regrets over the loss of Flight Lieutenant Pool and Sergeant Leech, both of whom are missing from the first patrol.

'Stirring' and newsworthy though the day had been, by the close of play the operation had actually been a disaster for the Allies. The Germans had reacted swiftly and some 1,096 Allied soldiers were killed, 1,943 captured, and 397 were missing. None of the intended objectives were achieved. The cynical suggest that this was a deliberate failure intended to prove to Stalin that the Second Front was not an option at this time. If true, the point was made at a high cost of young lives, most of whom were Canadian. It is interesting to note that when the liberation of Europe was eventually mounted, no attempt was made to seize a French port. When the time came, so as to avoid another Dieppe, the Allies towed a prefabricated harbour in sections across the Channel. Disastrous though Operation *Jubilee* had been, vital lessons had been learned.

From an aerial perspective, 11 Group believed that it had achieved considerable success. Nearly 100 enemy aircraft were claimed destroyed, and 170 probably destroyed or damaged. Actual German losses were forty-eight destroyed and twenty-four damaged. Unpalatable though the thought may be, RAF losses of ninety-seven aircraft to enemy action and three more to flying accidents, with sixty-six others damaged, made Dieppe a victory for the *Jagdfliegern* and German flak gunners. To further confirm the point, the RAF lost forty-seven fighter pilots, against the Luftwaffe's thirteen. In total, the RAF had flown nearly 3,000 sorties, the enemy 945.

Johnnie: 'Dieppe? It was a bloody tragedy. The Canadians on the ground were slaughtered. Someone said afterwards that it was a seaborne "Charge of the Light Brigade". Even the German gunners felt sorry for the Allied soldiers as they pounded them to pieces. Did it achieve anything? As usual we had over-claimed, so although LM hailed it as a great victory, the truth has since come out. I recall that while in combat that day I was rebuked for my swearing over the R/T by Pat Jameson!'

It was the last time that air fighting on this scale would be seen on the Channel coast.

Thursday, 20th
No diary entry.

We have no record of Johnnie's flights between this date and 6 September other than those recorded in the 610 Squadron ORB. From the ORB we know that at 1712 hours, Squadron Leader Johnson (EP254, DW-B) led 610 Squadron on a 12 Group Wing operation – covering the withdrawal of American B-17s returning from bombing Amiens. The 'Flying Fortresses' were seen withdrawing across the Channel, so Wing Commander Jameson led the wing on a patrol at 30,000 feet, east and west of Cayeux. Twelve FW190s were seen 2,000 feet above 610 Squadron, inland, so the Spitfires maintained their position, preventing the Germans achieving an up-sun position from which the bombers could be ambushed. Two 190s flew in front of the squadron as bait, in an attempt to draw the Spitfires away, which Colon Leader ignored, followed by two more enemy fighters.

Johnson reported:

> We held our position and a further pair of 190s. No 2 did not appear to see us as we were up-sun of him and I attacked him with a 1½ second burst of cannon and machine gun from his port beam, closing from 150 to 120 yards.
>
> I did not see any strikes but E/A pulled vertically upwards, fell over, and commenced a lazy, vertical, spin. I then broke away and did not see E/A again, but Wing Commander Loudon DFC watched it spinning for several thousand feet and is of the opinion that either the pilot was killed or the controls shot away. On his evidence, and pending development of the cine film, this a/c is claimed as probably destroyed.

Friday, 21st
Leave commences with Cocky.

Johnnie: 'After Dieppe, I went grouse shooting with Cocky Dundas, who was related to half the aristocracy of north-east England, or so it seemed to me. Anyway, all of them seemed to have a bloody great house and a grouse moor! They were all his second cousins, the Halifaxes, the Allandales, and what have you. He'd write and ask whether he and I could have a walk on the outskirts, but they would always write back saying "no, you can't walk the outskirts but you can come and join us in the butts and do it properly", and so on. So that was that. Great week, that was, shooting at Lord Allandale's, whose son was a prisoner.'

Having returned to Ludham, it was a quiet day for 610 Squadron with only one patrol by a pair of Spitfires.

Saturday, 22nd
No entry. Another quiet day for 610, just two uneventful 'stooge patrols flown'.

Sunday, 23rd
Ludham. The Pusher killed by an MT lorry when running across the perimeter track. I had him buried under the trees near 'A' Flight Dispersal and on a bit of board we painted 'The Pusher 610 Sqd'.

The AOC came down to Coltishall today and I went over there to meet him. He was in good form and seemed very pleased with 610. He said 'I thought I'd come along and congratulate you and the Squadron. Excellent show last Wednesday.' I had a chat with him about Doug Collinge and the numerous postings that we had to provide from the Squadron. He said that he would try and do something about it.

Today I recommended Crow for a Bar to his DFC.

Again it was a quiet day from a flying perspective, two sections of 610 Squadron Spitfires flying two more uneventful patrols.

Monday, 24th
No entry. Only a scramble and a shipping recce flown.

Tuesday, 25th
No entry. A scramble, followed by a shipping recce and a sweep over the Dutch coast, all of which were uneventful. Johnnie did not fly.

Wednesday, 26th
No entry. Only an uneventful convoy patrol and a scramble flown.

Thursday, 27th
Norfolk/Yorkshire
Leave commences. Day 1.

After lunch at Matlask, Cocky and I pushed off in the little Morris in the direction of Yorkshire. Ricky Stoop rolled up for lunch and I have never seen such a complete transformation in a chap. He has just returned from Malta, has lost a couple of stone and looks lean and fit, indeed the burns in his face (he was shot down) rather add than detract from his appearance.

The little Morris ran like clockwork and we made such excellent time that we decided to go right through up Yorkshire. Tea with Mrs Fixten at Rauceby Golf Club (memories of two years ago!). A couple of pints outside Newark and we were in Doncaster by 7, where we checked in at Punch's. Contacted Ken Holden and we all drank and dined together and talked a lot of shop over the brandy – a very pleasant evening.

Another unremarkable day back at Ludham.

Friday, 28th
Yorkshire. Day 2.
(Valerie turned up at the aerodrome on Wednesday evening.)
After breakfast we paid the score (just over £7 for one evening!) and drove on to Barnsley where I bought a book about 66 Squadron 'Ten Fighter Boys', which I have delved into and is bloody awful. Kendal who was at ITW, EFTS, FTS, OTU and for a short time in 616 with me is responsible for a chapter of jargon, but I won't criticise as at the end a footnote has been added saying that he lost his life when attending a convoy on the North Russian route. The last thing to be heard of him was on the RT when he called up and gave a fix for the German airman of an 88 he had shot down. A swim this afternoon in Archie's lake; to Barnsley to meet Andrews and Robin who weren't on the train, dinner with Hughie's charming parents and very early to bed.

At Ludham, Spitfires scrambled to investigate an unidentified radar plot which was found to be a Stirling, followed by an uneventful shipping recce.

Saturday, 29th
Yorkshire. Day 3.
Andrews, Robin and (hell!) four very high lobsters reported at 4 am this morning – a very excellent effort as he was a couple of hours late leaving Ludham and missed his first trains. After breakfast today we packed the guns into the Morris and drove up on the moors when we were soon joined by Lord Wharncliffe, Mr 'Arry Whitaker, a Sheffield millionaire and the

'stooge' of the party, Lady Vera Blare or Clare, and several other gentlemen. A very enjoyable day - about eighteen brace were shot, a three-ham lunch session and then some more drives, and after a couple of whiskies we went for a swim in the lake - and by God it was cold. An excellent dinner at Dale Cottage, the guns cleaned and to bed first after 10 pm. Wrote Paula.

For 610 and 485 Squadron there was a Wing show, led by Wing Commander Loudon. The Spitfires met twelve Bostons at sea level off Orfordness, twelve miles from the enemy-occupied coast climbing to 10,500 feet, the Bostons descending to 8,000 feet to accurately bomb the docks at Ostend. Heavy flak was experienced and one Boston was hit, turning on its back and diving vertically. No enemy aircraft appeared, so again there was no combat for 610 Squadron.

Sunday, 30th
Northumberland. Day 4
   Pouring with rain this morning but after running the Dundas's to church Hugh (Cocky), Andrews and I set off for Northumberland in the little Ford. We made very good time, dropped in at Caterwick? for a couple of beers and then proceeded to [illegible] where we had an excellent lunch with Lord and Lady Zetland and Olive Snell's daughter. Away again after the port and full speed for Hexham, which we reached at 4 pm and were unable to get in at any hotel. We appealed to the Police and were put in touch with a farmhouse at Hayden Bridge. Cocky and Andrews stayed there and as there was no accommodation for me I managed to get in at the Deneholme Hotel in Hexham.

Olive Snell was a celebrated portrait artist who became an official war artist attached to the RAF, painting Johnnie and many other Fighter Command luminaries.
   At Ludham only a convoy and a local patrol were flown, both without incident.

Monday, 31ˢᵗ
Northumberland. Day 5.
Lord Allendale
Allen Heads
Hexham
Northumberland.

Cocky and Andrews left the farmhouse and transferred their quarters to Deneholme – Miss Whittaker wouldn't accept a penny. We met Lord A. who invited us to shoot and stay with him for a couple of days commencing tomorrow which we readily accepted. A day's rough shooting but the grouse were very wild and generally we could not get within a hundred yards, but we did manage to bag five birds.

A few beers in the local, we challenged the locals at darts and thrashed them pretty soundly, doubles and hundreds being commonplace.

Dinner at 1715 with a bottle of Burgundy to assist the grouse, which were too well cooked. Afterwards all the staff came into out room and we drank champagne and beer. Slept like a log.

Sections of 610 Squadron flew two patrols over the Dutch coast, escorted a Motor Torpedo Boat, and scrambled once, all without incident.

During this month, 610 Squadron received seven of the improved Spitfire Mk VCs, and flew 873.20 hours, 461.35 of them operational. Combat claims made during August 1942 increased the squadron 'bag' to 123 destroyed, 41½ probables, and 41 damaged.

September

Tuesday, 1st

Northumberland. Day 6.

Left the Deneholme Hotel today after breakfast and again they would not accept any payment. Bishy said he was making a lot of money and this was the first time he had the pleasure of entertaining a couple of RAF types. Met Lord Allendale's shooting party at 0915 and then we set off for the moors. What a glorious and exhilarating day! I shot badly to begin with but the last three drives produced 7, 6 and 5, and his lordship was duly impressed. His daughters Ela and Felicity. Cocky's left hammer is u/s, so that tomorrow he will have to use mine.

A game of poker after dinner which raised my finances by 12/6!

59½ brace.

Only routine and uneventful scrambles were flown from Ludham.

Wednesday, 2nd

Northumberland. Day 7.

MRS BARNETT

HALTON CASTLE Retriever Puppies?

CORBRIDGE

Another glorious day although not quite so fine and sunny as yesterday. Lady A was out today and both she and her son Richard pulled off some very fine shots. Cocky borrowed my second gun but unfortunately that packed up after the first drive (one barrel) so that he didn't have much success.

40 brace today.

A telegram from the Adj that Crow is posted. He has got his squadron – Typhoons, being newly formed at Snailwell. Gaudard (the Frenchman) killed himself while carrying out low aerobatics this evening, a thing I had warned him about previously – just the same as Paddy Davidson.

Another game of poker this evening, Ela and I holding our own.

610 Squadron flew a routine patrol and shipping recce.

Thursday, 3rd
Northumberland. Day 8.

My eighth day of leave and our last day up here. We drove out to the butts in pouring rain and the birds came down wind at a tremendous speed. We were soon all absolutely drenched and it was no little relief when we knocked off at 1 pm for a quick whiskey and lunch. After this I drove to Halton where I saw a very nice litter of 9-week-old Labradors and chose one at seven guineas: 'Sally'

A bath and then goodbye to the Allenheads and the return journey commences. A few beers in Durham and then on to the Bridge at Caterwick, where we spent an enjoyable evening on the drink – in fact the Manager threatened to throw the pair of us out at 2230.

Fifteen brace until lunchtime and then the day was washed out.

Only one routine scramble was flown by 610 Squadron.

Friday, 4th
Yorkshire. Day 9.

Sally behaved very well and only pissed on the floor once in the night, and both Hugh and I think she will develop into a top notcher. After a good breakfast of mushrooms and bacon we set course for Yorkshire and after a couple of pints in Cawthorne village we were at Dale Cottage in time for lunch. Over to Wareley in the afternoon to see 'Archie', collect Robin and leave Sally with Clarke, one of the Earl's keepers.

Back to Dale Cottage for dinner and almost immediately afterwards I excused myself and shot off to bed. I understand and get on quite well with FJD (Hugh Dundas's father) but I'm afraid that FMD (mother) has me weighed and found lacking to some degree - at least that is the impression I gather. She is an exceptionally brave and strong-minded woman – very regal and conscious of the family history and breeding. What place has a grammar school educated policeman's son at her table?

This is an interesting comment by Johnnie. At this time, a distinctly unequal society existed in Britain. According to the social historian Martin Pugh, during the 1930s 80 per cent of the population was defined as 'manual working class by their occupation, 15 per cent middle class and 5 per cent upper class. While millions of people survived on a typical weekly wage of around £3 10s, and many on less, great fortunes were still being amassed, especially in urban property, finance and the consumer industry.'

Education was the key to advancement, but the quality of schooling depended entirely upon parents' ability to pay fees. Public schools, like Eton and Harrow, were considered 'training grounds for leaders of the nation'; indeed, 68 per cent of Conservative MPs between 1920 and 1940 had public school backgrounds, 27 per cent of them being Old Etonians. MPs from working class backgrounds never exceeded more than a third, and were exclusively Labour. Moreover, of 271 civil servants earning over £1,000 per annum in 1939, 190 came from public schools, as did fifty-six out of sixty-two bishops, and thirty-three High Court judges. Likewise, in the forces, until very recently commissions had been the exclusive preserve of those educated at public schools.

The problem was that only the 5.2 per cent of the population occupying the top strata of Britain's socio-economic pyramid could afford the fees, and similarly only 5 per cent of Britain's children benefited from a public-school background. In 1918 there was an attempt to narrow the gap and provide better opportunities for all when it became compulsory for local authorities to provide grammar schools – a cheaper alternative, modelled on public schools, but still fee-paying – so only the well-off middle classes could afford this.

In Johnnie's case, his father's occupation meant that the family occupied the 'Manual worker' bracket, working class, and he owed his grammar school education to his better-off uncle. Conversely, the Dundas family were upper class, from the top 5.2 per cent. Hugh's father was the director of a colliery, and wealthy, sending both Hugh and his elder brother John (also a Spitfire pilot (killed in action on 28 November 1940) to public schools. Johnnie, therefore, was not considered a social equal, which Lady Dundas apparently did not entirely conceal.

Nonetheless, this did not prevent Johnnie and Hugh becoming lifelong close friends as well as comrades in arms, at this time of the same rank.

The war would bring the classes together in the forces and elsewhere, accelerating social change, and in the case of the RAF especially, advancement became more about a man's ability and experience than social class.

At Ludham, there was no operational flying.

Saturday, 5th
Ludham. After breakfast Andrews and Robin left for London and eventually Ludham. Hugh and I left Dale Cottage and made good speed to Rauceby

where we had our packed lunch and a bottle of whisky with my good friend Leslie Frazer, whom I have not seen for two years (when I was at the Hospital with my shoulder). Already I am beginning to throw off the constraint which has enveloped me for the past week. I have stayed with Lord Allendale, Lord Wharncliffe and a very old and distinguished family (the Dundas's). I have had lunch with a Marquis and a Marchioness and I have not been altogether happy as, I must face it, I am not of their clay and have felt protected only by the sheer sense of my rank and war record in RAF... [scratched out with pen].

Arrived Matlask 5:30 pm, a cup of tea, thanks to Hughie and on to my Squadron at Ludham.

Wing Commander Loudon had led the wing, including 610 Squadron, over Dieppe, covering the withdrawal of Flying Fortresses after bombing Rouen. There were no engagements.

Sunday, 6th

Ludham: Yesterday I arrived back just in time to learn that Flight Sergeant Creagh and Sergeant Greggory had intercepted a Messerschmitt Me 210 over the Thames Estuary and had shot it down into the sea. Bloody good show. Creagh was shot down over Dieppe and it'll do him a world of good apart from the fact that that it is the first 210 to be shot down over this country.

Last month we put in almost 900 hours (at least a hundred more than anyone else) in addition to shooting down three Huns, one probable and five damaged.

To West Malling and a Wing show with 411 and 485, Johnny (Loudon) leading with my Squadron at the bottom. Our job was to meet the Fortresses returning from France and escort them back over the Channel – this was carried out. Return to Ludham just before dusk. Rang Paula, but she was on duty and could not see me. A lot of folk have seen the film I made at King's Cliffe - what price fame Johnson?

Johnnie flew five times today, to and from Coltishall, then to West Malling for the wing commitment, then back to Ludham (EP215). Some FW190s were seen shadowing the bombers over the French coast, but there were no engagements.

Monday, 7th

Ludham. A letter from Bob Bowen in West Africa, he has met Nipple, Jeff West, Roy Marples, Derek Beedham – what a bunch – remember the Kirton days last winter? I am sure that Bob doesn't know he has collected a gong, so I have written to him quoting the Air Ministry Order reference number. A letter also from Peter Clapham – he says – 'if you want to keep in touch with the old man, come over soon the sands are fast running out.'

Group IO [intelligence officer] over for a chat and a yarn this evening. Crow also came over in a Typhoon, at the moment his Squadron consists of his Adjutant and himself.

This evening I drove to 73 to see Paula – she has three elder sisters and for the moment I was rather confused but she did take my breath away when I eventually saw her, I thought she looked absolutely marvellous (you're slipping Johnnie!).

There was no operational flying for 610 Squadron today, Johnnie leading a squadron formation practice, landing at Coltishall, then returning therefrom (EP215).

Tuesday, 8th
Ludham. Laurie, my new Flight Commander, arrived today. He has just arrived back from a glamour boy trip in America. Previously to that he was a F/C in 222 and got himself a gong there. Kerville (an Australian) also joined the Squadron from 253 today. I remember him from 616 days as he was in 'A' Flight for some time and had rather a raw deal there – we shall have to see what we can do for him now.

A Black this evening. Max and Johnnie were entertaining the girls so I went over to C and before long was getting well under way on a mixture of whisky, gin and rum – at 8.30 I pulled out and drove to the Ferry where Paula was waiting for me. A few more drinks, a game of darts and at 10 pm I took her home. She checked in at 1 am and coming home I fell asleep and the next thing I remember I was arse upwards in a field having rolled the van over a ditch and hedge.

Johnnie did not fly today, but some sections of 610 Squadron provided escort for a damaged MTB in relays.

Wednesday, 9th
Ludham. With the help of a couple of Jocks, we righted the car which did not appear to have suffered much hurt and I must say these two boys were excellent. They straightened out the dents, found a decent way out of the field and within half an hour I was under my own steam

again. Damage: a missing filler cap and a broken near side window not to mention a couple of slightly buckled wheels.

No letter or news from V – I should imagine it is all over – a good thing too as not as not one of my friends that met her liked her – Neville, Cocky, Nip, Maisie, Colin Gray and a dozen others.

Paula came out to Wroxham to meet me again this evening, apparently, she got into hot water because she was so late last evening – 1 am when she arrived. However we made amends this evening as she was home well before 10 pm.

Johnnie flew once, a 'Squadron Balbo' (EP215) but the weather was 'u/s', although that evening two sections flew a shipping recce and a Jim Crow to the Dutch coast.

Thursday, 10th
Hutton-Cranswick

Cocky came over for tea and after a change of clothes we climbed into a couple of Spits and set course for Hutton Cranswick, where the Bull was on the tarmac to welcome us. Shortly afterwards the AOC and Tim Maurice arrived from the wrong direction, and I must say old God had a cheeky word for both Cocky and I (later on he told Cocky that he was under consideration for a Wing abroad). Basil Embry and Johnnie arrived a few minutes afterwards in a Mosquito, and after an excellent diner we went to the gym and saw some really excellent boxing. A Polish Corporal, who was like a steel spring, impressed me immensely – he had his English opponent out for the count in the first round.

Adjourned to the Mess for a few more drinks, a few card tricks by the AOC, an astounding game of poker and so to bed after a typical 'Ken-organised' evening.

Johnnie flew to and from Digby sector station, then to Hutton Cranswick (EP215). One section flew a shipping recce, while six other Spitfires provided escort to MTBs.

Friday, 11th
Ludham. Left H/C after breakfast and I managed to lead Hugh and self at least 20 miles to the West of Norwich.

Very little else of interest during the day. In the evening I drove into Norwich and saw Paula at No 73. I apologised to Mrs Ingate for keeping her up so late on Tuesday, but she said that's OK! (anytime old boy).

Johnnie's only flight was returning from Hutton Cranswick (EP210). Two sections flew an uneventful shipping recce.

Saturday, 12th
Ludham. Poor weather today. The new Station Commander (Group Cpt Harvey) arrived yesterday so I flew over to Coltishall to pay my compliments. He seems to be an extremely efficient and able Station Commander but rather devoid of a keen sense of humour – however we shall see, we shall no doubt see. He and the Wing Co came over after lunch for our inspection, and I must say he asked a lot of questions I knew f.a about and those I did I answered them badly.

'A' Flight and one other section released after tea today and all the boys cracked into Norwich. I felt fairly tired so I went to bed at 9 pm – rang Paula up, read, and eventually went to sleep.

Sent Neville's kit off to his father at Manchester today.

Johnnie flew twice, a formation practice, landing at and returning from Coltishall (EP215). Blue Section flew a shipping recce, reporting flak ships off Texel.

Sunday, 13th
Ludham. Over to Coltishall for a few sherries with Max Aitken, Roger Frankland, Johnnie London and Cocky. Became roped in with the Wing Co and the new Group Capt for lunch. The Group Capt seemed rather more affable, but we haven't quite decided on the policy yet. Chose some further *Rhubarb* targets which we will attack on the next suitable day.

Took the chaps down to the Ferry in the evening for a few quick beers.

Crowley-Milling awarded Bar to DFC.

Johnnie flew to and from Coltishall (AR528), then to and from Saltby (EP215).

Monday, 14th
Ludham. Jim Vincent's cottage at 9.45.

A day's partridge shooting with Mr Rennin and son (the Essex amateur boxer). Marbent Woods, an estate agent and Jim Vincent. Shot pretty well, not a lot of stuff about but I came home with a fair-sized hare and a brace of red-legged partridge, rather on the small side.

After tea I took four of the chaps out on a stooge patrol over the sea but the only good it did was to give us all a little dusk flying.

The Squadron carried out a practice Wing Show today – Laurie leading the Squadron – it appears to have been a balls-up one way and another.

56 Squadron got their first Hun today since they have been equipped with Typhoons – A Ju 88 shot down by the Finch and his No 2.

To bed at 9 pm.

Johnnie's log book is unavailable for the period 14 to 23 September 1942 inclusive, but we do know from the ORB that the uneventful 'stooge patrol' was flown over the Smith's Knoll area (EP245).

Jim Vincent was a legendary Norfolk countryman who fished and shot on the famous Broads. Particularly well-known for his pike-fishing exploits there, Vincent will always be remembered by pike anglers for inventing the so-called 'Vincent Spoon', a lure still in use today. In addition to shooting, Johnnie fished, so was in good company.

Tuesday, 15th
Ludham

Owing to a great many complaints I called a mess meeting to thrash out the question of the food, a lot of the chaps have been moaning particularly about breakfasts and suppers. We had a good old pow-wow and as a result Race was instated as Messing Officer. The Poggi spoke up and said there was one thing that he insisted upon and that was retaining control of that Bar. He had opened the mess and built up the bar, he had run a bar for years, he had managed to get this one very well supplied etc, whereupon Halton (the Canadian) leapt up and proposed Laurie as the Bar Officer. I took the count and Laurie won the day.

Poggi was in a frightful temper, called me a shit, said I had put the Sqd up to it and that I would find he (Poggi) would now be very spiteful.

Met Paula down at the Ferry. A Flight of 68 Squadron also throwing a bit of a party down there.

450 hours of flying to date (this month).

Johnnie led Yellow Section on an 'offensive patrol' to the Dutch coast (EP245) but only fishing boats were seen. Blue Section flew a shipping recce and were fired upon by light and heavy flak from the Dutch mainland, but were unscathed.

Wednesday, 16th
Ludham. For the first time in many moons (in fact since my 616 days) I rose at 0530, drove down to 'A' Flight and was off on a dawn patrol by 0600.

The Squadron called for readiness at 1000 hours for a 12 Group Circus. Briefly, the intention is for ourselves and a Mustang Squadron to bomb the docks at Den Helder on Texel Island – just 140 miles of grey North Sea either way! We met the Bostons six or seven minutes early over Cromer and promptly set course for Texel. The weather gradually worsened towards Holland until about 10 miles off the coast cloud was 7/10 - 8/10 at 2,000 feet, whereupon the Boston Leader called and said that we was returning, so we promptly returned with him and were met by the Typhoons when halfway home.

A stroll round the Tallower's farm (one rabbit) and then on to the Ferry with Sam and brother where we eventually met up with Johnnie L, Laurie, Ady, Reg etc – leaving just before 12 pm.

Johnnie first flew a 'stooge' patrol with Sergeant W.J. Stark, nothing doing, then on the aborted escort sortie (EP245).

Thursday, 17th
Ludham. Poggi is becoming unbearable, instead of a man of 59 he is behaving like a child of 12. Sulking and moping about the whole day long. Unless things improve we shall have to look into the wretched business.

Took Laurie, Pierre, Sammy and Doug into the Castle where we joined up with 56 and drank some of the worst whisky that I have ever tasted. We then came back to the Sergeants' Mess and drank more whisky, rum and beer. It knocked me up for a couple of days.

Shot four partridge on the aerodrome, of which Sally picked up two – 11 weeks.

Johnnie made no operational flights today, on which only two uneventful scrambles occurred.

Friday, 18th
Ludham. Squadron Party. Squadron Formation to Ijmuiden, no e/a seen but a very large convoy of 17 merchant and escort vessels preceded by six armed trawlers. We were fired at by one of the flak ships but no one was hit.

When back over the English coast I ordered the Squadron to tighten up and as a result Malton (one of the new Canadians) ripped a large slice out of my rudder and elevator, but 'B' flew steadily in to Ludham where I landed successfully.

A Squadron party at the Ferry and at 10.30 we broke it up and repaired to the Mess where all the Squadron NCOs were entertained. Game pie and roast duck for dinner, plus sherry, Burgundy, port etc. A very excellent show I thought. Guests – Group Captain Harvey, Max, Johnnie, Crow, Rodger, Cocky, Michael Ingle-Finch and Mac and Large (616) Jonah, ? and George (Max's RO).

My tummy was rather u/s but I lasted the evening out.

During the morning, Johnnie led the whole squadron on an offensive patrol, looking for trouble over the Dutch coast, but again nothing doing.

Saturday, 19th

Ludham. Herbert Woods rang up yesterday and asked me to shoot with him today but I felt so bloody awful I had to call it off.

"Flash" Pleasance (successor to Wing Co Gough) and Foseman down from Group to discuss my views of the Matlask Air Firing Course, which I consider a waste of time. They both think the course a good thing but they listened to my views and, I think, were half convinced that I had something.

A visit to Ops room at 7 pm and then on to Park Lane (Norwich) to see Paula.

Telegram from American Pilots' Association inviting me to a 'Banquet' at the Savoy on Thursday evening.

Max, Johnnie and Cocky also invited.

Johnnie, unsurprisingly, did not fly. Several sections patrolled uneventfully.

Sunday, 20th

Ludham. Lunch at Coltishall with Wing Commander Loudon. Arranged three *Rhubarbs* after lunch, but the Group Controller wouldn't give his permission as he said the weather was going to close right down - of course it didn't but improved rather towards the evening.

To bed at 9 pm with rather a troublesome cold.

No flying for the ailing Johnnie today on what was in any case a quiet one, with only one section patrolling with no contact.

Monday, 21st

Ludham. A letter from Wing Co Pleasance: my cine film of a FW190 destroyed over Dieppe. As this was seen by at least three members of my Squadron he can go and stuff himself.

Three *Rhubarbs* today.

Huiden & Stark - To Texel. No targets attacked.

Pearson & Musgrove – Alkmaar. No targets attacked

Pappy & Pierre Pabiot – Barge neat Petton, hangars at De Koog aerodrome.

About 21 WAAFs from 'A' Watch Operations visited the Squadron today and all had a trip in the Maggie. We then brought them down to the Mess for a noggin or two and then on to the Ferry until 2230.

Johnnie led the squadron on an offensive patrol that morning, reporting shipping off the Dutch coast but no contact (EP245). Late afternoon, the *Rhubarbs* were flown, Johnnie and three other pilots covering Red, Green and Blue Section, but no enemy aircraft appeared.

Tuesday, 22nd
Ludham. A game of rugger today, an inter-flight 'do' with 'A' Flight winning by a couple of tries. The Wing Co came to collect his Spitfire and said to be prepared for a move, as he has heard that one is imminent.

There was no operational flying today from Ludham today.

Wednesday, 23rd
Ludham. Shooting all day with the Tallowers at Horning. Poggi, Coff and I. Returned to Ludham at 5 pm and found nothing of interest in the office, so was changing when Adj rang up and asked me to come along as there was an important signal in. I thought either 11 Group or overseas and was angered and disgusted to find that it was the most northerly aerodrome in Scotland – Castletown in Thurso. Decided to go and see the AOC tomorrow. Into Norwich to see Paula, out to the local for a beer and then back to Park Lane where we had a big chat with Mr & Mrs Ingate.

Johnnie did not fly operationally. Red Section flew a shipping recce, reporting movements off Ijmuiden.

Thursday, 24th
Ludham. Took off at 0440 and proceeded to Holland on an Intruder Patrol. Claimed a railway engine damaged – 12 Group are flapping again about permission etc.

After breakfast flew to Hucknall where I managed to get transport to Watnall. Saw the AOC about the Squadron move. He said how sorry he was but there was nothing for it – he had tried to argue with the C-in-C but he, the latter, was adamant, although he had promised we should only be there a few months. Paul asked me to keep in touch with him and to see him after Xmas.

Set off for Northolt and the American party but decided to have lunch at Wittering with Basil Embry, Jamie and Peter Clapham. After lunch not feeling too grand so I returned to Ludham and after tea went to bed feeling bloody well fed up with Fighter Command in general.

Johnnie's 'Intruder Patrol', at dawn, was a solo sortie, shooting up and stopping the train near Schagen (EP215). Other pilots flew the usual scrambles and shipping recces, but there was no contact.

Johnnie: 'We had expected to be posted back to 11 Group, having been in 12 Group for a while. We were fed up, in fact, with all those long sea crossings on these pointless but extremely hazardous *Rhubarbs*. Instead we were posted to Castletown, on the northern tip of Scotland – we couldn't have had a posting further from the action! I even went to see the Commander-in-Chief, Air Chief Marshal Sholto Douglas, about it, and consequently got my arse kicked for my trouble, so to Castletown go we would!'

Friday, 25th

Ludham (sands running out). Had to see the Group Captain today about my intruder job and although he was quite cheerful he asked me for a report on the patrol, so I expect there will be a bollocking from the 12 Group. Poor old [illegible] also on the carpet too.

Became engaged to Paula; a party at the Ferry with Marjorie, Alan Sawrie and a few more of the boys. Under the champagne fountain.

Johnnie's only flights were to and from Coltishall (EP215). On the personal front this was another significant day indeed, Paula Ingate, whom Johnnie had met just the previous month, having accepted his proposal of marriage.

Saturday, 26th

Ludham. I have a bloody good Canadian in the Squadron, Malton, who I am developing into a first class No 2.

Cocky and his boys in 56 gave the Squadron a farewell party this evening in their old Mill House by Matlask. A very good evening with plenty of liquor, good food and a few games of rugger.

Flew to Castletown (which will shortly be our new home) with Laurie today. Called in at Drem for a cup of coffee and then to the north. Some snow

181

on the higher mountains and we found it very cold and bleak at Castletown. Called in at Hutton Cranswick on the way home but unfortunately the old Bull was out.

Party in Cocky's Mess for my Squadron. We challenged 56 at rugger and nipped them by two tries to one on their own ante room floor.

Johnnie's were a series of transit flights to Castletown and return (EP215). Only one section undertook a patrol, which was typically uneventful.

Sunday, 27th
Paula's party.

Johnnie flew once today on a 'Squadron Balbo' (EP215). Several other operational flights took place, again with no contact.

Monday, 28th
Into N and to the flicks with Paula.

Johnnie did not fly. Only one scramble took place, but no enemy aircraft sighted.

Tuesday, 29th

No entry, and no flying took place.

Wednesday, 30th
To Yarmouth with Max, Johnny and another of Max's Squadron to dine with the Navy. A few double whiskies at Ludham and then on to the MTB berths where we drank a quantity of duty-free liquor. From the Ward Room we pushed on to the Star where we had an excellent dinner on the Navy.

A very glamorous blonde by the name of Sylvia turned up to accompany Max and after a few free pints in the Star we slipped back to Ludham, where we all had bacon and eggs.

A bloody awful scene with a drunken Poggi in the Mess before all my guests.

Johnnie did not fly today, and two patrols were uneventful. During this month Johnnie had added 10.20 operational flying hours to his total, plus 2.05 at night.

October

Thursday, 1st

Party in the Sergeants' Mess. Met Paula in the Ferry and then on to the Mess via my boudoir!

A good party, introduced Paula to most of the Sergeants present. 'Fraid Hvinden put up a black with the Army when under the influence.

Johnnie made no operational flight today. Red Section, Flight Lieutenant Collinge and Sergeant Edden, flew long-range Spitfire Mk VBs on a Jim Crow, reporting only 'genuine fishing boats'.

Friday, 2nd

No entry today. 610 Squadron was ordered to Martlesham Heath, from where Johnnie (EP245) led his Spitfires to cover the withdrawal of Flying Fortresses from St Omer, together with 485 and 411 Squadrons. The operation was successfully undertaken without incident. This was a significant sortie, being Johnnie's 100th operational flight.

Saturday, 3rd

Ludham. Standing-by for Operation Aflame. Group Cpt Harvey over this morning to talk on security etc. The road party had left Ludham ten minutes when the operation was again postponed.

With P/O Malton, P/O Coffin and F/Sgt Westbrooke to shoot over at Harry Bexell's farm. A very good day walking.

8 brace of pheasants

5 Partridge

1 Hare

All Squadron personnel confined to camp, so we organised a game of Poker and I went to bed at 0130 £5 up on the day.

Johnnie made no operational flight, and none of note took place.

Operation *Aflame* concerned a proposed combined services operation, in which it was planned to drop dummy paratroopers on Berck-sur-Mer while simultaneously No 12 Commando landed by sea, to confuse and convince the Germans that a major landing was underway – therefore provoking the Luftwaffe into action. Perhaps fortunately for the commandos, the raid never went ahead.

Sunday, 4th

'Aflame' put back again 24 hours. A practice interception on Cocky and afterwards we landed at Coltishall and enjoyed a very excellent lobster lunch with Max and Johnnie Loudon.

Practice interceptions on Lancasters in the afternoon.

Again, we have no record of Johnnie's non-operational flights until 13 October 1942, so no details are available of the afternoon's affiliation exercise. White Section, Sergeants Peart and Stark, flew an uneventful Jim Crow, representing the day's only operational sortie.

Monday, 5th

Doug Collinge, Pappy Wright and Smithy recommended for the DFC. I think Pappy and Smith will get theirs but am a little doubtful about Doug as he hasn't clobbered anything in the air.

In the afternoon, Barry, F/Sgts Westbrooke, Yates, 'Sally' and I drove to Harry's farm and had a walk around but it turned out to be a disappointing trip as the four of us only shot a hare, rabbit and a pigeon.

Into Norwich with Alice and Peg (met Paula) to see Bing Crosby in 'Holiday Inn', a bloody good film which we all thoroughly enjoyed.

Heard today that the Yanks may be taking over this Section – if so our dreaded trip to Castletown may be cancelled.

610 Squadron's only operational flight was a 'stooge patrol' by Flight Lieutenant Collinge and Pilot Officer Malton, which passed without incident.

Tuesday, 6th

Duck shooting with Harry today.

Again, the only operational flight was made by Collinge and Malton, another patrol on which there was no contact or sighting of the enemy.

OCTOBER

Wednesday, 7th
Ferry with 68, 56 & 610.

There was no operational flying.

Thursday, 8th
To Biggin Hill

Stayed in bed today until 12 noon. What with rugger, a run yesterday and the thrash last night I feel bloody awful. Ops came through that we were to be prepared to move immediately to Biggin Hill. The Wing Co came over to brief us and with the news that the Group Capt has a splintered bone, Max a sprained ankle and Cocky is almost dead!!! The gallant 610 are still on their feet. After lunch we received instructions to crack down to Biggin so I led the first twelve straight there and Watson came in immediately afterwards with the reserve six. Found Wing Co Thomas the Wing Leader and Group Capt Hallings-Pott (of Hawarden) the Station Commander. We learnt after tea that the Big Show (to Dieppe) is off, owing to the poor sea conditions.

A good evening in the Biggin Hill bar on beer and brandy.

According to the ORB, 'After several postponements (one of which involved a chase to recall a road party who had started out before the recall message was received) a considerable part of the Squadron moved temporarily to Biggin Hill by air (Spitfires and transport), to take part in some hush-hush operation. But they were out of luck; the operation was cancelled.'

Wing Commander Eric Thomas DFC & Bar, the Biggin Hill Wing Leader, was a very experienced pilot, having flown with 19 Squadron before the war and helping introduce the Spitfire to operational service when the unit became the first to receive the new fighter on 4 August 1938. Having spent a spell as a flying instructor at Cranwell, Thomas returned to 19 Squadron in August 1940, a few days later moving on to 266, then 222 Squadron, serving as a flight commander with the latter at Hornchurch. During the rest of the Battle of Britain, Thomas displayed great skill and courage, destroying a number of enemy aircraft. The following year, scoring more victories, he commanded both 611 and 133 Squadrons before taking over the Biggin Hill Wing in early August 1942. Wing Commander Thomas had led the Wing on the Dieppe raid, himself destroying a FW190. Awarded the DSO in 1943, he was invalided out of the service in 1944, suffering from tuberculosis, and sadly died prematurely in 1972.

Friday, 9th

London. The biggest daylight Bomber raid of the War. 108 Fortresses to LILLE. We took off in the Biggin Hill Wing with 340 and 65 (led by Thommie) to provide the well-known withdrawal support. The Squadron were at their best and I was very proud of the whole bunch. We saw the Yanks coming out of France by the dozen and chased the odd 190 that were about. Thommie was heading the Squadron with his nine and shot down a 190 which Aunt saw go in, he also claims a damaged. Both he and Group Captain Hallings-Pott were delighted with the show the Squadron put up.

Into town with Johnnie, Alan, Laurie, Musgrove and Jonal.

The New Yorker, ?, Wellington, Shepherds etc.

Meet Peter Powell, Dizzie Davies, Gibbs and missus and a few other acquaintances.

On that day, the 92nd, 93rd, 97th, 301st and 306th Bomb Groups of the American Eighth Air Force sent a record total of B-17 Flying Fortresses and B-24 Liberators to the Lille steel works. The 610 Squadron ORB reported: 'The Squadron helped provide cover for the withdrawal of over 100 Fortresses which bombed Lille by day – an operation that made the headlines as our biggest day bombing raid of the war and one in which sensational successes were scored by the Fortresses against enemy fighters. 610's part was comparatively quiet, however. Only Squadron Leader Johnson (EP245) fired his guns and he did not make any claim.'

The American bombers claimed fifty-six enemy fighters destroyed, twenty-six probably destroyed and a further twenty damaged. The more experienced British, in the main, treated these claims with scepticism. We now know that the more aircraft are engaged, the greater the number of claims, actual losses being much lower, because the speed of combat often deceives the human eye. Imagine, then, several hundred American gunners blasting away at fleeting enemy fighters. How many of them simultaneously fired at the same target and genuinely believed that they were personally responsible for the enemy's destruction? It is easy to understand, therefore, why the over-claiming on this day was so high. Nevertheless, it was a great propaganda coup and President Roosevelt himself broadcast the results to his people. Although figures were later revised to twenty-one destroyed, twelve probables and fifteen damaged, it is now believed that the Germans only in fact lost two fighters. Four American bombers were shot down and forty-six were damaged. This was the first mission for both the 93rd and 306th, as a result of which bombing was poor. Many bombs fell outside the target area, resulting in civilian casualties. Nevertheless, the raid proved that heavy bombers could penetrate enemy occupied territory with but moderate losses – in daylight. The Americans reasoned that with experience their results could only improve. It is important to understand that the bombers' operational radius was still dictated by that of their fighter escorts. RAF Bomber Command's early wartime sorties in daylight, without fighter protection, had already proved how essential escorts were, all the way to the target and back.

Saturday, 10th
London
Shooting with Mt Pennin and son. Pleasure Boat. Hickling 9 am
'Wellington'
'Studio Club'
'Shepherds'

To Bentley Priory at 0900 for an interview with Sholto Douglas. Saw Groupie first, who said the move (to Castletown) was definitely on, and then Alan, Laurie and I shot on to see Sir Sholto. He promised that our stay at Castletown would not exceed six months and that I could go and see him again in February.

Back to town where I ordered a new suit from Burberry's – Gave them a Bankers Order for £3 a month and bought a couple of shirts. Lunch at the Carlton, saw a very excellent film 'In which we serve' and then on the beer at Shepherds, Ritz, Wellington and the Studio Club.

There was no operational flying today.

Sunday, 11th
London. 3 am. I have just rung up Paula at Norwich and I think she's wizard! (drunk when I wrote this!). Returned from London, leaving after breakfast and calling in at the Trevallin's en route for a cup of tea and a yarn. Len Trevallin is now back in England, is a P/O and being trained at Leconfield, should like to get him in my Squadron.

On the road again after half an hour and the V8 went like a diva to Newmarket where we had a snack lunch at the Golden Lion, or is it the White Lion? All the same it was quite good. Reached Norwich by 1530, called for Pauline at 73, and after yet another cup of tea I took her back in the V8 to Ludham, where we had tea in my room and later gave a small dinner party to Poggi, Sammy and Coffin. The pheasants were far too rich and poor Andrews had to dance round for eggs and bacon but he rose to the occasion and dragged me out of a difficult situation.

Again, there was no operational flying.

187

Monday, 12th

No entry, and only routine scrambles flown.

Tuesday, 13th

No entry, and only one routine scramble flown. Johnnie's only flights were to Saltby and return (EP245).

Wednesday, 14th

No entry. Johnnie 'and thirty others' were flown in a Harrow transport aircraft from Ludham to Doncaster, then onwards to Castletown. It was a disappointing posting, tempered only by the Commander-in-Chief's promise that the sojourn would only be for six months. Johnnie: 'But still, we had a good time up there, plenty of game about. We were up there to protect the fleet at Scapa Flow. Not surprising, really, because from what I could make out the buggers rarely left the anchorage!'

Thursday, 15th

Castletown

Goodbye to Poggi and Ludham today. The Harrows landed just before noon and within three quarters of an hour we were all loaded inside and within 90 minutes were at Doncaster for lunch. Airborne at 1500 hours and landed at Castletown just before 1800. Colford, Sandy and one or two of the groundcrew were all very sick.

Pouring with rain and we all felt very miserable and depressed but after a good hot meal and a warm fire we began to cheer up a little.

Early to bed.

Wright, Smith – travelling by car

Malton, James – travelling by Tiger Moth.

There was no flying as 610 Squadron moved into new quarters.

Friday, 16th

Castletown

A good look round the Station today and there is room for a great deal of improvement. 'B' Flight has twenty-nine panes of glass missing from the dispersal room and over two months ago there was a fire there which messed the place around somewhat. Sick Quarters are a positive disgrace and the poor Doc is almost heartbroken, but after seeing the Station Doc I am not in the least surprised. He is a dirty great untidy lumbering mountain of a man who chain smokes his way through the day – a slacker!

Saunders, the Wing Commander, is a quite anaemic type who looks as though he has got too big a wife. I am afraid that most of SMQ officers regard an aeroplane as the last thing essential on this Station.

Flew my aeroplane today and what a terrible condition it is in. The main planes are thick and heavy and it is quite the dirtiest aeroplane I have ever seen.

This was not a great start to the squadron's tour at Castletown. Johnnie flew an air test and a sector recce (BL888). There was only one uneventful scramble, flown by Pilot Officers Pearson and Hvinden.

The station commander was Wing Commander Gerald 'Sammy' Saunders DFC, who had taken a short service commission in 1935 and was one of the Few. Posted to 65 Squadron at Hornchurch in January 1936, he first flew biplane fighters before converting to the Spitfire. By the time of Dunkirk he was a flight commander, opening his account as a fighter pilot over the French coast. He remained with 65 Squadron throughout the Battle of Britain, taking command a day before it finished. Exactly what his duties were beyond September 1941, when he was posted away, is unclear, and discovering that he was station commander at Castletown at this time is new information.

Saturday, 17th
Castletown

As I am getting married in less than four-weeks' time I had a look around for somewhere for Paula to stay – that is if she comes up this way at all! All the available accommodation in the village is full although there is one house that might be suitable.

Shooting today with F/Sgt Westbrooke round the local area.

6 rabbits

2 snipe

Flew my aeroplane again and after seeing Sandy slipped down into Echelon for a complete strip down and overhaul.

One loses track of the days up here – the papers rarely arrive and the days drift aimlessly by with little contribution to war effort.

There was no operational flying. Johnnie flew an air test (BL888).

Sunday, 18th
610 Squadron:-

S/Ldr J.E. Johnson. DFC and Bar

'A' Flight	'B' Flight
F/Lt COLLINGE	F/Lt LAURIE DFC
P/O WRIGHT	P/O SMITH
P/O CREACH (RAAF)	P/O PEARSON
P/O PABIOT (FRANCE)	LT. HVINDEN (NORWAY)
F/O STUTZMAN (POLAND)	P/O BARRY
F/O CASTULA (POLAND)	P/O WATSON
P/O MALTON (CANADA)	P/O MUSGROVE
P/O SOMES (CANADA)	

Johnnie did not fly and nor were any operational flights recorded.

Monday, 19th

A good afternoon shooting with Doug, Coffin and Westbrooke.

7 Rabbits

2 Snipe

2 Grouse

1 Partridge

Which cost me a bloody soaking as I fell in a deep flooded dyke.

Johnnie did not fly. A convoy patrol and two scrambles were flown without incident by other pilots.

Tuesday, 20th

Sgts Pear, Stark and Brown posted to Malta – rather a shaky do as their personal kit has not yet arrived.

Two Polish F/Os posted to the Squadron.

Our personal kit arrived today from Ludham.

Johnnie flew once, a sector recce (BL628), the only operational flights being a dawn and dusk patrol with nothing to report.

Wednesday, 21st

Castletown

Squadron Formation very good, as usual. Sgt Jameson (Canadian) on his first flight, or rather an attempt, appeared to bang open his throttle very coarsely and within fifty yards swerved off the runway and cart-wheeled over. The aircraft was completely written off but the wretched chap escaped practically uninjured.

Rugger

610 squadron, 5 pts SHQ 5 Pts

(A good game – we were lucky to draw)

Dinner with the Group Capt (Grail) and W/C and Mrs Saunders in Thurso. Quite the worst dinner I have had for some time but Saunders had a bottle or two of good whisky which we soon polished off.

The Major, Sam, Reg, Westbrooke and I.

1 Teal on Loch Heiton

Johnnie flew once, on the 'Squadron Balbo' (BL288), otherwise the only operational sorties were again the dawn and dusk patrols.

Thursday, 22nd

Castletown

Two new English Sgt Pilots posted to the Squadron from Hawarden.

Shooting in afternoon with G.L. Grove, Laurie, Reg, Major Miller and Barry.

3 Hares

1 Rabbit

2 Grouse

1 Snipe

4 Mallard Duck

Dinner with the Grp Capt, Wing Co and Mrs Saunders, Alan and Doug – in the Ladies Room.

Johnnie did not fly. Five convoy patrols were completed without incident.

Friday, 23rd

Castletown

Up at 6 am to catch the morning flight of duck.

1 Mallard

1 Teal

1 Unidentified

Johnnie flew an aerobatic practice flight (AB860). Two more uneventful convoy patrols took place.

Saturday, 24th

Castletown

Squadron Balbo at 1030. Very good again but had a few words with the Wing Co, relating to taking off on the wrong runway and his [illegible] V Squadron Balbos. The conversation became very heated and abusive language was used against me to which I replied in the same vernacular. Afterwards in the Mess with Wing Co. Peak and S/Ldr Cain he was very affable and we had a few beers together.

Paula rang up when I was in my bath this evening – my dirty past has reared its ugly head again and I am in the shit again – must fly down at the first opportunity.

To SKITTEN with W/C Saunders, Alan, Doug and Reg Pearson for a house warming – left at 3 am more drunk than sober and felt bloody awful the next morning – for the first time in many moons I was not out of bed until 1030 am.

Johnnie's only flight was the 'Squadron Balbo' (AB860). Dawn and dusk patrols were flown, nothing to report.

Sunday, 25th
Castletown

My aeroplane out from Echelon.

After lunch took off for Norfolk but only managed to get a few miles the other side of Inverness when I had to turn back – a bloody great front looming ahead of me.

Duck Patrol this evening. I don't go much on this aerodrome for night flying – lighting inadequate and runways too small.

Swapped my main jacket with S/Ldr Cooper for a full-length RFC flying coat – a good bargain from my point of view.

Johnnie flew twice, an air test and aerobatics (BL888). Only routine patrols were carried out.

Monday, 26th
Weather test again as far as Inverness but definitely u/s so that once again I had to postpone my trip to Norwich.

Johnnie's aborted 'Weather Test' to Inverness lasted fifty-five minutes (BL888). Only a dawn patrol was flown.

Tuesday, 27th
Norwich

Left Castletown after breakfast and flew down the Scottish coast in dirty weather which gradually improved as I approached England. Slipped across the [illegible] by Box Rock and on Southwards down the Northumberland Coast. Flew over Allenheads where Hughie and I spent such a good leave in August with the Allendale family. Had to land at a bomber aerodrome, Croft, as I was getting pretty short of fuel and it took the inefficient bastards over an hour to refuel me – bloody disgraceful. On to Hutton Cranswick where The Old Bull was waiting to give me lunch.

Off again at 3 pm for Ludham where I found old Sam and Group Captain Harvey inspecting 107. Had a long chat with God and after tea and a bath I pushed off to Norwich in Poggi's car where I found Pauline patiently waiting at 73. A long chat with she and then we both chased old Bishop Herbert but were unable to get in touch with him.

Johnnie's three flights were transit to Ludham (BL888). No operational flights took place.

Wednesday, 28th
Norwich

Firewoman Ingate on duty, so Mrs Ingate, Doris and I spent the morning shopping and I made a smart hole in my bank account. Fixed up the wedding at the Registrar's Office for Saturday 14 November at 1130, and then on to London and Blackpool for the honeymoon.

Saw a Great lobster lurking in a fishmongers shop so I bought it for £23 and we had it for tea – very good too.

Paula and I saw a flick and then she had to return to work at 2100. Picked up Doris from the [illegible].

Back at Castletown 610 Squadron flew a number of uneventful patrols.

Thursday, 29th
Norwich

A whole day with Pauline. After breakfast we drove to Ludham where the weather forecast was bad, so I decided to hang for a few more hours before returning to Castletown. Drove on to see Jim Vincent where I was lucky enough to buy a couple of hundred cartridges with a promise of a further 500 in a few weeks' time. Then on to Harry's farm where we spent a very pleasant afternoon after the pheasants.

6 Pheasants

With Pauline acting as beater. An excellent high tea and on again to the Ferry where we spent a pleasant hour with Sam, Brother and Reg and eventually home to 73.

No operational flying took place at Castletown.

Friday, 30th

Drove Pauline to the Fire Station and then slipped on to Ludham where I took off for Castletown at 1030, but the weather was bad and within twenty minutes I was down at Matlask.

Started on the beer stakes with Cocky and Michael at the Buckingham Arms and then back for the sherry stakes with Bill, Basil and one or two other types. After lunch Bill flew my Spit and I rolled my old car V8 and completely wrote it off. Nearly pranged Bill's Bentley but finished up at an angle of 45 degrees on the bank.

To Blakeney with the CO and two flight commanders. Several pints of beer, darts with the locals and then to finish the day Cocky rolled the Standard when we were within sight of the camp. We righted it, pulled off a door and threw it into the ditch and proceeded on our way.

An enjoyable day.

Johnnie's only flight was to Matlask (BL888). Various uneventful patrols were flown by 610 Squadron.

Saturday, 31st

Took off for Castletown at 1130 feeling decidedly ropey and thinking that it would be a good thing to get myself away from the Coltishall Legion before the rot sets in. Landed at Drem, another hour to refuel and then on again to Castletown, arriving here at 1500 after an extremely enjoyable four days leave.

Johnnie's two flights were returning to base (BL888), from where only a routine dawn and convoy patrol were flown.

November

Sunday, 1st

Fired my guns and cannon. (not in anger!).

Johnnie's firing practice was his only flight today (BL767), on what was another quiet day with only two uneventful patrols flown.

Monday, 2nd

Castletown. Shooting – Coffin, Westbrooke, Preane, Danny, self.

3 Hares

2 Snipe

2 Rabbits

1 Green Plover

Johnnie did not fly today. 610 Squadron flew a variety of convoy and other patrols, all without incident.

Tuesday, 3rd

Castletown

Letter from all my old Staneley acquaintances, Pita Kela, Jim Churn, Eddie and also one from Len Trevallin. Also today had a letter from Lord Titchfield's keeper – one George King who informs me that there are 30 [illegible] to be shot at his Lordship's Scottish home - Bernidale - after 16 November.

Had a really beautiful letter from Pauline, she really does write wonderful scrolls and I can read them over and over again.

Arranged for some bomber officiation with a squadron of Hampdens from Wick. Their boys steam across to Norway from Wick looking for the *Tirpitz* at a steady 130 knots and carrying a bloody great torpedo – and this in the fourth year of the war – its bloody disgraceful! The Wing Co in charge says that if he even has to have a crack at anything big he entreats that not more than one of the squadron will get back and as a protest he will resign before he takes off.

Johnnie flew twice, the bomber cooperation flight and a thirty-minute 'beat up' (BL767).

The Handley Page Hampden, known by its crews as the 'Flying Bedstead' because of its ungainly appearance and cramped interior, was a twin-engine bomber obsolete by 1942. Indeed, the aircraft had been withdrawn from daylight operations by Bomber Command. Unfortunately for 144 and 455 (Australian) Squadrons, both were transferred to Coastal Command in April 1942, converted to torpedo bombers and based at RAF Leuchars.

In September 1942 both squadrons sent detachments to Vaenga in Russia, there to hand aircraft over to and train the Soviets. Sixteen of 455's aircraft were lost en route. It is likely that the unhappy Wing Commander would have been the CO of one of these squadrons, although neither's ORB mentions such a cooperation exercise, the flight not being an operational one. The *Tirpitz* was a formidable German battleship of the *Bismarck* class, based in Norway as a deterrent to Allied landings. After attacks by British midget submarines and numerous air attacks, it would be the famous 'Dambusters', 617 Squadron, who would eventually sink the *Tirpitz*, dropping 12,000lb Tallboy bombs from their Lancasters on 12 November 1944.

Wednesday, 4th
Castletown. A lovely day and quite the best we have had since being in this Group. I took off in the early morning and flew along the NW tip of Scotland round Cape Wrath and not very far from the Isle of Lewis. Had a look at the snow on the mountain crests and the frozen lochs in the valleys. Not a bump or a tremor in the air – a really ideal day for the job.

This evening Doug Alan and I entertained the Wing Co and his wife to dinner and we also invited Sqn/Ldr Cameron who has just arrived here from King's Cliffe with his RAF Regiment Squadron. A good evening - hare soup, fresh plaice caught from Thurso this evening, grouse, duck, woodcock and snipe and pineapple – cost us about 15 bob each.

Johnnie flew twice, testing machine guns and cannons, and air-to-air firing (BL767). Two sections flew uneventful patrols.

A 'bob' was a pre-decimal shilling (5p), so that dinner was 75p a head!

NOVEMBER

Thursday, 5th

Castletown. Doug Collinge, Pappy Wright and Smithe have now been recommended one month for the DFC. No news yet.

Aerobatics – I have now mastered the vertical roll and the roll off! and Air to Sea firing at the cork target in Dunnet Bay.

We were invited to a party at Wick this evening but my tummy was out of sorts, so Doug, Alan and South pushed off with the Wing Co and Mrs Station Commander.

I didn't think they had too enjoyable a time as they had to buy their own booze which was rather a poor show.

Johnnie flew two firing practice flights (BL767). A number of convoy patrols were flown, all uneventful.

Friday, 6th

Castletown. To Inverness to see Air Vice-Marshal Collyshall CB DSO & Bar MBE MC DFC & C&C.

'My Brother Sylvest.'

'Row of 40 Medals on his chest'.

Had a long chat with the old boy and he gave me permission to fly the Moth and the Master down to Coltishall to take two or three of the boys to the wedding.

Wired the Mayfair about accommodation for Pauline and I, and had a very prompt reply this evening which Doc Kains took for me. Not a bloody word from the Dorchester – I wired them yesterday.

Johnnie's only flights were to and from Inverness. Several more uneventful patrols took place.

Saturday, 7th

Castletown. Air to Sea firing and Formation & Aerobatics with Fallow and Worley – both pretty steady. Shooting on draw at Sinclair's land with Coffin, Malton, James and the Doc.

1 Hare (the size of a donkey)

2 Brace Grouse

To the Dunnet in the evening with Alan, Stuart, Reg, Jones, Collins (ex 411) and a bloody good sing-song in the Ante Room afterwards.

Johnnie flew once, as described above (BL767). No operational flying took place.

Sunday, 8th

Castletown. Lots of Air Firing at today.

Self – fifteen hits on the 20' drogue: at the moment, Doug holds the record with thirty-eight. Another foraging party out today, led by Alan to skirmish for the Wedding Breakfast.

2 Hare

3 Grouse

1 Woodcock

1 Duck

Doug Collinge and Smithy awarded the DFC, no news of Pappie's recommendation.

Johnnie flew three firing exercises (BL767). Only one patrol was flown, nil return.

Monday, 9th

Another shooting party today led by myself using Reeve's beautiful Holland & Holland twelve bore – a beauty.

Doug Alan and I went round to the Wing Co's home this evening to meet Shona Sinclair and a convalescent Dutch pilot from 167 who is staying with her (according to Reeves) in a house on a local hill. Quite a good party with lots of whisky on the Wing Co.

3 Hares

3 Grouse

1 Woodcock

1 Partridge

1 Snipe

2 Plover

Johnnie did not fly today, and the only two operational patrols were uneventful.

Tuesday, 10th

Castletown. Poor day with bad visibility and low cloud. Doug took some of his Flight out on the moors to try and clobber another brace of grouse.

2 Grouse

1 Hare

The weather cleared at tea time so I lurked off on a look-see round the Islands. The Squadron gave a party for me at the Dunnet this evening and a very good one too with the Wing Commander and Reeves present.

We sang steadily from 8 pm until almost 1 am without repeating ourselves and mopped up a fair quantity of ale. Barry was in good voice, Aunt and

Creagh were the champs at hand clasping and I threw the Wing Co a couple of times in a cock-fight.

Johnnie flew an aerobatic practice today (BL767). Only one routine patrol was flown.

The ORB recorded: 'This day the Squadron had a real excuse for a party. The CO, Squadron Leader J.E. Johnson DFC & Bar, having decided to take the flip (whence there is no return) into matrimony and the date of take-off (or 'prang' as you like it) being imminent. Officers and senior NCOs, with the Station Commander, Wing Commander G.A.W. Saunders DFC, and Station Adjutant, Flight Lieutenant Reeves, as guests, chose the Dunnet Hotel as rendezvous. Much signing – and not a little 'partaking of refreshment', as the old saying has it! And so, for Squadron Leader Johnson, the beginning of farewell to bachelordom.'

Wednesday, 11th
Castletown. Leave commences - officially tomorrow. Left Castletown at 1045 after arranging for Sammy and Reg to follow in the Tiger and Alan and Aunt in the Master. Made good time to Acklington despite fact that Ops were flapping like hell, 'weather u/s at destination.' etc. Refuelled at Acklington (the usual finger in on the Bowser) and then on to Hutton Cranswick to be greeted by a cheerful Tommy Raeton.

Lunch with Ken and then the pair of us set off – he to escort me as far as Lincoln where we found an absolute front – quite impossible. I tried to sweep down the coast but simply couldn't make the grade, so returned to H.C and spent a very good evening with Ken, [illegible] and a Brown job at a good little Yorkshire pub.

Johnnie's flights were all attempting to reach Ludham (BL767). A number of convoy patrols were flown but no action.

Thursday, 12th
Hutton Cranswick. Weather again completely u/s so after waiting until lunchtime I decided to continue my journey by train. Ken rang up Tim Maurice about Pappy's gong and Tim told us the whole story – he kicked Pappy's out and put up Doug and Smithy – the old bastard. But he outlined a scheme whereby it is pretty certain to go through – he is going to write me about it. Tim also told us some grand news – today Cocky has been promoted Wing Commander and given the job at Duxford, predecessors Prosser Hanks and Denys Gillam.

This Station is very much after the Holden manner – everything scrumptiously clean and the Station runs like clockwork; he seems to be very popular although I should think it is a difficult and tough job looking after an Allied Squadron.

Arrived at Norwich an hour late to be met by Pauline and a very drunken 50 Squadron and Johnnie Loudon. Took Pauline home and then back to Matlask for eggs and gammon!

Relieved to have got back for his impending wedding, Johnnie would not fly again until 26 November 1942. 610 Squadron's CO was missing nothing at Castletown, as only further uneventful operational sorties were flown.

Friday, 13th
Matlask. A lunchtime session at the Ferry with Cocky and Taffy on light ale. A cup of soup at Ludham, borrowed Poggi's car and into Norwich, after picking up some hack etc at Ray's of Wroshaw. Back to Ludham to collect Poggi and then on to Matlask, changed, had another bowl of soup and back to the Ferry to find Alan, Reg [illegible] and Aunt. A very good last bachelor evening with cock fights and others! Reg thought we were going to break the place up so he turned is all out at 11 pm. Tore back to Ludham where Poggi got us a meal and then we bedded down in front of the Ante Room fire for the night.

Saturday, 14th
WEDDING DAY. A few light ales and an odd whisky in the Bell, and Pauline and I were married at 1130 and how wonderful she looked. To the Haymaker for the Wedding Breakfast. Present – Cocky, Ken, Max, Johnnie, Michael Ingle-Finch, Alan, Sammy, Aunt, Reg, Ernie, Ross, Nat Moins, Sam and brother, Mr & Mrs Maeny, Reg from the Ferry, Jim Vincent too, and 50 or 60 of Pauline's friends and relations.

Took Pauline, Marjory and Gran back to 73 Park Lane, and the others turned up after a bit of a session at the Bell – said goodbyes and after being pranged in Poggi's car eventually arrived at the Bull at Barton Mills where we spent the night.

The 610 Squadron ORB recorded the nuptials: 'Squadron Leader Johnson married at the Registrar's Office, City Hall, Norwich, to Miss Paula Ingate, youngest daughter of Mr & Mrs Sidney Ingate, 73 Park Lane, Norwich. His old friend Wing Commander HSL Dundas DFC was best man. Squadron officers present, who gave the occasion something of an international flavour, were Flight Lieutenant W.A. Laurie DFC, Pilot Officer R.W. Pearson, Flying Officer G.S. Malton (Canada) and Lieutenant A Hvinden (Norway).'

Other guests included Wing Commander The Hon Max Aitken DFC, son of Lord Beaverbrook, and Lord Lovett.

Paula Johnson remembered:

> We met at the Samson and Hercules Ballroom in Norwich. I was dancing with a schoolfriend of my brother's called "Ham" when Johnnie, who was then based at Ludham, cut in. He asked my name and I told him. He replied that he had seen the name "Ingate all over Norfolk!" Our family owned several small businesses in East Anglia, including a marine garage at Bungay, but my mother wanted to move to Norwich, so we moved to the city. We spent a delightful evening together on the occasion of our first meeting, upon conclusion of which Johnnie drove me home. I knew straight away that he was the right man for me, that there could be no other. Not long afterwards Johnnie asked my father for permission to marry me, promising to always take care of me, which he did. After our wedding there was a sit-down Wedding Breakfast for thirty at the Haymarket, the food provided by local farmers. My sister had been to Woolworth's and bought toy Spitfires which were placed on every table – Max Aitken roared with laughter and exclaimed "We don't need to return to base, we have a squadron right here!" Johnnie and his pilots were a real band of brothers, all quite mad, of course! In fact I became known as "Paula" because of Douglas Bader. My real name is Pauline, but he said "We can't have that, the 'Perils of Pauline', you must be called 'Paula' to go with my wife, Thelma!" I remained in Norwich throughout the war, where I worked for the Fire Service. At the time there was a saying, "Careless Talk Costs Wives". Johnnie was very protective and didn't want me on the station.

Sunday, 15th
(DING DONG. MY WEDDING DAY!!)
(Makes you think Johnson!)

Left Barton Mills after breakfast and drove steadily to Laughton where we had lunch with the Trevallon's and a chat with Joe Heath.

Rang up the Mayfair and discovered that Finch, true to his word had reserved our rooms there. After tea we saw a couple of good flicks at the London Pavilion and then we returned to the Mayfair via the Piccadilly for dinner and bed – rang up Nat who made a bloody nuisance of himself by ringing up every half-hour.

Monday, 16th
Mayfair. Breakfast in bed and then we fixed an appointment at Pearl Freeman's for 1130 tomorrow – photographs. Onto Burberry's where Mr Green gave me a fitting for my new suit and then a stroll down Regent Street, Marble Arch, Park Lane and eventually to Shepherds where we had a couple or four beers with Johnnie Loudon, and afterwards an excellent lunch upstairs – lobster for me and a beef steak pie for Pauline. To bed for a couple of hours in the afternoon while Pauline had her face lifted and her hair set, as maybe she thinks she is not already beautiful enough. A few Martinis in the American Bar where we met 'Corky', now DSO & DFC, who was at one time in DB's original Squadron, 242. Nat turned up just after 8 and took us to the Rendezvous in Albemarle St. Then we went into Knightsbridge where we met a rather unpleasant Jew and his woman, and the whole gang of us had supper in Regent Street. To bed at 1230 with my baby, Pauline.

'Dicky' Cork was a Lieutenant and pilot in the Fleet Air Arm, who was amongst those navy pilots who volunteered to reinforce Fighter Command for the Battle of Britain, throughout which he served in Squadron Leader Douglas Bader's 242 Squadron. Becoming an ace during the summer of 1940, Cork was recommended for the DFC but in fact the Navy insisted upon the Distinguished Service Cross, as awarded to their own officers. After the Battle, Cork went to Coastal Command briefly before joining the aircraft carrier HMS *Indomitable* and fighting in the Far East and Malta, for which he was appointed to the DSO. In 1944, Lieutenant Commander Cork was killed in a flying accident at China Bay.

Tuesday, 17th
To Melton Mowbray after an unpleasant half hour having our photographs taken at Pearl Freeman's. Then a terrible time finding my way out of town and particularly as the blasted car clutch had almost gone. Lunch at a wayside pub and steady on to King's Cliffe, where we picked up Ross and brought him on to Melton for the evening. To the George where we knocked back a few quickies and then early to bed.

Wednesday, 18th

Melton Mowbray

Quiet day spent at home with Pauline. Took Poggi's car down to Garners to try and have the clutch trouble repaired but it has definitely gone and they cannot repair it without spare parts. Saw Mr Walker my bank manager and fixed up about my overdraft and Pauline's allowances.

An evening with her Leader and missus & Mrs Morrell.

Thursday, 19th

Melton Mowbray – Manchester

To Blackpool! To see Nat and Co. Saw Johnnie Townsend at 10 am and fixed up an insurance on the little Morris. Drove into Leicester with Johnnie and licenced the [illegible]. Had lunch and then set off for Manchester via Denby, Ashbourne, Leek, Macclesfield. Stayed at the Grand, saw a flick and quite the worst dinner I have ever seen in any hotel.

Broke the bed!

Friday, 20th

Manchester – Blackpool

Left the Grand at 11 am and up to Blackpool via the old route of Tom Heynes and Jack [illegible] days – Middleton, Prestwick, Bolton and Preston. Slipped into the Metropole and ran bang into Nat in Leslie's Bar, a few beers and then onto the Empress for lunch.

After lunch Nat took Paula to do a little shopping and bought her about ten pounds worth of clothes and silk stockings to say nothing of perfume, soap and a handbag.

To the Palace in the evening to see a variety show and then in Leslie's we ran into Norman Donnigen of 56 Squadron.

Saw Bob Clayton from the old Aero Club days.

Saturday, 21st

Blackpool

Black Market shopping with Nathan. Eggs, Butter, Steaks etc. Saw the Jew Donnigen again in the Casino and booked a table for this evening with Nat's help.

Nat lost 'half a hundred' on the dogs this afternoon. Small stuff & Paula collected her dresses from Fred Tipping of Cleveleys.

Sunday, 22nd

Blackpool

To Poulton with Nat: saw Wilfred [illegible], Alf Bithnell and two or three others of the old hands. Back to the Metropole via the Cabin where Pauline joined us and then some lunch.

This evening we dined with some of Norman Donnigen's friends and relations at the Casino.

Blackpool is simply unaffected by the war, plenty of food, steaks, eggs, lots of money about, dog racing, football, shows and hundreds of young men with far too much money and spending it too – perhaps so that the Income Tax folk won't hear of it. In fact I should say that the place is about 10 per cent war winded.

Monday, 23rd

Blackpool – Manchester – Melton Mowbray

Left the Empress and rather pleased too as the place was beginning to get on my nerves a little with its dirt and lack of clean linen.

Followed Norman to Manchester and had a look at his firm in Cheetham – someone measured me for a blazer – I wonder if I shall get it. Lunch at the Victoria with the Donnigen brothers and then straight down to Melton via Macclesfield, Leek, Ashbourne, Denby and Six Mills. Laden with steak, eggs, fish and new clothes for Pauline.

Tuesday, 24th

Melton Mowbray

Quiet day at home with Pauline and playing cards with Dad.

Wednesday, 25th

Melton Mowbray – Norwich

After lunch said goodbyes to Mother and the old Dad and set off for Norwich via Stamford, Peterborough, Wisbech, Kings Lynn and East Dereham, arriving there just before dark. To the flicks with Pauline and her Mother to see 'Mrs Miniver' and myself shooting a line in a Ministry of Information flick.

Thursday, 26th

Norwich – Castletown

Said goodbye to Pauline and drove Poggi's car unsteadily to Ludham and there was no sign of Aunt in my aeroplane. Edwards of 107 very kindly lent me a long-ranger and I set off for the North flying through some very dirty weather before I reached Drem. Refuelled there and arrived at Castletown at 1900 hours to find things very much the same as when I left fifteen days ago.

Johnnie's flight was in Spitfire Mk V AR509.

Friday, 27th
Castletown. Air to Sea Firing. While I have been away, Sandy has put up a black and for his sins is Duty Pilot for three days. This evening went to Loch Haluim with Reeves and Sally to wait for the duck flighting off. It was very cold with driving sleet and rain but we found some protection from a rubble wall and I had a few useful shots at teal and mallard, dropping one or two a few feet away in the lake which were both retrieved by the 5 month old Sally.

Reeves and I split a Mallard duck for dinner this evening – very good too, not in the least muddy.

Johnnie flew once, as described (BL760). There was no operational flying.

Saturday, 28th
Party at Wittering.
Party at Kirkwall.

To Grimsetter in the late afternoon with Pappy Wright and we had to fly through some dirty weather in order to get there. A few quick beers with the Belgian CO of 129 and then on to the mess at Kirkwall, where we had a few quick beers with the Groupy and the AOC, followed by a light supper.

On to the dance which proved to be quite a jolly affair and the old man was quite whistled by 2 am, although he certainly put a spot of liquor back as did the CO of 129. Met some of the 102 boys from Skaebrae and one or two other types lurking around.

Johnnie also flew another cooperation flight with Hampdens (EN898). Again, no operational flying took place.

Sunday, 29th
Returned from Grimsetter and very pleased to be back. What a bloody God-forsaken desolate place it is. If we ever have to move there it will be the end.

In addition to flying back from RAF Grimsetter, near Kirkwall, the Orkney's capital, Johnnie also flew a cine gun practice (EN898). There was no operational flying again, but the AOC 14 Group, Air Vice-Marshal R. Collishaw CB DSO OBE DSC DFC visited Castletown, addressing all 610 Squadron's pilots at Dispersal.

The squadron presented Johnnie an onyx cigarette box to commemorate his marriage to Paula.

Monday, 30th
Visit by the AOC to 'A' Flight where he chatted with all the pilots for some ninety minutes and talked a pretty average amount of cock.

Johnnie did not fly, and again no operational sorties were made. In this entry he is at odds with the ORB, which records the AOC's visit as having been the previous day.

December

Tuesday, 1st
Official opening of the new Bar in the mess by the pranged Doc Kaird, who arose from a sick bed and hobbled down on crutches. Last evening the Squadron gave me a beautiful wedding present in the form of an onyx table cigarette case finished in silver and gold, and this evening the Station HQ officers slipped me a silver watch-box holder.

We had a terrible evening and the bar was finally closed at 0300 hours. Couldn't get up the following morning and had to have my lunch in bed.

Johnnie did not fly for the next two days, and neither were any operational flights made by 610 Squadron throughout that time.

Wednesday, 2nd
Castletown. Visit of an ENSA concert party to the station – they came back to the Mess for a drink after the show and as there were a few officers wives present we had a bit of a party. Bar closed at 0230 hours, and high time too as I had organised a great tie and hair cutting contest.

Managed to get up the following morning at 0930 and had the shock of me life when I saw Sammy's hair – he looks worse than any convict.

Thursday, 3rd
Quiet day. Saw what I took to be some geese on Loch Meilan, so we organised the Tiger Moth and with Sammy flying at a steady 45 I confirmed one and damaged two others. We dashed down in a dinghy and Feathers gallantly volunteered to retrieve the bird, but after about ten mins with his hands in the icy cold water he had to come ashore and I managed to get the thing back. A great controversy still rages as to whether it is a swan or a goose but we are going to keep it for ten days and then have a bang at it.

Johnnie flew twice, a 'runway test' and squadron formation practice in line abreast (BL760).

Then, extraordinarily, with Flying Officer Malton flying the Tiger Moth with Johnnie toting his 12 bore in the rear cockpit, 'Two swans/geese destroyed'!

A section of two Spitfires flew an uneventful dusk patrol.

Friday, 4th

Smith and Skbinski shooting at Langdale. One Hind each.

Johnnie flew twice, to and from Inverness (BL767). A number of patrols were flown, all without event, but there would be no more operational flying for several days.

Saturday, 5th

No entry and no flying.

Sunday, 6th

Squadron Balbo at 1430 for 'B' Flight to escort 'A' Flight to Tain for Operation *Goliath*. I have never seen the Squadron flying in such bloody awful formation and when we eventually arrived at Tain told them so in no uncertain terms.

Afterwards brought 'B' Flight back to Castletown – we had to fly most of the way up the coast owing to the wretched day.

Johnnie flew four times, two aileron tests then to and from Tain (BL767).

Operation *Goliath* was an army cooperation exercise in which the squadron was to support 'German' troops 'in action' around the northern shore of Loch Ness.

Monday, 7th

Tain. Flew down to Tain with Michael Dewey to see how the boys of 'A' Flight were progressing under Pappy Wright. The weather down there was almost u/s and Tony Rooke, Coffin and I shot down to the Mess for a cup of coffee and then on to The Royal at Tain, where we found some excellent draught beer. Drank steadily from 1100 to 1500 hours and then back to the Mess for a curry. Pappy rang up and said that Group Cpt Somerville was at flights – a shaky do as we could hardly stand, Rooke swayed on his feet, Coffin lumbered past and I thought the safest place was in the air and accordingly clambered into DW-B and took off. Another good party in the evening at the Royal and eventually Stavert, Coffin, Sammy and I slept there.

Johnnie flew twice, to Tain, and to escape the Group Captain, participated in Operation *Goliath* (BL767). Two operational patrols were flown from Castletown, both uneventful.

Wing Commander Tony Rook DFC was a pre-war auxiliary pilot with 504 'City of Nottingham' Squadron, with which he flew Hurricanes during the Battle of Britain. In 1941 his Flight was expanded to become a new squadron, 131, and sent to Vaenga, near Murmansk, in support of the Soviets. Later he was decorated with the AFC for training work and commanded 504 Squadron when re-formed post war. His brother Michael was also one of the Few and a decorated fighter pilot but was killed after the war in a flying accident.

Another of the Few mentioned by Johnnie is Flight Lieutenant Michael Stavert, who had joined 610 Squadron from 1491 Fighter Gunnery Flight on 4 December 1942 as supernumerary having flown during the Battles of France and Britain, scoring combat victories, with 1 and 504 Squadrons; he survived the war.

Tuesday, 8th
Two or three [illegible] in the army today in the vicinity of Loch Ness and at 1300 hours I brought 'A' Flight back to camp and 'B' Flight took over, returning just before dark. Took Sally out this evening to the eastern end of the loch but we didn't see a thing.

Johnnie flew on two Operation *Goliath* sorties, then back from Tain (BL767). Two patrols were flown from Castletown, nil return.

Wednesday, 9th
A very pleasant afternoon's shooting with Reeves round Ham, Many Lochs and St. John's Loch.
    4 Green Plover
    3 Snipe
    2 Rabbit
And a couple of duck which we couldn't find as they were runners/ swimmers and bunked off.

A day or two ago a hind turned up from Lord Titchfield's place at Langdale and I am making arrangements for a Squadron party at the Dunnet on Tuesday next.

Johnnie flew a bomber affiliation sortie (BL767). There were no operational flights.

Thursday, 10th
Xmas Cards

Mother	Mrs Oakley
Ross	George King
Pauline	G/C Somerville
Peter	Smithy
Thelma Bader	Supt Stapleton
Jim Vincent	Trevallions
Poggi	Holbowa
Harry Bleenell	Woolley
Tawallen Bros	
Reg at The Ferry	
616 Sqd	
Cocky	
Ken	
F/Sgt Rauderson	
UACs Burton & Radcliffe	
JV Booth	
Nat Morris	
JH Smithson – Australia	
Mrs Arthur Race	
Herb Woods	
Johnnie Townsend	
Len Leader	
Wing Co Parker	
Max Aitken	
AVM Collyshaw	
GC Harvey	
Wing Co Rooke	

Johnnie flew a cannon and machine gun test flight (BL767). There was no operational flying.

Friday, 11th
Pappy, Pierre, Coffin and self out for the day on the moors.
2 Grouse
1 Snipe
1 Hare
3 Curlew

Party at the Sergeants' Mess. A good do, most of the officers pissed including Creagh who cut his lip badly, the Doc who wanted him to go to Sick Quarters, Cooper who just sat down quietly, Sammy who brought a red lamp home, Pearson who fell down and ruined his uniform in the mud and myself, who as the Adj says 'wasn't in your usual fighting drunken mood.'

Johnnie's sole flight was firing at a drogue (BL767). Several patrols were flown with the usual nil return.

Saturday, 12th

Castletown. Doug returned from leave and to celebrate this I beat him up in a game of squash. An Anson belonging to the Shipping Recco flight ditched in the Sea off Duncansby Head owing to engine failure (there may be other causes too!) but the crew either clambered or swam ashore – set up Doug, Sandy and Creagh to follow a Court of Inquiry.

Johnnie flew once, a 'squadron scramble' (BL767). There was no contact on any of the day's patrols. At 1600 hours, Exercise Crab II began, lasting until 0800 hours on 15 December 1942: 'Purpose of exercise was to test Station security against enemy guerrillas. Strengthened night guards were maintained, mainly at dispersal points, and several "brushes" with intruders occurred.'

Sunday, 13th

Appointed Doug, South and Sandy to form a Court of Inquiry re the Anson prang.

Group officers up for two or three days.

The festive season approaches and I am at present £30 overdrawn and over half a month to go!

Johnnie did not fly. There were a number of uneventful patrols.

Monday, 14th

Operation *Crab*. Miller ran in my office this afternoon in a hell of a flap screaming out that the aerodrome was surrounded by enemy troops and what should we do? What an incompetent fool the man is, an example of a regular officer with 22-years-service in the Scotch Guards.

I sent off a flight of six Spits to beat up the 'enemy' positions, and Reeves and I took off in the Tiger with a Verey pistol and cartridges to show the boys the enemy strong points. Unfortunately on the fourth attack Reeves set fire to a haystack and we promptly returned to base and landed. Saw the farmer – one Sinclair – who was very decent about the whole thing but we shall have to report the damage.

Doug thrashed me at squash and later I rang up Paula but she wasn't on duty – just my luck as the line was loud & clear.

Johnnie's only flight was in the Tiger Moth (DE626), writing in his log book 'One haystack destroyed by one Verey light!' There was no operational flying.

Tuesday, 15th

Little flying today – weather u/s and blowing a gale. We adjourned to the Dunnet where the preparations were well in hand for this evening's party.

We all looked up there about 1930 and our guests were Cooper, Reeves, Bailey, A. Brown. The hind that Smith shot was roasted deliciously and we all tucked into a bloody good feed.

Rang Pauline up about 2230 but was only just able to hear her and as there was such a noise going on we didn't say a deal to each other.

The rest of the officers dining at Castlehill ate the swan that Sammy and I shot and all swore by it.

Johnnie did not fly, and nor did he for five days. There was no operational flying either. At the party, the squadron enjoyed their dinner of hind and 'found much to admire in Squadron Leader Johnson's grand manner as he dispensed the portions with the air of a proud father ministering to the needs of an outsize family.'

Wednesday, 16th

Castletown. Weather u/s again today, low cloud and blowing a gale with gusts up to 60-70 mph. No flying, so to get last night's beer out of my system I decided to spend an afternoon out with the Gun.

Self, Reeves, Barry, Neil – 7 Golden Plover, 2 Snipe

S/Ldr Cooper left early this morning as I decided to send him on leave pending his posting. Steady evening in the Mess with no beer drinking by way of a change.

Thursday, 17th

Castletown. Shooting again with Doc, Chastula and Sammy at Loch Bushter but although we had some excellent sport and knocked down five big

Mallard, we only succeeded in picking up one as the others were wounded and had crept in the banks.

To the Dunnet this evening to pay the £10 Bill that we owed for the party. A session with Marton, the Rolls-Royce specialist, on the menu. Very drunk when we staggered back.

Friday, 18th
Inverness

Party at 14 Group HQ. Arrived at Inverness and had dinner at the Caledonian – awful.

To the Group Party and there met AVM Collyshaw, SASO, Groupers Sommerville, Wing Co Rook, Kain, Coates and various others. Took a violent dislike to a Canadian type called Boswell who was bumbling the AOC and I'm pleased to record that the old man ordered him to bed, but the bastard didn't go. Some fell by the wayside, Reeves and Smithy at 0600 but we ate a pretty fair breakfast at 08.30. Lunch with the old man, then we brought the Wing Co and his wife home.

Saturday, 19th
Returned from Inverness with the Wing Co and his wife. Hit Castletown at 2100 hours.

Sunday, 20th
Flew my new a/c 'B' and found her delightful.
45 minutes dual instruction to Doc Cameron in the Tiger.

Johnnie flew his new Spitfire on a formation and air test flight (BL659). There was no operational flying.

Monday, 21st
Took off at 1030 with the idea of seeing Pauline for a few hours and buying her Xmas present. Refuelled at Acklington and hit Ludham just in time for lunch with Poggi.

Found Poggi in poor form as all his sins have caught up with him and he is going to be reduced to Flying Officer and posted to Church Fenton.
Rang up P. and as she is on duty for the rest of the day I decided to slip down to Duxford and spend the night with Cocky. A good evening with Cocky, Crowley-Milling, Jerry Bail and two or three other Duxford types. Slept on Cocky's bedroom floor with Robin.

Johnnie's three flights were transits, first to Ludham, then Duxford (BL659). 'Robin' was Cocky's retriever.

Tuesday, 22nd
Norwich. Flew back to Horsham St Faith in bad weather and was with my darling by 1130. A quiet day; flicks in the afternoon and dinner at the Castle in the evening with Bill Hudson, his wife and Michael Ingle-Finch.

Johnnie's only flight was from Duxford to Horsham (BL659).

Wednesday, 23rd
Hutton-Cranswick. A fine day so I decided to return and P. saw me off at Horsham. Flew across the well-known Wash (shades of 616 at Wittering) and on up the Lincolnshire Coast, by the Humber Estuary and up the Yorkshire Coast with the weather gradually closing down. At Middlesbrough it was very bad so I decided to retrace my steps and eventually landed at Driffield with not more than 10 gallons.

Scrounged a lift down to Hutton-Cranswick and spent a very enjoyable evening with Ken Holden and his wife, Mary, and some of the [illegible] squadron.

[When I was refuelling at Ludham I looked across the familiar aerodrome and the first thing I saw was the wooden prop marking the grave of Pusher, I could still read 'The Pusher, 610 Sqd'].

Johnnie's only flights were transit (BL659).

Thursday, 24th
Took off at Driffield at 1030 hours and was at Peterhead shortly after 12. Refuelled and was very pleased to hit Castletown in time for lunch with the boys. Thankful to get back as the weather forecast was bad and I had visions of a lovely solo Xmas.

That Christmas Eve, Johnnie flew two transit flights and an air-to-sea firing practice sortie (BL659). There was no operational flying and nothing of any significance had occurred in Johnnie's absence from Castletown.

Friday, 25th
Staggered out of bed after a mild session last night, just in time to play SMQ at rugger. We licked them thoroughly. After a bath and a change we all cracked

round to the Airmens' Mess to wait upon them at their Xmas lunch. On to the Sergeants' Mess where we enjoyed another session and a sing song and eventually back to our own Mess for lunch at 1500. Half an hour in bed and then on to 'B' Flight where we held a small party – airmen, sergeants and officers – consuming 18 gallons between us what with 'Schooner Races' etc. Back to the Mess, change into Best Blue and on with the party until 0700 on Boxing Day!! F/Lt Will was captured and dragged into my car as per Operation *Sammy*, but he jumped out at the Guard Room and was not re-taken.

Johnnie did not fly on this Christmas Day. Two operational flights were made, a convoy and a local patrol, no contact.

Saturday, 26th
Up at 1130 and could not face lunch as I thought I was going to die. Reeves, Jack and I went for a stroll, shooting over the moors this afternoon.
1 Partridge
1 Green Plover
1 Dozen Eggs

Sunday, 27th
Quiet day, a little flying and some dusk landings and fairly early to bed after taking ten bob off Sammy at 'shares'.

Johnnie flew twice, a 'Squadron Balbo' and firing practice (BL659). A dawn patrol was flown, nothing doing.

Monday, 28th
A gale sprang up this afternoon and as a result there was no flying. To the Station Cinema to see 'How Green was My Valley' but the gale was so violent that we could not hear the thing.
Found some good Harris Tweed in Thurso, Tarry tells me it's the real thing.

Johnnie flew once, firing practice over the sea (BL659). There was no operational flying.

Tuesday, 29th
No flying again today. Gale and snow with gusts up to 70-80 mph.
Bridge this evening with Father Brown, Dutton and Tarry.

Getting fed up with this place – there is so little to do after dark and not enough to do before dark.

Wednesday, 30th

Alan to Duxford to collect my greatcoat, see Rhodda and contact Peter Clapham at Wittering. Doug's Flight beat up a squadron of Hampdens from Wick.

A Spitfire is missing from a flight between Inverness and Skae Brae and as a flare was reported off [illegible] Head last night, Sammy and Tarry in the Master, and Doug and I in the Tiger, carried out a search but we didn't see a thing.

Two letters from Pauline.

A very strange sort of year this has been. With 616 at Kinton under Colin Gray, my Flight at Goxhill and Johnnie Walker coming over to visit us, to King's Cliffe where HS Brown takes over command, sweeps from West Malling with either Jamie or Prosser Hanks leading. Tess Ware killed, Strouts and Lepel Cointet missing.

Johnnie flew twice, firstly local flying practice (BL659), then in the Tiger Moth (DE626) with Flying Officer Cameron, the SMO, on the fruitless search for the missing Spitfire pilot; it would be Johnnie's last flight of 1942.

Thursday, 31st

(continued from the 30th) Bob Bowen given a gong and myself a bar. The rumours of my taking over 610, Valerie, and the frequent visits of Cocky and I to each other. Dozens of Parties, 'B' Flight – Joe Crofts, Smithy, Paddy Davidson (killed), Red Winter, Miller, Welch, Neville (USA) etc.

To 11 Group and Kenley but I am only there a few days when I am whipped back to 12 Group to take over 610. The journey North in the Morris with all the luggage and Pusher, and the stay with 56 at Snailwell.

Ludham, 610, Pauline, Poggi, Pusher killed, Dieppe with Creagh rescued from the drink and Peter Poole and Leach missing, sweeps from West Malling and then the posting to 14 Group. Visit to C-in-C, wedding day on the 14/11 with HSLD (Cocky) as best man, honeymoon and back to Scotland for Xmas and the New year.

And so ended 1942 and what is Johnnie's only surviving diary. The following month, Johnnie attended the Fighter Leader Course at Chedworth, and the

Commander-in-Chief honoured his promise: after six months at Castletown, 610 Squadron returned south, relieving 131 Squadron at Westhampnett on 20 January 1943. Johnnie: 'While at Castletown we had received a number of replacement pilots, so these chaps were keen to see action, to prove themselves. It was an exciting time for the Squadron, a challenge which 610 was ready for.'

All of that, however, and Johnnie's subsequent command of the Kenley Wing, is another story…

Bibliography

610 Squadron Operations Record Book   AIR27/2107
616 Squadron Operations Record Book   AIR27/2126
610 Squadron Combat Reports   AIR 50/172
JEJ's Personal Combat Reports   AIR50/402

The foregoing documents have been digitised and can be downloaded from The National Archives: nationalarchives.gov.uk

JEJ's Pilot's Flying Log Book (copy, Johnson Papers).

Caldwell, D, *The JG26 War Diary Volume I*, Grubb Street, London, 1996
Johnson, AVM JE, *Wing Leader*, Chatto & Windus Ltd, London, 1956
Sarkar, D, *Spitfire Ace of Aces: The Wartime Story of Johnnie Johnson*, Amberley Publishing, Stroud, 2011
Wynn, K, *Men of the Battle of Britain*, Frontline Books, Barnsley, 2015

Also see the author's website: ourfinesthour.net

Other Books By Dilip Sarkar

(in order of publication)

Spitfire Squadron: No 19 Squadron at War, 1939-41
The Invisible Thread: A Spitfire's Tale
Through Peril to the Stars: RAF Fighter Pilots Who Failed to Return, 1939-45
Angriff *Westland: Three Battle of Britain Air Raids Through the Looking Glass*
A Few of the Many: Air War 1939-45, A Kaleidoscope of Memories
Bader's Tangmere Spitfires: The Untold Story, 1941
Bader's Duxford Fighters: The Big Wing Controversy
Missing in Action: Resting in Peace?
Guards VC: Blitzkrieg 1940
Battle of Britain: The Photographic Kaleidoscope, Volumes I-IV
Fighter Pilot: The Photographic Kaleidoscope
Group Captain Sir Douglas Bader: An Inspiration in Photographs
Johnnie Johnson: Spitfire Top Gun, Parts I & II
Battle of Britain: Last Look Back
Spitfire! Courage & Sacrifice
Spitfire Voices: Heroes Remember
The Battle of Powick Bridge: Ambush a Fore-thought
Duxford 1940: A Battle of Britain Base at War
The Few: The Battle of Britain in the Words of the Pilots
Spitfire Manual 1940
The Sinking of HMS Royal Oak *in the Words of the Survivors (reprint of Hearts of Oak)*
The Last of the Few: Eighteen Battle of Britain Pilots Tell their Extraordinary Stories
Hearts of Oak: The Human Tragedy of HMS Royal Oak
Spitfire Voices: Life as a Spitfire Pilot in the Words of the Veterans
How the Spitfire Won the Battle of Britain
Spitfire Ace of Aces: The True Wartime Story of Johnnie Johnson

219

Douglas Bader

Fighter Ace: The Extraordinary Life of Douglas Bader, Battle of Britain Hero (reprint of above)

Spitfire: The Photographic Biography

Hurricane Manual 1940

River Pike

The Final Few: The Last Surviving Pilots of the Battle of Britain Tell their Stories

Arnhem 1944: The Human Tragedy of the Bridge Too Far

Spitfire! The Full Story of a Unique Battle of Britain Fighter Squadron

Battle of Britain 1940: The Finest Hour's Human Cost

Letters From The Few: Unique Memories of the Battle of Britain

Index

INDEX

227

INDEX

INDEX